D1282367

MEN AND THINGS

MEN AND THINGS

BY

J. A. SPENDER

Essay Index Reprint Series

BOOKS FOR LIBRARIES PRESS

FREEPORT, NEW YORK

First Published 1937
Reprinted 1968

PR
6037
P 45M4
1968

LIBRARY OF CONGRESS CATALOG CARD NUMBER:
68-8496

PREFACE

THE first part of this book and several of the Essays in Part II are now published for the first time. Of the remaining pieces, most have appeared in the *Westminster Gazette* and *News Chronicle*, to the proprietors of which I am indebted for permission to republish them. I have also the permission of Messrs. Methuen to reprint the chapter on the Indian Durbar from the *Indian Scene*, published by them in 1912, and of Messrs. Ernest Benn to include the passage on the "Descent into California" from *The American of Today*, published by them in 1928. Two of the Essays in Part II have appeared in the *Fortnightly Review* and *Hibbert Journal* respectively. The pieces in Part IV are survivors, more by accident than design, of a great many that went into the oven at the end of the day's work. Most of them first saw the light in the evening *Westminster Gazette*, and I have dated some of them because their interest, if any, is precisely that they "date."

J. A. S.

1937.

CONTENTS

PART I

PORTRAITS

PART II

POLITICS AND HISTORY

PART III

THINGS SEEN

CONTENTS

PART IV

SIDE ISSUES

PART I

PORTRAITS

A

I

GREY OF FALLODON

I

Balliol, February 1882.—Two young men—myself in my first term and another youth a little senior—sitting together behind the "oak" which served as an outer door to their respective sets of rooms—both armed with pokers, their backs against the inside door, their heels hard pressed against the "oak." Much battering without, but the defence unbroken for the first hour. Then sounds of holes being bored in the oak, through which red-hot pokers are passed, and countered by blows from cold pokers within. The oak visibly weakening under this treatment; then a sudden rush bringing it down and overwhelming the defence. The heaviest man in College (17 stone) serves as a battering ram, and just behind him and sprawling on top of him, comes a tall slim youth shouting "Now we've got him." "Him" was my companion. I did my best to the end, but he was beyond my help. There were six of them, and they bore him away and worked their will on him. Being quite new to the College I knew none of them.

Queen Anne's Gate, 1925.—Viscount Grey and J. A. S. talking over old Balliol days.

J. A. S.: Balliol was not quite the prim intellectual establishment it is sometimes supposed to be. When it started ragging it was in the first flight. I remember a night in February, 1882, when I was a fresher and stood siege with Lord W. against a party which battered down an oak in the front quad.

Grey: Yes, that was really a fine rag. *I* led that party.

3

Dec. 21, 1901.

MY DEAR SPENDER—I see you express surprise that I should have agreed with Rosebery's (Chesterfield) speech, and this strikes me as the most damnable misconstruction either of Rosebery's speech or of my speeches. Let me have it out with you for once. (Follow four sheets written on four sides, very emphatically " having it out.")

I put these two fragments from the past at the head of this chapter, because it seems to me that Lord Grey's character is in danger of being somewhat over-sentimentalized in public memory. Prof. Trevelyan's biography dwells very rightly on its softer side, and the biographer's business would indeed be a dreary one if he could not find relief from the solemn task of presenting his subject in the full-dress of public life. Grey was all that Prof. Trevelyan shows him as being in his charming portrait of him—a lover of birds and the country-side, an observer of genius, a finished and gifted performer in any accomplishment that needed supple wrist or faultless eye, whether it was casting a fly, or timing a stroke at (real) tennis. To be with him in the country or to watch him at any of these favourite pursuits was a delight, and for the time being, both for him and for you, the curtain seemed to have fallen on any other sort of existence.

On this side of him he had devotees who seemed to be unaware that he was anything else. When the form of the memorial to him came to be discussed, one enthusiastic bird-lover pleaded to the end for a statue in one of the public parks in which he should appear with a fishing-rod in one hand, while he fed his favourite ducks assembled at his feet out of the other hand. Of the subscriptions sent in, actually the major part went in the end to the Ornithological Institute at Oxford. The bird-lovers, whose hero he was, seemed to be almost unaware that he had serious claims to be commemorated on other grounds.

Grey's own habit of speaking as if this was his real life,

the life he would have chosen, if he had been free to choose, played into the hands of opponents and critics who wished to make him out a dilettante in public affairs. Bacon observed of the great men of his time that they were in the habit of complaining of the dreadful lives they lived; and this, he said, they did to "abate the edge of envy." This was far from Grey's intention; he did quite honestly, when he was a young man, dally with the idea of turning his back on politics and living the quiet life in the country with his wife. He told me once that he was "converted" from this by Arthur Acland, the well-known Minister of Education in Gladstone's 1892 Government, whose exhortations to young men to take a serious view of their public duties were among the strongest influences on several of them at that time. "Converted" was the word he used, as if it were really some inward and spiritual process. Whatever it was, it seemed to awaken in him the latent hereditary instinct for public duty which was in his Grey blood.

There were moments in his life in which the two things were in a rather uncertain balance, and all through it his love of the country was strong enough to save him from any competitive striving to shine in public life and win its prizes. He had none of that passion for the red boxes which I have known persisting in otherwise blameless public men to the end of their days; no one ever heard him talk about his "career," or even speculate on his own future. Yet, to speak as if he gave grudgingly to public life hours snatched from fly-fishing and bird-watching is a travesty which, if it were even approximately true, would expose him to very just criticism. One might as well depict the late Archbishop of Canterbury, who also was a fisherman and a lover of nature, as perpetually fleeing from his sacred duties and lamenting the hard fate which chained him to Lambeth or Canterbury when he would so much rather have been watching the spring in an English wood or landing a salmon at Bonar Bridge. Since archbishops also are God's creatures, it is possible that they do occasionally yield to these thoughts, even on a Sunday morning. Grey undoubtedly had sharp attacks of them, one of which, as his biographer records, brought down on him some plain speaking from the breezy Birrell; and enough could be culled from his letters and *obiter dicta* in moments of depression to give colour to certain caricatures of him which his enemies and critics put into circulation. The truth was that love of the country and living things was one of the deep necessities of his nature, and the source from which he drew strength and refreshment in his public work. But to that public work he was resolutely and even sternly dedicated, and no one spared himself less in performing it. To be absorbed in it was actually his salvation after the death of his first wife.

2

There is no need to labour the point. The voluminous records we now have tell their own tale about Grey as about all the other principal figures of this time. For eleven years continuously he held one of the greatest positions of trust— in some ways the greatest—in the European world, and if there is anyone else who can be set beside him either for length of service or steadiness of purpose, his name has yet to be revealed. Taking the eleven years together, I doubt if any similar period can be found in which a British Foreign Secretary made so few mistakes in following out a given line of policy, or was so seldom compelled to retract or retreat. The great series of dispatches that bear his name may well, both now and hereafter, be the pride of those who value the good repute of their country. If nothing else remained, they would prove Grey to be a master of his craft. Let it be admitted that they have the simplicity which the foolish may mistake for ignorance. Not a trace can be found in them of the twisting and turning, the chicane and double-dealing that deface so many of the parallel records of Ministers in other countries. If the general judgment of the world is that British policy was honest and honourable in these years, it is largely to Grey that we owe it. The great collective calamity of the War was defeat for him as for every reasonable man. But if war had to be, no man did more than Grey to secure the unity and unanimity of his countrymen, to fortify them with powerful allies, and to ensure them against the immeasurable catastrophe of defeat.

To Prince Bülow and the tight-rope performers of his school Grey always seemed too good to be true. Could anyone be so simple, they asked, as to think of policy as if it were just an affair of standing by your friends and keeping your promises? Could any man of the world, let alone an experienced statesman, really think it possible to reduce armaments or attach serious importance to abstractions like the "Concert of Europe" and "International Law"? Was it not obvious that he was all the time engaged in encircling Germany, and doing it steadily and remorselessly at the behest of King Edward? Let him only confess it, and they might respect him and admit that his strokes were well timed and, according to their own standards, correct. But his air of moving on a superior moral plane, talking as if honour forbade things that all clear-sighted objective politicians knew to be the normal and recognized way of conducting affairs—this really was intolerable.

It was, nevertheless, just Grey's simplicity on these points that made him the power he was. He had one predominant idea throughout—that to let Germany conquer France would be disastrous for Europe and eventually for the British Empire. Therefore, to resist all German efforts to drive wedges between Britain and France, and especially the effort to extract a pledge of neutrality from Britain in the event of war between Germany and France, was a cardinal necessity of British policy. If sentiment came in, as undoubtedly it did, it was to reinforce this idea. The notion that France was being bullied because of her friendship with us brought him at once to her side; the evident belief of the Germans that we could be frightened out of our friendship with France or prevented from making friends with Russia, by threats from

7

Berlin, hardened him in his resolve to keep both friendships. He would be friends with the Germans, but not on the condition on which they seemed to insist, that we should break with other friends. The Kaiser kept saying that the right way to treat an Englishman was to plant your fist in his face. There could hardly have been a worse subject for this treatment than Grey. Was he to be frightened into betraying his friends and going back on his word? We see it all coming to the boiling-point in the final German bid for our neutrality in the last days before the War. Couldn't they understand that for us to bargain with them on these terms would be an indelible disgrace? No, they could not understand it. It was, from their point of view, a perfectly legitimate way out for them and for us. Hadn't they offered substantial compensation? What else could we want? Bethmann-Hollweg was unfeignedly astonished at the wrath in London.

The whole controversy seemed to be summed up in this final explosion. On the one side was the hard realist brought up to believe that the affairs of nations were beyond the good and evil of any homespun morality; on the other the British Foreign Secretary bringing the public-school spirit to bear on great affairs. He and his opposite number in Europe were playing the game by quite different rules. The one said that no one could be so simple, the other that no one could be so cynical, as the other seemed to be. Grey simply could not understand the German "objectivity" which, as Marschall von Bieberstein openly avowed, construed treaties by an unwritten clause—*rebus sic stantibus*—and left the signatories at liberty to treat them as scraps of paper when keeping them proved inconvenient. His European critics could not believe that anyone calling himself a Foreign Secretary could be so innocent as to expect great nations to be bound by engagements made in different circumstances which were obviously to their disadvantage. It was impossible, said the Germans, that anyone could have such fine feelings as Grey affected in the business of practical politics;

8

it was impossible, said Grey, that anyone could be so rude as the Germans without intending to pick a quarrel. "Their way of beginning a conversation," he told Roosevelt in 1911, "is to stamp on your foot to attract your attention, when you aren't looking, and then they are surprised and very annoyed when the conversation doesn't go smoothly afterwards."

3

A little group of the English said at the end that Grey had led them into a trap, that he had so shaped his course as to put us under an obligation to intervene, when we might have stayed out. He had practised a "secret diplomacy" behind the backs of his colleagues and the country. The records are now plain for all to read, and from first to last there is no trace in them of any material fact which was withheld from Cabinet or country. Those who search them for evidence of sinister hidden forces will waste their labour. The secret of Grey's diplomacy was that there were no secrets in it. Whether the British people were right or wrong in deciding to intervene in August, 1914, they had in their possession all the material facts necessary to a judgment. The forces at work were what they seemed to be; if we could be taken back to August, 1914, with our present knowledge, the case would be restated in almost the same terms as in Grey's simple and massive statement of it in his speech to the House of Commons, August 3, 1914. But Grey and his critics were always at cross-purposes on one point. When he spoke of freedom, they interpreted him as meaning freedom to stand out, whereas in his mind it was always freedom to come in, if Parliament and the country so decided.

But whether it was to come in or stand out, this freedom carried with it certain limitations which a Foreign Secretary was bound to keep in mind. Grey never kicked against these pricks. He took for granted that the British people would not have compulsory military service in time of peace, that they would not let him turn the Entente with France into a military alliance, that they would not part with their liberty to decide for war or peace on the merits of the case when the time came. He would have resigned and risked breaking the Government if it had failed to provide a sufficiency of sea-power, but he would not be drawn into argument or risk schism and friction on any of these other points. As abstract propositions there might be argument for or against them, but a British Foreign Secretary, and especially one who was serving in a Liberal Government, had to accept certain things as inherent in the national character and tradition, and shape his policy accordingly. Hence his characteristic conclusion that in handling French and Germans he was always at liberty to warn the Germans of the risks they were running of British intervention, but not at liberty to pledge British assistance to the French. This was his line from January, 1906, to July, 1914. If national unity was to be achieved in the event of war, it had to be by the free choice of the British people in circumstances which they judged to be compelling, and their Foreign Secretary must so steer as in the end to have a case which would command a unanimous, or all but unanimous, consent.

In spite of all the changes of the post-War years, the chief difficulty of British foreign policy remains still what it was in Grey's time. How far are we a Continental Power in the sense that our neighbours in Europe understand the expression; how far can our friends in Europe rely on our acting as they in like circumstances would act; how far can the hostile be warned that we shall take the field against them if they break the peace? The question came again and again to Grey as it comes to his successors, and both he and they have so far been compelled to answer "wait and see." League of Nations and Collective Security yes, but qualified by the conditions that a decision to act shall be unanimous, which brings us back to the old points. Grey and Asquith, like Mr. Eden and Mr. Baldwin, were half in and half out of Europe, a little more than half in by virtue of the Entente on the

Western side, but extremely anxious to keep out on the Eastern side.

Grey's frontier, like Mr. Baldwin's, was the Rhine. Only with great reluctance was he persuaded to preside over the London Conference in 1912-13 to deal with the affairs of the Balkans. He had great success in that, and all Europe applauded the discovery of his skill, knowledge and impartiality—so unexpected in the British dilettante. But in August, 1913, we see him winding up this Conference, turning with relief from the tangled affairs of Eastern Europe, concentrating on the West, and making a last effort to end the British-German quarrel on exclusively British and German ground. The logic of the alliance system which was to make the assassination of an Austrian Archduke in a Bosnian town of vital concern to Great Britain was not revealed to Grey or to any British statesman. Had the country been consulted a year before the War, it would almost certainly have said— as Mr. Lloyd George did twenty-two years later—that not a British battalion should be mobilized for an Austrian quarrel. The criticisms of Grey in this period are not criticisms of one British Minister, but of what may be called the standardized British policy from the Napoleonic wars to the present time. Any British Minister who broke away from it would have wrecked his party and divided the country. By none would he have been more fiercely assailed than by some who have persuaded themselves after the event that they were in favour of this course.

All that can be said against Grey on the score of "secret diplomacy" is that he too easily took for granted that his colleagues were as well acquainted as he was with the very open secrets of Europe—secrets that had been debated a dozen times in the House of Commons, and were discussed daily in the newspapers. I myself was more than once bitterly reproached by Cabinet Ministers in these years for knowing things which they said were unknown to them, and which they supposed had been disclosed to me by Grey. They were quite wrong. Grey told me nothing which he was not ready to tell everybody who cared to ask. My knowledge, such as it was, was gained from sources which were equally accessible to them; the only difference between them and me was that my particular work in life required me to follow these affairs from day to day and, so far as I could, to repair the gaps in my knowledge, whereas they were absorbed in the business of their departments, to which foreign affairs were only a side-issue. If these men complained that Grey kept foreign affairs to himself, he on his side used to say that he found it extremely difficult to interest them in these affairs. They were abundantly supplied with papers, but only a few read them.

4

Grey's critics twitted him with his inability to talk French and his refusal to travel about Europe. So insular, so British, so unlike the enterprising and far-ranging Foreign Secretaries of a later date! Possibly even Grey would have had to fall in with the new peregrinating fashion if he had been in office after the War, and certainly he must have gone to Geneva. But he had his own reasons for remaining at home, and they were at least carefully considered. It was not at all convenient to talk high politics with Sovereigns and Ministers on their own ground, as you had to if you went with King Edward on his visits to foreign courts. Mere civility might require you to say pleasant things which would expose you to a charge of hypocrisy, if you failed to live up to them afterwards; it would in any case be very difficult in this courtly atmosphere to say the things you wanted to say. Royal visits and return royal visits were, as he said in his *Twenty-five Years*, a perpetual anxiety to him. The French had to be reassured when King Edward visited Germany, the Kaiser appeased when he went to Paris and did not immediately go on to Berlin. Both Paris and Berlin wanted to know exactly what had happened when he visited the Tsar. It was better for the Foreign Secretary to keep his distance from these royal and imperial occasions. Let Haldane go to Windsor and do the talking when the Kaiser was there.

A very sincere dislike of getting into uniform and performing the ritual proper to these occasions reinforced these ideas, but they were part of his deliberate practice. To the end of his life he looked back on his visit to Paris with King George in April, 1914, as having involved him in the tiresome and quite unnecessary complication of the "naval conversations" with Russia. The French said it would be convenient to them and help Russia to feel that she was not being left in the cold, if the British and Russian naval authorities might discuss the parts to be taken by their respective fleets in the event of Great Britain taking part in a war. There seemed to be nothing in it. "To my lay mind," says Grey, "it seemed that in a war against Germany the Russian fleet would not get out of the Baltic, and the British fleet would not get into it. But the difficulty of refusing was obvious; it would offend Russia by giving her the impression that she was not treated on equal terms with the French; it would be ungracious to the French," who were his hosts. So the permission was given and the admirals were allowed to talk. It seemed a harmless courtesy on the spur of the moment, but immediately the word went out that a naval conversation had been concluded between Britain and Russia; Berlin became greatly agitated; questions were asked in Parliament, and Grey was driven to answers which though "absolutely true" were not answers to the questions put to him. Since he was a very honest man, nothing gave him greater mental discomfort than being driven to these subterfuges. But what was he to do, if M.P.'s would insist on putting these questions? By all the rules of the game these military arrangements were part of the *arcana imperii* which no one discussed in public—indeed to do so would have been a betrayal of Russian and French, as well as British, confidence. Grey's after-reflection was that it would never have happened if he had not been in Paris and been

13

placed in a position in which it was impossible for him to say no to his hosts.[1]

In June, 1907, I had an interview with the Kaiser in Berlin, the main theme of which was the neglect of his country by Englishmen. He wound up somewhat vehemently, "go back and tell your Government people to come to Berlin; tell Sir Edward Grey to come." I duly passed on this message on my return, but Grey said, naturally enough, that he would wait until the invitation came to him through the regular channels. I learnt in after years that the Kaiser considered himself to have invited Grey to Berlin, and that he had taken some offence at not having received an answer. Grey, in fact, never received any invitation except this verbal message which, officially and diplomatically speaking, had no existence. He could not have followed it up except by proposing himself to stay with the Kaiser—a thing unheard of in the practice of those times, which would have set all Europe agog with gossip and rumour.

Grey seemed to take a special pleasure in professing himself unable to speak French, and he greatly exaggerated his incapacity. He certainly had no great accomplishment in the language, but he could get on as well as most of his colleagues under the spur of necessity, and was by no means tongue-tied in the many conferences with French Ministers which he attended in the first months of the War. I have spent evenings with him and Cambon who never spoke English, well as he understood it, and, as many of us suspected, could speak it if he chose. Grey was quite fluent and intelligible, if without scruple where genders and tenses were concerned. But the point is of very little importance. Unless he is quite perfect in a foreign language, a responsible Minister engaged on important transactions should speak no language but his own. Much misunderstanding has been caused by the-not-quite-

---

[1] I was supposed to have been Grey's agent in this business. During the War I received a copy of a German newspaper containing an entirely apocryphal account of my supposed dealings on Grey's behalf with the Russian naval attaché.

perfect insisting on speaking the language of a foreign Ambassador or visitor. They nearly always say a little more or a little less than they intended to say or than they would have said in their own language. I have heard experienced Foreign Office officials of the old school say that no Foreign Secretary except Lansdowne was to be trusted to speak either French or German when precision was necessary or desirable. Cambon, the French Ambassador, understood this, and it was a large part of his success that he gave himself the advantage of speaking in his own language.[1]

5

In a letter to his friend Wilfrid Ward, quoted in Prof. Trevelyan's Life, Lord Hugh Cecil, no mean judge, described Grey's speech on August 3, 1914, as the "greatest speech delivered in our time or for a very long period . . . the greatest example of the art of persuasion I have ever listened to." Persuasive is the right adjective for Grey's quality as a speaker. Of all the men of his time he came nearest the Greek definition of the orator as the man who persuades others that he is likely to know (τὸν εἰκότα εἰδέναι). Professional orators and star-performers were often at a loss to understand why everybody wanted to hear Grey, why they flocked into the House when it was known that he was up, listened breathlessly in great halls to his quiet and even homely expositions of world affairs. There was no spice, no "punch" in it, only an even flow of quiet argument, as in a circle of friends by the fireside, and such fairness to opponents, such allowance for their points of view, as to fill the fighting politicians with despair.

It was just for these reasons that he was so persuasive. Grey at his best seemed to be the voice of things speaking for themselves. He was not trying to convince you or convert you; he was telling you what he knew and leaving

[1] Schouvaloff, the famous Russian Ambassador, said that Lord Salisbury talked "Foreign Office French."

you to form your own judgment. His talk had the same quality; he never sought to win in argument; what he said about the War—that, if there hadn't been an opposition to it, there ought to have been—he felt about most political questions. This doesn't mean that his opinions were luke-warm or even necessarily moderate. On the contrary, he was an advanced Radical on many questions of domestic policy. Indeed the peculiar tenacity of his views, the "Grey obstinacy," as some called it, followed from his having weighed all the opposing arguments before making up his mind. He was for that reason one of the few men who were never fogged or distracted by seeing all sides of a question. Argument with him generally followed the same course. "Yes, all that is quite true, there are very strong reasons against the course I am taking, but the balance of advantage is in doing what I propose, and if we do it, we mustn't wobble between for and against."

I have never known anyone who had so sure a touch in answering unexpected questions. In all the eleven years in which he was bombarded with "supplementaries" in the House of Commons, he never got himself into any serious difficulty with rash or ill-tempered impromptus, often as he was tempted by questioners whose only object was to make mischief. In any advice that he gave, whether to a Party on public questions or to a friend in his private affairs, there was the same quality of cool, clear wisdom which, whether you liked it or not, nearly always put things in a new light. When it was said that Grey disagreed, all wise men stopped to think.

He had a circle of devoted friends, but he was not of the hearty disposition which makes for popularity. He would not stop to gossip in the lobby or engage in small talk with men he did not know. This was not pride or stand-offishness, but partly an intense preoccupation with his work, and partly a natural modesty which made it impossible for him to realize that he was a person of importance who could give pleasure to humbler mortals merely by passing the time of day with them. But let the humbler mortal take the initiative and rush his guard, and no one was more forthcoming or readier to give his best. In this he resembled Asquith, who was one of the same disposition and laid himself open to the same reproach. To the end of his days Asquith could never be made to understand what sort of towering figure he was to the rank and file, and how much pleasure he could give and how much opposition disarm by a smile or a nod or a little practice in the more innocent demagogic arts. Both men would have had fewer critics if in this respect they had been better politicians.

6

In 1924, when he had decided to write his own memoirs, the deterioration of his eyesight had gone so far that it was impossible for him to collect or assemble the necessary documents, and he asked me to do this for him. It was not a very easy job. There were piles of them, and the work of selecting, classifying and annotating so admirably accomplished in the subsequent years by Dr. Gooch and Prof. Temperley, had still to be done. I remember my despair when a whole cupboard-full, which had escaped notice, was suddenly discovered at the last moment. But Grey had an extraordinary memory for the salient occasions, and his clue through the labyrinth was clear and unwavering. Once more I was struck by the simplicity of his outlook, his quickness in discarding unessentials, his sense of the whole. In spite of failing eyesight he wrote every word of *Twenty-five Years* with his own hand, for he never could dictate even a paragraph when it was a question of writing a book. As the sheets passed through my hands, I more and more felt it to be the kind of masterpiece which comes from the deep roots of character, truthful, self-searching, utterly free of vanity and vindictiveness, meeting the great occasions with the grave emotion which is so much more than rhetoric. It seemed treason to touch it, even to suggest a few necessary amendments where memory had failed.

Eight years later, when I had finished my own study of the post-War Documents, afterwards published under the title of *Fifty Years of Europe*, he came to stay with me and my wife in the country, and we went over the ground again. I had prepared a little list of questions on which I was in doubt and we took them one by one through a long morning. By that time he could read only for a short time and with great difficulty, but he was immensely interested in certain passages that I read to him from the German and Austrian documents and from the memoirs of Conrad von Hötzendorff. His attitude was always the same. Nothing was to be suppressed, nothing said in his favour which was not wholly borne out by the evidence; I was not to treat opposition to him as malicious or factious; on so great occasions and in circumstances of such difficulty there ought to have been opposition if there was not. It would be no credit to the English people if one represented them as capable of being led by the nose by him or by anybody else. Again the old questions came up—might the War have been prevented, if he had done this or not done the other, did he go wrong at any point; yes, certainly at one point in thinking that Germany could control Austria, whereas it was evident now that she was being driven by Austria. But would it have made any difference if he had known it and tried to put the brake on Austria? Never was a man so entirely free from that passion of self-justification which seems to overtake most of the eminent when they look back on the past, so sincerely anxious to see things *sub specie historiae*, and to do justice to old friends and colleagues.

In those days I had a garden with a little wood in it, and in the heart of the wood a pond to which the kingfishers came. When we had done, we went and sat by the pond in the hope that he might just see the flash of blue if they came that day. We were disappointed; they did not come, and we were left anxiously debating whether Tennyson meant the kingfisher when he spoke of the "sea-blue bird of March," and Grey trying to remember whether he had ever seen a

kingfisher in March. The very last letters I exchanged with
him were about a chaffinch's nest found in my garden. The
birds had decorated it with blue and yellow confetti picked
up after a village wedding. He sent it to experts and asked
me to look out for any others similarly adorned.

7

I find it very difficult to think of Grey enshrined in history
or becoming, as he undoubtedly will, one of the central
figures in the controversies of these tremendous years, discussed as Chatham, Pitt, Castlereagh, Canning are discussed.
He had, indeed, the beautiful presence which is appropriate
to such characters, but he never dressed for the part and had
no touch of the theatricality which enters into the make-up
of most historical figures. A great simplicity and an unaware-
ness, which at times was almost a weakness, of the part he
was playing in the world, and of the trust reposed in him,
were his abiding characteristics. It is common to speak of
public men as being spoilt or unspoilt by success. One could
never think in these terms of Grey, for he so obviously never
gave a thought to the effect on his personal fortunes of anything that he did or that might happen. I have heard him
called self-absorbed, and it is true that he had a habit of
retiring upon himself at moments of great stress, and then
only a few intimate women friends seemed able to bring him
comfort or sympathy. But self-conscious or exacting or
jealous he never was in the slightest degree, and no one
could have been kinder or more considerate in the little ways
that give graciousness to friendship. That so upright a man
should have suffered such cruel adversities as he in the course
of his life seemed a peculiar inversion of natural justice.
On these occasions one saw him engulfed for a time, then
coming desperately ashore to take up his daily life. He was
splendidly stoical about his blindness, and only very rarely
let one know what it meant to have this curtain fall between
him and the world of nature and the world of books. The

last blow seemed to have fallen when his fingers failed him to read Braille. Suffering and responsibility left their mark on him, adding something of melancholy and something also of gravity and nobility to his character, but to think of him as a melancholy or unhappy man would be altogether wide of the mark. He had long periods of great happiness, and to the very end had sudden bursts of high spirits which brought back the youth one had known forty years earlier.

I bear in affectionate memory his little idiosyncrasies, the little traps he set for your ignorance of natural facts, and hearty laugh when he had caught you out, his habit of testing you by whether his ducks would eat out of your hand, or his squirrels come into the room when you were there; whether you liked the same bits of Wordsworth that he did, whether you could name his vintage clarets, or shared his taste for Himalayan blackberries. He loved the good things of life, but was curiously austere in certain things. He hated being waited on, insisted on packing his own bag, and even when he was half blind absolutely refused to take servant or secretary with him when he travelled. Walking with him in London was a constant anxiety, for he plunged ahead into traffic which he could only half see, and trusted to luck to bring him across. Worse still, bicycling with him in the country. One breathed a prayer of thankfulness on getting back safely to Fallodon after one of these excursions to the moors. To follow him uphill was a fair test of heart and lungs; to be behind him as he coasted downhill, rounding corners at full speed, swerving suddenly to avoid carts and other obstacles which he only saw at the last moment, was shattering to your nerves, though apparently without any effect on his.

I saw him in a nursing home in London just before he returned for the last time to Fallodon. He was a very ill man but still cheerful and hopeful. There had appeared in a London newspaper that morning a most painful attack on him which had filled his friends with indignation; somehow he had got to know of it and had insisted on its being read to him. He asked me if I had read it, and I was obliged to say I had. He seemed unruffled and begged me not to be disturbed by it or to try to answer it, but said finally "if there is anything in it you really think I don't deserve or any point of fact that ought to be put right, tell me when you come again next week." That was my last word with him. Before the next week he had seemed to gain strength and the doctors allowed him to be moved. On the morning of the day fixed for me to come again I had a telegram from him, "Better, going home," and ten days later a message by telephone from Fallodon to say that he was unconscious and dying.

II

HALDANE

I

THE case of Haldane will probably rank with that of Aristides among the classic instances of national ingratitude, but in some ways it is even more puzzling. What was it in this man which excited such irrational feelings in his political opponents? It is impossible that intelligent men like the leaders of the Tory party, who insisted on his exclusion from the coalition of 1915, should have taken seriously the legend that he was a pro-German. The fact that, in paying a tribute to his old teacher, Lotze of Tübingen, he had said that his spiritual home was Germany was no doubt a tempting morsel for unscrupulous jingo journalists inciting the mob against him. But to suppose that educated and eminent men who had filled high places and sat for years on the front benches in Lords and Commons actually regarded it as evidence of treachery to the national cause would argue deeper depths of ignorant Philistinism than their worst enemies could impute to them. Unread as some English public men may be, they cannot all of them have been on this level. Moreover, most of them had seen Haldane at work, seen him deliberately and laboriously organizing the British army in such a way as to enable it to act on the continent of Europe in concert with a potential ally, who was clearly France, against a potential enemy, who could only be Germany. It stands on the record that the greatest of English generals went first of all on his return from France after the victory of 1918, to the house in Queen Anne's Gate where Haldane lay forgotten and neglected, and there left a copy of his Dispatches inscribed "to the greatest of British War Ministers." Yet this was the man on whose ostracism the leaders of the Tory party insisted to the point of refusing to serve their country in one of the most critical of its emergencies unless he were excluded. One could have understood it if they had insisted on the omission of certain others whose resistance to the War had been prolonged to the last minute of the twelfth hour in August, 1914, but it was well known that throughout the terrible twelve days' pre-war diplomacy Haldane had been a staunch supporter of the line on which Asquith and Grey were steering.

The excuse made afterwards was that facts were facts—that Haldane was, in fact, so suspected by immense numbers of people that his inclusion in a National Government would have been a serious disadvantage at that moment. From this point of view whether the suspicions were just or unjust was said to be of no consequence. Haldane had incurred them and he must pay the forfeit. The suspicions would, I believe, have counted for nothing if they had not been endorsed by these eminent people; it was they who had given the dog his bad name; it is they who will chiefly be held responsible for having hanged him. But the question remains to be asked, ought Haldane's Liberal colleagues, and especially his intimate friends Asquith and Grey, to have consented to this sacrifice?

Grey was desperately unhappy about it, and to the end of his life reproached himself for not having resigned in protest. Asquith held that the formation of a non-party Government was a national necessity at that moment, and that, when he had exhausted his efforts to overcome the prejudice of the Conservative leaders, he had no option but to yield. The friend had to be sacrificed to the country. I believe Asquith was right, but his dislike of doing unpleasant things led him on this, as on several other occasions, to do them abruptly and ungraciously on the final compulsion. He might have been expected to assure his old friend of his unaltered belief in him in a letter which he would have been free to publish. Prof. Trevelyan shows in his Life of Lord Grey that Asquith did actually exchange letters with Grey with the obvious

23

intention of publishing them, so that the facts might have been conveyed to the public together with a glowing testimonial to their late colleague. A discreet official appears to have convinced them that the publication of these letters would have started a new and bitter controversy in the popular press, which would have been a bad send-off for the new Government and no service to Haldane. Possibly he was right, but this plan having miscarried, Haldane slipped away without a word from his old Chief. No one who knew Asquith or saw him at this time could have attributed this to lack of feeling; the truth was, rather, that he felt too deeply to be able to dress up the occasion with the conventional apologies and excuses. He would see Haldane and tell him. It was long before he did see him, and by then a wound had been inflicted which was past healing. These things happen between the best of friends, and there is no more to be said about them.

Haldane bore himself with unruffled dignity, but he could scarcely be expected to forget. When the War ended, he considered himself at liberty to act in complete independence of his old friends, and he somewhat astonished them by joining MacDonald's Labour Government in 1924. I fancy he suffered some disillusion in the subsequent months. The proceedings of that Government in August and September of that year must sorely have tried his sense of legality. But if so, he was far too loyal to communicate any doubts and misgivings to his former friends. To them he said, and continued to say to the end of his life, that his main interest in joining the Labour Government was to promote the cause of Education. Never was there more unsparing and dis-interested zeal in that cause than he showed in these last years. He would take journeys of hundreds of miles to address meetings of a few score of workmen with no reporters present. With his health visibly failing he would undertake engagements of this kind crowding thick on one another in all parts of the country, just as in the old days he had gone from town to town recruiting for his Territorials. Often in

these years I have spent an hour with him in his long upper
room in Queen Anne's Gate, and each time borne away
with me the same impression of mellow wisdom, disinterested service, and gentleness of character, surviving all
the vicissitudes of his public life. Our talk was usually
prefaced by a solemn discussion of the merits of various
brands of cigars, and the choice from his great store, of
that which seemed appropriate to the day and hour. Even
when his health was failing and movement was pain to him,
he insisted on coming the whole way down the steep stairs
from his upper chamber and letting me out at the front door.

2

I return to my question. How was it that such a man
kindled such angry feelings? How could such a myth
have grown up about this disinterested, public-spirited and
essentially gentle character? The mystery deepens as one
tries to recall the real Haldane, as one knew him, through
all those years, from his beginnings in the 1886 Parliament
down to the end. There is no more serviceable asset for a
public man than to be personally liked by opponents as well
as friends, and none more damaging than to be disliked.
Haldane might be supposed to possess every quality which
would ensure liking. He was socially acceptable without a
trace of snobbery, he gave charming parties, he never talked
maliciously, he was highly respected in his profession, he
had a considerable, and perhaps exaggerated, reputation as
a philosopher, he had plenty of money and one of the best
cooks in London—all things thought adornments in public
men at this time. And yet—it must be said—he had throughout his career a singular capacity for irritating both friends
and opponents. Tempers ran high during the Boer War,
and, as a leading Liberal Leaguer and Imperialist, he naturally
came in for his share of denunciation from the pro-Boers.
But when that hatchet was buried and peace had been
made between the sections, he alone remained unforgiven.

Massingham could hardly hear his name with patience;
C.-B. thought him the author of all mischief in the Liberal
party and blamed him far more than he blamed Grey for the
mortification put on him when the two summoned him to
go from the Commons to the Lords in December, 1905.
"Serve him right," was a very general comment when C.-B.
finally appointed him to the War Office—which in those
days was supposed to be the grave of reputations. And
C.-B. undoubtedly had in his mind the supposed penitential
nature of that appointment. "Master Haldane" had been
a thorn in his side for the past nine years, and even though
"Master Haldane" had to have a Secretaryship of State,
the least desirable was ample reward.

But again, why "Master Haldane" and not "Master Asquith
or "Master Grey"? The answer was, I think, that Haldane
had come to envelop almost everything he did in an air of
mystery which seemed specially to aggravate C.-B. He was
really a very simple man, and the mischief he was up to,
if it was mischief, was none other than his political associates
were doing openly and avowedly, but he had a habit of
fetching a long compass, as Bacon puts it, to quite simple
conclusions. One of his friends said that if you took him to
Hampton Court he would think it necessary to approach the
State chambers by way of the Maze. Having got the
reputation of a mystery man he seemed actually to nurse it.
One of the happiest moments of his life was when Balfour
employed him on a secret mission to Cardinal Logue on the
seemingly innocent subject of Irish University Education.
He went at midnight, muffled up to the eyes, after taking
the most careful measures to make sure that he would
not be observed going or coming. His precautions on these
occasions were often so elaborate as actually to advertise
his proceedings. Instead of passing the time of day, his
intimates accosted him with "what mischief are you up to
now?" and he received the question with a chuckle. It was
his secret joke to be thought an intriguer when he was up
to nothing at all.

It became in time a rather expensive joke; people whose sense of humour was not quite equal to it took him at his word. The impression was heightened by his habit of using metaphysical language on very slight provocation. The extreme mistiness of his own language, as it seemed to unsophisticated listeners, contrasted with his perpetually repeated injunction to "cultivate clear thinking." C.-B., whose knowledge of German philosophy was limited, called him Schopenhauer, and when he became Secretary for War waited with lively anticipation for the reactions of the Generals to the philosopher's touch. He was disappointed if he expected sport. Within a few weeks "Schopenhauer" and the Generals were on the best of terms, and the former was displaying that extraordinary competence in administration which distinguished him not only from philosophers, but from many Ministers of his time. Within a year he had accomplished a task which had defeated all his predecessors, and given order and coherence to the scattered limbs of the British army. What is more, he had disarmed pacifists and economists by producing economies, and had persuaded the Prime Minister, who was an old Secretary for War and a devout Cardwellian, that the ark of his Covenant, the linked battalion system, held the place of honour in the new structure. On this understanding the reconciliation between the two men was complete.

3

Having brought this new thing to perfection, Haldane proceeded to wrap it in a cloud of words. Again, it was really quite simple, and its merit lay in its simplicity; but, as explained by him, it so puzzled his colleagues and mystified the House of Commons that all but a few experts gave it up in despair and left him in possession of the field. Pacifists said angrily in after years that they had had no idea what he was about, but everything was in his speeches and it was not his fault if they failed to pierce the veil thrown over it by military terminology in the mouth of a metaphysician.

This was his characteristic way of expressing himself and it served him admirably. The cranks and carpers who would ordinarily have prolonged debate over a whole session fled from the scene, and left him to complete his military revolution in a few sittings. When he had finished with the War Office, he wanted to go on to the Admiralty and implant the "true doctrine of the General Staff" in the breasts of the Sea Lords. But Admirals are a little different from Generals, and at that point Asquith cried halt.

Pacifists and little-Englanders might have complained of these activities, but it is impossible to discover anything in them which could have lent itself to his Conservative assailants in the subsequent years. They first got their opportunity in the "Haldane Mission" of 1912, when he went to Berlin and talked intimately with the Kaiser, Tirpitz and Bethmann-Hollweg to see if it was possible to find a way of abating the naval competition. Nothing could have appealed to him more than the circumstances of this Mission. He was to go, as Asquith told the King, "in his capacity as Chairman of the London University Commission to obtain first-hand knowledge of the German method of clinical teaching," and, when there, to drop in upon the Kaiser and the Chancellor and have a heart-to-heart talk about the two navies. The Press was to know nothing about it; the University Commissioner was to go quietly and slip away after dusk, and if anyone asked, he was to supply them with details about German clinical teaching.

Of course everybody did very soon know all about it, and within a few days of his return the story was all over London that he had been flattered and deceived by the Kaiser and had brought back to his colleagues falsely reassuring information about German intentions. As a matter of fact his conduct of this business was from beginning to end impeccably discreet and correct. When the new German Navy Law was handed to him he made no comment on it, but on his return took it straight to the Admiralty, which sat up all night on it, and then pronounced it to be worse than the worst they had expected. As to the political equivalent—practically the rupture of the Entente—which the Germans asked in return for even a small abatement of the naval competition, he was solid with the majority of the Cabinet that it could not be conceded. Nothing, from beginning to end, could have been more irreproachable than his conduct of this business. Why, then, should it have been added to the score against him? The only answer I can think of is that, as usual, he himself wrapped it in an air of mystery. He put his finger to his lips and spoke in a whisper about those midnight sittings with the All-Highest and Tirpitz. He expressed the hope that his mission might have saved one Dreadnought and so be "worth a return ticket to Berlin." Had it been any other man, no one would have thought any more about it except possibly to condole with him when this modest hope was disappointed. But since it was Haldane, it went down on the record as one more proof of his all-but treasonable gullibility where Germans were concerned.

It was a disaster for the country as well as for Haldane himself. When the War broke out, he was the man who should have been at the War Office as Secretary for War. He knew by heart the military machine that he had built up, and Kitchener never came near understanding the use or intention of some of its principal parts. I remember Haldane's despair in those early days when Kitchener scattered his General Staff, treated his Territorials as if they were doddering old men, and destroyed at a stroke the organization provided for their expansion and for the supply of their needs. Also his horror when he learnt that the Expeditionary army had been sent to France without its hospital service. Haldane as Secretary for War, and Kitchener as Chief of the Staff, would probably have been an ideal combination. Haldane was one of the very few civilian statesmen of this time who understood the military mind in both its qualities and defects, and knew how to work the war machine in such a way that civilian and military got the best out of each other.

It needed just this kind of mediator to avert the angry

misunderstanding between the two which in the later years became so great a scandal and disservice to the national cause. I have a memory of Haldane in respectful talk with a tongue-tied, verbally incoherent, but extremely able soldier. How patiently he worked at him, how skilfully he brought up the buried treasure, without breaking any of it, with what good-will they parted, and what mutual desire to meet again! Haldane was in all these respects an extraordinarily modest man, and entirely free from that worst vice of politicians of putting the dialectically unaccomplished in the wrong when they are essentially in the right. He knew the value of the able inarticulate and could never be imposed upon by voluble superficiality.

Outwardly he came more and more to resemble a benevolent French abbé of the old school, and he had many of the corresponding qualities. He was man of the world, mystic and realist, an ideal father confessor and confidential adviser. No trouble was too great for him when it was a question of helping a friend; here the benevolent conspirator found congenial opportunities, and it was literally by accident that one occasionally stumbled on the good he had done by stealth. To the end he drove himself hard. If he accepted a Lord Chancellor's pension he would earn every penny of it as a Law Lord, and live up to his exacting standard of preparation for the day's judicial work. One saw him failing and remonstrated, but it was no use. He had never learnt to idle and had to give the whole of him to the last. History will do him justice.

III

KNOLLYS AND ESHER

I

I AM often asked who—apart from the notorious public characters—were the most influential men in my lifetime, and in the little list prepared in answer to this question two names stand near the top, those of the two Viscounts—Knollys and Esher; Knollys, King Edward's principal Private Secretary; Esher, confidant and handy-man to both Crown and Government in three reigns. To both I was greatly beholden during the twenty-six years in which I was editor of the *Westminster Gazette*, and so many of Knollys's letters passed through my hands when I was writing biography in the subsequent years that I seem to have a rather special knowledge of him. To lunch with Esher and Knollys, and to find John Morley at the same table, was one of the pleasantest interludes between office hours in the twelve years from 1902 to 1914.

Knollys was a man of great but cool and quiet ability. He was not in favour with courtiers, who seemed to think it improper that a Liberal, as he undoubtedly was, should be near the person of the King. But this was what was most needed at this moment, for a continuance of Queen Victoria's Conservative partisanship into the new reign would very seriously have prejudiced the monarchy and brought it into dangerous collision with the Liberal and Radical forces which were then gathering strength. But though a Liberal, Knollys was above all things a Constitutionalist, with a keen and even jealous eye for the legitimate power and influence of the Constitutional Monarch, which he saw endangered quite as much by Conservative obstinacy as by Radical extremism. Being the ideal Private Secretary, he would have been horrified to see anything attributed to his initiative, yet after twenty-five years we may reasonably suspect that it was he who gave King Edward the advice (which finally prevailed with King George) that he could legitimately refuse to create peers for the passing of the Parliament Act on the strength of the Budget Election of January, 1910, but that he would be obliged to consent if the Government obtained a sufficient majority at a second Election directed to that issue, and the peers still resisted. In Knollys's mind the whole series of events from the rejection of the Budget up to the passing of the Parliament Act were a continuous chain which was not broken because a new King was on the throne. The second Election, which King Edward had required, had taken place under his successor in December, 1910, and in his view King George was bound to accept it as settling the issue—as presumably his father intended to do.

It is now universally agreed that King George's action was constitutionally correct, but at the time courtiers and aristocratic persons who shrank from blaming the King vented their wrath on Knollys, and charged him with having betrayed the Royal citadel to a Radical Government. He took it all with great composure, and it was not the least of his services to the Crown that he had the correct measure of the badness of the advice offered by courtiers to kings. Reading the German Emperor's account of the talk he heard at Windsor when he came to King Edward's funeral, we may be thankful that Knollys was on the scene.

The principal Private Secretary acts as a buffer between the King and his Ministers, and among his multifarious duties is that of conveying his master's disapproval of rhetorical excesses which he thinks unbecoming in his Ministers. Thus, when Asquith throws his shield over Lloyd George for his Budget speeches in 1909, Knollys writes sharply to beg him not to pretend to the King that he likes the Limehouse style, for the King did not believe it, and it only irritated him. Limehouse, in the King's opinion, was Billingsgate, and there was no more to be said about it. The offenders were always apologizing and always repeating their offence, whereupon the King became peremptory and said, through the mouth of his Secretary, that he really must insist on the Prime Minister keeping his colleagues in order. The King evidently within his right in requiring that his name should not be used in political speeches, but it was more doubtful whether he could claim the same respect for the House of Lords. Was it unconstitutional for a Minister to call the House of Lords "Mr. Balfour's poodle"? Knollys thought not, but certainly it was unbecoming in a Minister, and a rebuke might go forward on that ground.

There were other large fields to be watched; Bills touching the prerogatives of the Crown were introduced without the preliminary formalities; appointments announced in the newspapers before being submitted to the King; naval and military changes made without his knowledge—small matters, but if allowed to pass without protest, establishing precedents which by degrees would eat away the royal prerogatives. Then, at least twice a year came the tiresome business of honours, requiring interminable correspondence. The Prime Minister had his list and the King certain nominees of his own. Each objected to certain persons in the other's list, and the King got some of his men by withdrawing his objections to some of the Prime Minister's men, and vice versa. All letters on these subjects and all correspondence with the Prime Minister or other Ministers had to be in the principal Private Secretary's own hand. Not for him the shorthand writer and the typist. Knollys's industry in these matters was unending; he was always writing, writing, writing; stacks of his letters are to be found in the archives of Prime Ministers. He had a quiet and rather sly sense of humour which found occasional expression in an otherwise straightforward exposition of facts, but he had to remember that he was the mouthpiece of the King, and humour in that context is apt to be misunderstood.

His great gift was a sense of perspective. *Nec deus intersit nisi nodus vindice dignus.* The King must preserve his rights, but he must not intervene except on fit occasion, or expose himself to rebuffs by encroaching on the territory of his Ministers. Knollys had short ways with the trivialities of routine and etiquette, and a steady eye for the greater issues. There could have been no more patient mediator between the King and the politicians, or wiser counsellor than Knollys in these difficult years. It would be absurd to say that he or anyone else foresaw the problems with which Parliaments were faced in the subsequent years, but he saw clearly that there would come a point when Parliamentary Government would break down if one party were in a position to do anything it liked when in power, and to place its veto on anything it chose when in opposition. This in his view was the danger-point for the Sovereign, and to keep it at a distance was his most constant endeavour. It is therefore no exaggeration to say that this frail old gentleman with the soft voice and piercing eyes was, for twenty years, one of the most important men in the British Empire. King George was fortunate in finding two men, Lord Stamfordham and Lord Wigram, who carried on the tradition when he went.

The King's secretaries are a race apart. It is second nature with them to suppress their personalities, to be neither seen nor heard except for an occasional mention in the Court Circular, yet to carry on a continuous tradition which without them might be broken in the changes of Governments or Sovereigns; to keep the boundaries and prevent encroachments from either side, to correspond on equal terms, as befits the King's spokesmen, with Prime Minister and Ministers, yet to do so without letting a trace of their own handiwork appear. It is against all tradition that their lives should be written or that they should leave records of any private activities which might enable their conduct or character to be distinguished from that of their royal employer. Yet again and again, when he comes to certain points in the reigns of Queen Victoria, King Edward or King George, the historian has to pause and bear in mind that on this occasion Ponsonby, on that Knollys, and on that Stamfordham, was the Private Secretary and trusty counsellor of queen or kings.

2

Though King Edward called him the "greatest of my public servants," Esher was never sealed of this tribe. For a few years under Queen Victoria, throughout King Edward's reign, and intermittently in subsequent years, he was a sort of extra Private Secretary to the Sovereign, but it was precisely his value that he was not attached to the Court or subject to its restraints. On one occasion, when he had been rash enough to speak disrespectfully of the German Kaiser in a letter to *The Times*, the latter retorted by expressing his surprise that this liberty was permitted to "the man who looked after the drains at Windsor." Since he was, or had been, Permanent Secretary of the Office of Works which performs this necessary function, the jape was not so wide of the mark. Indeed, Esher's rise to royal favour was actually by way of this office, to which he had been appointed after being five years in Parliament and serving as Private Secretary to Lord Hartington during Gladstone's 1880 Government. His friends were greatly puzzled at his persistence in seeking this apparently not very desirable appointment and rejecting all others. But he seems to have been shrewd enough to perceive that it offered unique opportunities for what Americans call "contacts" with those whose palaces were in his department, and since he was extremely acceptable and well-informed, he was soon admitted to intimacy on other subjects than drains and repairs.

Putting it thus might seem to imply that he was a snob, but that was exactly what he was not. He was deliberately choosing the career which he thought best suited to his abilities. He had a just measure of courtly hangers-on, and if he gained favour, it was not by any sycophancy to royal personages. To Queen Victoria he made no secret of the fact that he was a Liberal and Home Ruler, and he earned

her displeasure by throwing himself with enthusiasm into
the arrangements for the public funeral of Mr. Gladstone,
which she thought extravagant and unnecessary. He greatly
admired W. T. Stead, whom the Court thought mad and
dangerous, and stood by him without flinching throughout
the most unpopular of his purity campaigns. He said once
that his old chief, Hartington, was incapable of being shocked
or surprised by anything; and he himself was—perhaps a
little too deliberately—of the same disposition. Communism,
Socialism, Vegetarianism, Anti-vivisectionism, Seventh Day
Adventism, Flat-earthism—he would examine them all dispassionately just to discover what was in them. If a married
woman ran away with another man, he had nothing to say
except that she should do it with her eyes open and not
pretend or whimper when "respectable" people objected to
respectability being flouted. How, with his ranging mind
and queer friendships, he managed to acclimatize himself to
the atmosphere of the Court was always a puzzle to his
friends outside, but he did somehow, and was, I believe,
a thoroughly good influence there, helping to keep the place
ventilated and opening doors and windows to the outside
world. Needless to say, the professional courtiers disliked
and mistrusted him; they thought him a trespasser on their
ground, and were at a loss to know what King Edward saw
in him. Οὐ φροντὶς Ἱπποκλείδη—Hippocleides doesn't
care—was his attitude to all these.

3

Esher was an extraordinary man, in some ways the most
extraordinary man of these years. I use the word deliberately,
for there was nobody at all like him, and unless it was Colonel
House, who played much the same part to President Wilson
as Esher did to King Edward, there never was anybody like
him. But House was entirely devoted to politics, and there
was a certain furtiveness in his comings and goings, whereas
Esher was a man of the widest accomplishments and moved

freely and openly in all circles, collecting the voices, listening
for the movements of opinion, storing up a fund of innocent
gossip and passing it on to King Edward, who loved gossip
and was insatiably curious about everything. The offers
he declined bear their own witness to his capacity and
acceptability. He was asked to write Disraeli's life and
said no; he was asked to edit the *Daily News* and said no;
he was offered the Secretaryship of War by the Tories, and
the Viceroyalty of India by the Liberals, and said no to both.
These glittering prizes had no temptation for him; he had
taken a cool measure of his own abilities, and having made
up his mind that his talents were not those of the public
performer, the debater or the orator, he was not to be lured
on to ground which he considered unfavourable. To pin
his fortunes to a political party was to go in and out of
office, and be for a large part of the time unemployed, as
he counted employment. To be Viceroy of India would have
ended his career in one grand set-piece. Continuity was
essential; given that, he had the utmost confidence in his
ability to influence events in his own way, and if there was
no place for him under the Constitution, he would make one.

He did make one, and by about the year 1903 had become
an all-round handy-man to both King and Government.
Balfour had the good sense to see that among his many gifts
was a quite remarkable capacity as organizer and administrator
and, though he was entirely without military experience,
appointed him to be one of a junta of three to reorganize
the army after the South African War. Out of that came the
establishment of the Committee of Imperial Defence, of which
he was to the end of his life the one permanent member;
and the accumulation of much material which was placed at
Haldane's disposal for the great reorganization of 1907.
When the Territorial Army was established, he became
Chairman of the London County Association, and could not
have worked more zealously in that capacity if it had been
his whole business in life. I speak from knowledge, for he
procured my election to that body as a co-opted member,

and I am still after thirty years Chairman of its Recruiting Committee.

4

My own relations with him in these years fitted in with his general scheme. At that time there was no regular means of communication between the Government and the Press. It was understood and thought proper that Ministers should communicate with *The Times*, but all communications with other papers had to be disguised and were thought to be slightly improper. Esher was not at all of this opinion. He thought that Opposition papers like the *Westminster Gazette* ought to be informed about matters which concerned the whole country, impending treaties, naval and military policy; and with Lansdowne's consent he conveyed to me the general outlines of the British-Japanese Alliance of 1902, and of the British-French Entente of 1904, a week or a fortnight before they became public. In the same way he used me quite frankly to convey from the Government side to the Opposition leaders facts which, in his view, ought to be common knowledge to both parties. There was a certain give and take in these matters, for he thought it equally important that King Edward should be kept in touch with opinion in the Liberal party, and I was able to help him occasionally in this part of his self-imposed task.

When King Edward died it was supposed that Esher would disappear, and indeed for a time he seemed to lose a little of his accustomed composure and cool judgment. In the stress of the Parliament Act he was, for once, more royalist than the King, and appears from his diary to have given advice which the King was too wise to follow. This for a time jeopardized his special position as liaison officer between the Crown and the Government, but he went on indefatigably with his work with the Territorials and the Committee of Imperial Defence, never wavering in his view that war was coming, and that we should need to have an instantly-ready army of 150,000 men to dispatch to France. Looking to his activities from 1902 onwards, the fact that we had such an army and that it was ready must to a considerable extent be set to his credit.

When the War came, he was once more the handy-man at everyone's disposal. The Government used him, the French used him, the soldiers used him. When anyone went to France he met Esher; Esher in a uniform apparently of his own design which caused much speculation. Was it the uniform of "the Constable of Windsor Castle," the position which he now occupied? Was it the symbol of the Committee of Imperial Defence, or something appertaining to the Order of the Bath? Whatever it was, no one grudged it. As usual, he was ready to go anywhere and do anything. When there was trouble with the French he would go and talk to Joffre; when there was friction between British Commanders he would smooth it out; when it had to be broken to the Commander-in-Chief that he was to be superseded, who could do it so tactfully and considerately as he? If there was anywhere I wanted to go, or anyone I wanted to see on my visits to the French front, Esher could always arrange it for me. Being the son of a French-speaking mother, he was perfect in the language and soon made himself almost as much at home among French statesmen and politicians as British. Once more, when it came to the test, there was no one with quite the same range of accomplishments.

But the first two and a half years of the War about exhausted his usefulness. Tempers got frayed, and however accomplished a smoother might be, it was impossible for him to keep on even terms with all the people who were quarrelling with one another. He had got wrong with Kitchener; Asquith grew impatient with him; he was supposed—quite wrongly I believe—to be up to some sort of mischief. When Lloyd George took control he faded out of the picture; the quarrel between G.H.Q. and Downing Street was beyond all smoothing, and Esher wisely did not try. Indeed, what could be done between the Prime Minister who was persuaded that he could win the War by moving the British army to the

Balkans or planting it on the road via Laibach to Vienna, and the Commander-in-Chief who was convinced that, if the Prime Minister had his way, the Germans would win the War? Esher advised his friend Douglas Haig to be a little more diplomatic in his dealings with Downing Street, but the gulf was beyond bridging, and he ceased to try.

The Esher Journals and Letters will probably be to a future generation what the Greville and Malmesbury Memoirs were to the last. But as a diarist, Esher was far more accomplished than either of his predecessors. Together with a mass of material bearing on politics, the history of the army and the constitutional struggles of these years, he presents a unique picture of the vanished world of London society in the last years before the War. He was widely read, wrote vividly, loved music, and was never happier than in the company of actors and actresses. Through it all he was a devoted husband and father, and if ever there were perfect relations between father and son, they were between him and his son Maurice, who edited the first two volumes of his diaries, but unhappily died before seeing them in print. Much as has been written about King Edward, there is no better portrait of him than that which paints itself in this record. We see the King in his circle—sociable, irascible, fundamentally good-humoured and warm-hearted, thoroughly enjoying life, keeping touch with all sorts and conditions of people, but without compromising the dignity of the monarchy. If a modern Sovereign is permitted to have a favourite, he could hardly have chosen a better one than Esher. Of very few King's favourites could it be said, as was said of him, that he never took advantage of the position for his own profit. I believe that Esher rendered great and lasting service to the country in the course of his long and active life.

IV

ALFRED KEOGH

WHEN the War ended there were speeches in Parliament commemorating the great soldiers; peerages were bestowed on them, and the more famous received large grants of public money. No one grudged them these rewards, but in the meantime there had slipped from the scene, unnoticed and unhonoured, the one man whose glory it was to have saved life and mitigated suffering in this terrible welter of death and wounds. I speak of Sir Alfred Keogh, the Director-General of the Army Medical Service, who lived in a modest retirement and failing health until his death in August, 1936. If a man's services are to be measured by the number of lives he saved, Keogh would easily, I think, head the list for his generation.

For, cruel and terrible as were the death and suffering inflicted by the Great War, scores of thousands are living today who, but for this man's efforts, would have been numbered among the dead. He it was who, working with Haldane, organized the service for the wounded and the careful measures for sanitation and hygiene which made the British Army an example in this respect to all others in the War.

In the South African War the death-rate from disease was appalling. In the Great War it was almost negligible in the British Army. If for that alone Keogh would deserve to be remembered. The preliminary work which assured this result was done for both the Expeditionary Force and the Territorial Army in the years 1908-12, when he was serving his first term as Director-General. At the end of that time he left the War Office and was appointed Rector of the Imperial

College of Science—an appointment which testifies to the regard in which he was held by the scientific world.

When the War broke out he took service as a volunteer with the Red Cross at Rouen, and there he waited in growing impatience to see the medical units which he had formed at work in France. Week after week passed, and they did not appear. His successors, who were well-meaning but unimaginative, had worked out a scheme for evacuating the wounded on the assumption that the railways would work as in peace time and enable them to be taken across the Channel and delivered to base hospitals in England within twenty-four hours of their receiving their wounds.

The reality was far otherwise. The so-called hospital trains, really horse-trucks in which men were slung one above another, were taking anything from eighty to one hundred hours to get to the coast, and wounds were being terribly aggravated by the torture and suffering of this kind of transport.

I have told in another book the story of a self-appointed mission to France which my wife and I undertook just after the battle of the Marne, on hearing of this breakdown in the medical service. My wife had for the previous sixteen years made herself responsible for a little fifteen-bed hospital by the sea at Tankerton for the treatment of wounds which had failed to heal after operations in the London Hospital, and she had learnt the facts or the alleged facts from her medical friends in London. For this particular purpose she had the great advantage of actual experience in nursing which had taught her the difference between "healthy" and "unhealthy" wounds, and she was able to obtain sufficient professional backing to save us from the imputation of being amateurs unused to war, who had lost their nerve on the first sight of its inevitable horrors. After a week spent in timing hospital trains, visiting such hospitals as there were, consulting doctors and surgeons, and going out with the ambulance service organized by the Americans in Paris, we came back with a carefully documented report and laid it at once before Kitchener and members of the Government. Kitchener needed some convincing, but when convinced, he acted with his usual promptitude, and within three days Keogh had been recalled from France and was back at his place at the War Office.

Somebody else would no doubt have been the agents of this necessary business a little later, if it had not fallen to us, but it established an intimacy between Keogh and ourselves which lasted to the end of his life. He sometimes stayed with us, and often spent his evenings with us during the four years of the War, and we were able to see the great medical service, of which he and Haldane had laid the foundations, growing under his hand. The chain of services from the surgeon's dug-out in the trenches to the casualty-clearing stations and hospitals in France, and finally to the military hospitals at home, all stages being linked up with ambulances, hospital trains and hospital ships, was a miracle of smooth-working organization, and its expansion to meet the needs of the immense improvised army which was shortly put into the field little less than a work of genius.

It was at first far from easy to convince the French that this provision was necessary. They said that we were pampering our wounded and providing a service which was beyond their means and would cause discontent in their army when compared with ours. But Keogh was ready with rigid proof that everything he required was necessary to keep the wastage of the army within bounds. Humanity apart, horse-boxes in which light wounds were infected with fatal gas gangrene were infinitely more expensive than the most luxurious hospital trains. The argument went on all through the autumn of 1914, but before the winter came everyone was convinced.

As time went on, Keogh gave me the opportunity of seeing both the French and the British medical services through all their stages from the front line (at least in the French front line, for the British would not have civilians in trenches) to the casualty-clearing stations and base hospitals;

and in the meantime my wife's little hospital at Tankerton was expanded to a fully equipped military hospital of 350 beds, of which she was appointed Commandant. Keogh came several times to Tankerton, and certain experiments which he wished to try out on a small scale were made there. When I went to France he sometimes gave me little commissions; for instance, I was to inquire about a new treatment for burns called "ambrine," which was being used in the French service. He prepared the way, for when I got to Paris I found a brief note from the French authorities to say that a car would fetch me the next morning to a hospital twenty miles distant, where I should see the twenty worst burns in the French army dressed with ambrine. I spent a miserable night wondering whether I could stand up against this test, but it was one of the strange things about war that it steeled you to sights which made you sick and faint in ordinary times. I survived the test, and learnt the technique by practising with my own hands on a terribly burnt back, and brought back a large sample of the specific for delivery to the British medical service.

In this way Keogh had his eyes open all over the field, being totally free from professional prejudice, and ready to take and test any new thing, regardless of the credentials of those who brought it, if only it offered a slight chance of alleviating suffering. Nothing in these years proved more useful to him and the country than his touch with the scientific world through his position as Rector of the Imperial College of Science. An ordinary medical department might have been stunned and baffled by the sudden emergency presented to it by the German gas attack at Festubert in March, 1915. The cry went up for an instant means of protection; it was feared that the whole defensive system might break down if it were not found at once. Keogh knew exactly what to do and where to look. He called to his professors at the Imperial College and they were on to it from the first moment, working day and night, risking their lives on experiments which had to be rushed without any of the precautions which might have been taken if there had been time. For the next three days the anxiety was terrible, but Keogh was quiet and confident. He knew his professors, he could ask them to take any risk, he was sure that they would find the counter before the end of the week. And they did find it, not only for the British army but for all armies. In a short time gas masks were going out by the million to all fronts, even to the Russian. There was a general impression in those days that England was behind other nations in applied science, but Keogh never would admit it. He was sure that his professors would be equal to anything, if they were put to the test, and he was right.

Having an equal footing in the medical world and the world of applied science and research, he was in a unique position to bring all under one roof for the service of the army. As the original R.A.M.S. was expanded to bring in the civilian surgeons and physicians, there was none of the friction which was predicted, or which might have been expected if the supreme control had been in clumsier or less efficient hands. All were merged in one service in which the ruling spirit was that of scientific medicine and surgery, seeking only the one object of curing wounds and relieving suffering. That research should go on all the time, that specialists should be used to the utmost advantage in the general team work, and the wounded be assigned (after the first stage) to specialist hospitals in which their particular injury would receive the best treatment at the most experienced hands, were principles on which Keogh worked throughout.

He would have been the last to claim the sole credit for the result. It was a co-operative effort which redounded enormously to the credit of the medical profession and its most distinguished men. But Keogh had the great faculty of enlisting cheerful service in all who worked with him. His own spirit was so loyal and modest, and so entirely disinterested, that self-seeking and self-advertisement could not live in his presence.

As the War went on the medical service worked so smoothly

45

that the army and the public came to take it for granted, and
knew little of the incessant planning and scheming or the
elaborate preparation against emergencies that it required
To a certain extent the great standstill of trench warfare
simplified the problem, but no one knew from day to day
when the tide of war might turn, or how it might flow
when it did turn. Casualty-clearing stations and hospitals
might have to be picked up and transferred miles in a night,
either might be bombed or shelled; all sorts of unforeseeable
emergencies had to be met in an orderly way. There were
no precedents, nothing like it had been seen in previous wars;
all wars had been attended with breakdowns and scandals in
the treatment of the wounded. It would be too much to
say that there were none in the Great War; but there were
very few, and hardly any of those few were within the
jurisdiction of the British medical service. Taking it from
first to last, that service was a triumph of organization, and
in certain respects—especially its provision of trained women
nurses—superior to any in the other armies. Nothing bore
the test of war better than the expansible skeleton organization
which Keogh was mainly responsible for building up between
the years 1908 and 1912.

When the test came he had just the qualities needed for a
great Director-General of this humane service—warm heart
and quick sympathy combined with courage and coolness
resourcefulness and complete freedom from red tape. On one
occasion in the Dardanelles campaign, when he was distracted
with anxiety about the evacuation of the wounded, he let me
take the whole War Office file and carry it to Balfour, who
was First Lord of the Admiralty. Instant measures were
necessary; I could explain it in five minutes, the official
routine would have taken ten days. I suppose Balfour ought
to have put me under arrest, but he was grateful and under
standing and eight days were saved. I was told afterward
that the affair came to the knowledge of the Dardanelles
Commission, and that the late Field-Marshal Lord Nicholson
expressed himself in high language about the conduct of the

Director-General in letting secret and confidential War Office documents pass into the hands of an irresponsible journalist. Suppose I had dropped it between Whitehall and Carlton Gardens, suppose I had let it pass into the hands of the enemy, suppose—most monstrous of all—I had conveyed its contents into the *Westminster Gazette*! The military imagination boiled at the thought of possible calamities only just averted by some unexpected—and never to be expected again—special Providence. The Director-General smiled and said he would do it again.

It has been said that the world knows nothing of its greatest men—which all depends on what is meant by "great" and "greatest." But it very often knows little of its most useful and helpful men, and Keogh certainly was one of these. If one were trying to enumerate the men who helped "the unknown warrior" to win the War, he, assuredly, would rank high among them. Had the army been devastated by disease as in the Crimean or South African Wars, had the wastage from wounds been anything like as great as in these former wars, it is quite probable that the War would not have been won. The toll was terrible enough, but all its horrors would have been far exceeded if the losses from disease and wounds had been on anything like the same scale relatively to the numbers engaged as in the wars of the previous century. That they were not so was largely due to Keogh, to his careful preparation in time of peace and his masterly handling of the system he had built up in the stress of wars. I saw most of the great Generals, British and French, in these years, but when I look back on the War, the figure which is most associated with it in my memory is that of Keogh, the chief repairer of its damage.

A grateful country awards his widow a pension of £187, 10s. a year.

MYRON HERRICK

IN January, 1928, I had the unusual honour of being invited to a great banquet given by the American Union Club in New York, and, bar the French Ambassador, I think I was the only non-American present. The banquet was in honour of Myron Herrick, then on the eve of returning for his last spell as American Ambassador in Paris, and my title to be present was that I knew something about Herrick which no one else in that great gathering knew, and a quarter of an hour was assigned to me to tell my tale.

Towards the end of September, 1914, after the battle of the Marne, my wife and I went to Paris on the errand which I have described in speaking of Sir Alfred Keogh. We some-how rushed the guard and got into Paris by a roundabout route, but being there we found ourselves helpless. The centre of the city was a desert, all the ways out were blocked, except to those holding special passes; the British Embassy was closed, even the British Consulate had shut its doors. My newspaper card as editor of the *Westminster Gazette* produced a polite wariness on the part of the French police and military authorities. Newspapers were under suspicion; there was a ban on correspondents; how had I avoided it, and in any case what was I doing there? I was a person to be watched, not aided and abetted.

Then someone said "try the American Ambassador," and we made our way to the Chancellory of the American Embassy. There we found a crowd of frightened people—men, women and children, refugees of all nationalities—who had got stranded in Paris and were imploring the Ambassador's aid to get out. The Germans had been beaten off for the time being, but no one knew when they would come back, and the sound of their guns and the droning of their aeroplanes was heard by day and night. By a common impulse these people had drifted to the American Embassy, which alone was open and at work in the diplomatic wilderness. Herrick and his staff were literally working in their shirt-sleeves, doing all the work of all the Embassies, keeping their doors open at all hours, and, much more difficult, being patient, courteous and kindly in circumstances which might well have taxed the serenest tempers.

The other Ambassadors had been instructed by their Governments to follow the French Government to Bordeaux. Herrick too had been instructed, but he had ignored his instructions. His argument was a simple one. The belligerents were bound to go; it was their business to keep in touch with the French Government; and in any case they could not run the risk of being captured if the Germans entered Paris. But why should he go? There were thousands of Americans in Paris, some of them very poor people who were obliged to stay. His duty was to stay with them and see that they got all the protection that was due to neutrals if the Germans should break through, and perhaps, as a disinterested observer representing the most powerful neutral, put a check to "frightfulness" if the Germans should be tempted to it. "If the Germans come," he told Galliéni, the Military Governor of Paris, "I will be at the gates to meet them, and I will tell them that I represent a people of a hundred and twenty millions and am here to watch." He had a plan to put an American citizen to reside in the Louvre and in every museum and treasure-house in Paris, and he had a little *affiche* printed which, in case of need, he had intended to nail on their doors:

SAUVEGARDE

AVIS

est donné par l'Ambassadeur des États-Unis d'Amérique que le local situé à Paris...........................
est occupé par M...................................

de nationalité Américaine, et, de ce fait, se trouve
SOUS LA PROTECTION DU GOUVERNEMENT DES ÉTATS-UNIS.

En conséquence, l'Ambassadeur demande que les
Américains habitant ledit lieu ne soient pas molestés
et que les objets s'y trouvant soient respectés.

L'Ambassadeur,
MYRON T. HERRICK.

In the meantime he and his admirable wife, who stayed
with him, had induced a large number of the wealthy,
luxurious and pleasure-loving American colony to stay.
As they came to him applying for their passports he said,
"Certainly you shall have your passport; it will be ready
for you at four this afternoon, if you will come again and
fetch it, but you have some hours to think, and please think.
God Almighty has put in your way the one chance you may
have in all your life of justifying your existence. You, Mr. A.,
can enlist in our American ambulance corps, and you, Mrs. B.,
have a place waiting for you in our hospital at Neuilly, where,
if you can only scrub a floor or make a bed, we want you
urgently. And if you don't like these jobs you can just
stand by and help some poor family to keep itself fed and
look after the children." When the afternoon came, a very
large number had decided to stay. It will always be to the
credit of the American Colony that its principal members sat
through these nerve-racking weeks when Paris seemed doomed
and only inch by inch the invading tide was turned back.

In these days the threat of "frightfulness" was a large and
deliberate part of the German strategy, and, in common with
all the neutral Ambassadors, Herrick had been warned by the
German Government that it was preparing punishment for
Paris in which it would be impossible to distinguish between
enemy and neutral. When it was learnt that he had determined to stay, these warnings were redoubled with no doubt
the deliberate intention of using him to spread panic. Shells
and bombs were to be poured on the city in incredible
quantities, horrors till then unknown were in preparation,

Paris was to be destroyed if it refused to surrender. In view of what happened afterwards these can scarcely be called idle threats, however much they may have been painted up to produce the desired effect. Herrick declined to play the part evidently assigned to him. He received all these warnings with composure and kept them all to himself. During the terrible weeks from the beginning of the Retreat till the Germans were thrust back beyond the Aisne, he was one of the great calming and reassuring influences, splendidly representing his country, and incidentally doing no small service—within the bounds of neutrality—to British and French. Among our American friends in these evil days Herrick, and with him that very gallant lady, his wife, whose labours at this time laid the seeds of fatal illness, deserve a warm place in our remembrance.

Herrick immediately gave us everything we wanted—a car and driver, armed with the white passes which enabled us to go everywhere and find out exactly what we wanted. On his recommendation I went out by night with the American ambulance corps, then working between Paris and the front, striving heroically to fill the gaps in the official medical service. By this time the whole American Colony had been mobilized under his guidance for ambulance and hospital work. Their hospital at Neuilly, working under incredible difficulties, bore terrible evidence of the medical needs of the fighting army. Herrick himself did not claim to be an expert in these medical matters. He blamed no one; he passed no judgment, but he put us in touch with the most competent medical authorities and begged us to go and see and form our own opinion.

On one of these days the first bomb was dropped from an aeroplane on Paris, and Herrick was very nearly the first victim. It fell within a few yards of where he was walking on his way back to the Chancellory after lunch. I had an appointment with him about this time, and followed a few minutes later and found him just finishing a dispatch which he passed over to me to read. I have forgotten its exact terms, but it has remained in my memory as a little master-piece of grave irony about the methods of modern war. I have heard him in after days, when we were discussing these times, express a mild wonder whether the killing of the American Ambassador by a German bomb in the first weeks of the War might not have been a greater service to humanity and the cause of the Allied and Associated Nations than any that he had been able to render. The occasion is marked in my memory as the great divide between the old warfare and the new. Up to this time very few people had seriously believed that the Germans would drop bombs on a defenceless city. They might bluster and threaten in the vain idea of intimidating the French people, but when it came to the point they would never venture to do it. Incredulity and anger were the immediate consequences. Herrick's advice to the Allies was on no account to retaliate in kind; he was shrewd enough to see that, as then practised, bombing exasperated without intimidating the enemy.

When I next passed through Paris the British Embassy and Consulate had been reopened, and Herrick's labours had to that extent been relieved. Grey had, in the meantime, thanked him warmly in a personal letter for his services to British subjects, and the British Government had presented him with a handsome service of plate. This gave him enormous pleasure; all the pleasure, he explained to me, that he could "possibly express within the bounds of neutrality." He was, I think, a little more discreet about these "bounds of neutrality" than his colleague in London, Walter Page. His sympathies were written all over him; you saw them in his face, you heard them in his voice, but he did not break in on the sequestered impartiality of Washington with eloquent expressions of his opinion. "You must remember," he used to say, "that according to the official instructions of my Government, I have to be neutral in thought." There was no mistaking the accent on "official."

The French came to love him, and well he deserved it. There never was more genuine grief for a foreigner in France than when he passed away. He was a very ill man—barely recovering from two serious operations—when he came for the last time to Paris. But he was still the splendidly handsome upstanding figure whom one had known fourteen years earlier, outwardly the perfect model of what an Ambassador should be, inwardly one of the kindest, simplest and wisest of men. His place is in the highest rank of Americans who served their country in these years.

VI

T. W. DUNN

(Address in Bath Abbey, Oct. 1932, on the unveiling of a Memorial Tablet to T. W. Dunn, formerly Headmaster of Bath College, who died at Cambridge, Oct. 7, 1930, aged 94.)

THERE are some teachers whom their pupils outgrow—to whom they look back as a mere episode in their lives and whom they remember with an indulgent and even half-humorous memory. There are others who are an abiding influence and presence in the minds of those whom they taught. These do rare and lasting service to their time and generation, and their works live after them. Of such was Thomas William Dunn, to whom in the Abbey Church of the City in which he did his life's work, we, his old pupils, are privileged to pay a debt of piety and gratitude today.

On such an occasion we search our memories for the dominant characteristic of our old Headmaster, and to me it is always the intensity of his character. Nothing in my early years remains more vividly in my memory than my first impression of him when he came to Bath in the year 1878. I was then fifteen years old. He was totally unlike any other teacher into whose hands I had fallen up to this time. He had none of the recognized marks of the trade—the starched dignity, the aloofness, the order-must-be-kept attitude which was thought proper in a headmaster in those days. He was vivid, original, intimate; he moved swiftly, gesticulated freely, flashed into sudden fervours of speech which burnt into the memory. All the tedium of forced learning seemed to vanish at his touch. There was no lesson which he did not contrive to make interesting; the least promising might start a train of thought which led to a fascinating soliloquy. Every hour spent in class with him became an adventure. No one knew, least of all he, where it might lead; he followed his thought with the flattering assumption that his boys could keep pace, though it took them from Greek grammar to the philosophy of Plato, and ended in a disquisition on the origin of species.

At the end of it all what most remains in my memory after more than fifty years is the unceasing debate which went on in the old school—in the classroom, in the School-house, in the Headmaster's study. He encouraged you to come out with your crudest thoughts, and suffered argument and even contradiction with a patience that bridged the gulf of years between boy and man, and made him the friend even more than the schoolmaster. And then at the end of the week he would gather it all up in some fervid discourse in the School Chapel. I would claim for my old school-master, especially in this place, that the foundation of his teaching was always religious. If ever his anger was stirred it was at the removal of the boundaries between right and wrong, or at any facile casuistry which might give a veneer to doubtful or shady practice. It was dangerous to come to him with even a hint of what the man of the world might think pardonable duplicity. "You wince and blush," he would say, "I see your conscience in your face." He would analyse conscience in a philosophical way, trace its roots and developments in its human framework, but always for him it remained something solemn and absolute, something for which a man was answerable to God.

With all his discursiveness he was the most practical of men. You had to know your lesson, and there was no evading him about that. Though he ascended to the clouds, he would always come down in time to be quite sure that the particular task prescribed had not been shirked; and anyone who thought otherwise was soon undeceived. He was an exacting teacher, with the passion for accuracy of the Cambridge scholar, and he would have you understand that the intellectual conscience was not far removed from the moral, that slovenliness and inaccuracy in the one sphere were very likely to be associated with carelessness and untruthfulness in the other. I own I have never felt quite the same sense of shame at any other literary offence as when convicted by Dunn of a grammatical blunder or a false quantity. But it was a fine lesson, and to know that that eagle eye was still on me has often been a steadying thought in the thousand and one temptations of after years. Among his many exhortations two specially have dwelt in my mind all through these years; one, to throw the whole of yourself into the task before you, τὸν προκείμενον πόνον, and not be always worrying and wool-gathering about what is to come after—which is the only condition on which people pursuing certain occupations—journalism, for example—can live at all; the other, never to say that you had forgotten when you had failed to do something he had told you to do. "Forget—pitiful excuse. *Quod curat meminit*. Never say that to me again."

It was, I think, the secret of his influence that he never dissociated the intellectual from the moral. At all hours of the day and whatever the subject matter, he was teaching his pupils the art of living, teaching them integrity, loyalty, disinterestedness; teaching by his own example, which was one of the purest devotion to his pupils, to the School, to his idea of education. If he valued the public-school spirit and tried to keep it constantly alive in the comparatively small numbers of Bath College, it was because he saw in it the symbol of devotion to a cause and the means of cultivating the loyalty to institutions, and finally to the public weal, which he held to be one of the main purposes of the good life. To betray or deceive your fellow-men for your own profit was, he kept telling us, the greatest of all crimes; the good man would take all risks and make all sacrifices rather than be false to his conscience, his beliefs, his idea of duty to God and country. The Memorial which hangs opposite the Tablet we are unveiling today is its own witness to the fruit of this teaching, but in many a humbler sphere it has been a sheet-anchor to his old pupils when, as happens to most at some time or other in their lives, they have had to make the choice between self-interest and their sense of right.

Dunn himself was uncompromising in this choice. His ideal of education was part of his conscience, and he fought for it to the end regardless of his own interest or the persuasion of practical people who begged him to make terms with the popular demand for utilitarian studies. He belonged, let it be admitted, to a generation in which the claims of science to be an integral part of education were very imperfectly recognized and in which the teaching of it in schools deserved a good deal of what the classical teachers alleged against it. But Dunn was no mere pedant of Latin and Greek. He saw in the ancient languages a unique instrument for training the mind, combined with a literature which took you to the fountain-head of modern thought, which was food for the mind and music to the ear. He loved good literature and was a sworn foe of the cheap and vulgar, and he lost no opportunity of training the taste of his pupils. But above all, he had in view a certain culture which should make the best of the thinking faculty, and make it in the end more useful even in the practical business of life than if it had been absorbed from the beginning in the art of bread-winning.

The conflict between these ideas of education goes on incessantly and will not be settled in our time. We may claim for our old Headmaster that he made a great stand for a noble ideal, and look back on the record of the School under his guidance with pride and gratitude. Necessarily, our thoughts are tinged with sadness because the thing he made has passed away. Its very excellence and its dependence on the personality of one man always threatened it with that fate. But all good work has an eternal value, and he laboured ever as in the great Taskmaster's eye. We who profited by his labours are here today to thank God who sent him to do this work, and to say that we remember.

VII

EVERYMAN

*(On the Dedication of the Tomb of the Unknown Warrior,
November 11, 1920)*

AT last we have found him—the man who won the War—
and the whole nation proclaims that he is without peer or
rival. Millions of words will be outpoured from newspapers
and pulpits, in the endeavour to express what he is, what he
means, what in his person we honour, and all will fall short
of what we feel about him. He is each and all of the
eight hundred thousand that laid down their lives, husband
to every widow, son to every parent, brother to every sister.
He died at every hour of every day of all the four years of
the nation's agony. He is the lost that was found, and in
him are all the nameless and unnumbered dead.

Memories of him crowd in on me. I see him on his way
to the trenches, chaffing his pals, swinging his legs in the
lorry which would be a veritable tumbril to the faint-hearted.
I see him marching with the discipline of the old soldier,
though his khaki is new, and singing as he goes; I see him
shaving before a cracked mirror at the door of his dug-out,
with the shells bursting on the hillside; and at all odd
moments brushing, cleaning, washing, polishing, so that he
may go smart, as a soldier should, in this world of blood and
vermin. I see him shattered and blood-stained, waiting on
his stretcher for the surgeon and still smiling. I see him
behind the lines, petting the children, chaffing the girls, taking
his French lesson; giving cigarettes to the German prisoner.
I see him at all times running to help, when the lorry is bogged,
or the horse down, or the shell has fallen.

Raked by machine-guns, blasted by shells, ploughing
through mud, holding grimly to the shattered trench, he
"does his bit," and that is all he wishes you to say about him.

PART II

POLITICS AND HISTORY

I

THE OLD POLITICS AND THE NEW

I

MUCH reading of what is called "left-wing literature" has set me thinking about the differences between past and present, and especially about the differences between the young men of my time and those of the present time. Youth would be very unadventurous if it were not in revolt against its elders, and there is no possible complaint to be made on that ground. *Et nos in Arcadia viximus.* We, too, were of the same disposition. Yet except on the assumption that youth must always be right and age wrong, something may be learnt by comparing the kinds and qualities of the youthful revolts at one time and another, and I am tempted to put down a few thoughts on that subject. If in some respects these take the form of a criticism by an old man of the ideas of young men, perhaps for once this reversal of the usual practice may be permitted as a contribution to debate.

Certain things strike one at the outset. We in the former time were stay-at-homes and kept our noses to the domestic grindstones; the young moderns are all over Europe, hob-nobbing with international revolutionaries in Moscow, Paris and Vienna, and bringing back news of the latest fashions in advanced thinking—fashions which incidentally make old Liberals look dreadfully dowdy. The moderns revel in abstractions and generalizations; we grovelled in the concrete. Their interest is in theories and doctrines; we wanted to know the facts. We listened respectfully to all the political theorists, heard our teachers dissect Socialism and Marxism, invited Henry George, William Morris and Ruskin to talk to us, and then turned to Arnold Toynbee, Alfred Marshall,

61

Canon Barnett and Charles Booth, who urged us to go and see for ourselves how the poor lived and whether we could do anything to help. Henry Smith, the famous mathematician, had said in his caustic way that an Oxford undergraduate's idea of a working-man was a hasty generalization from his scout (*i.e.* the servant appointed to wait on him in College), and we felt the sting of this gibe. In the next few years hundreds of us were living in Toynbee Hall and other University settlements, serving on Boards of Guardians, helping in relief work in the black winters of distress, doing our little bits in Charles Booth's great Survey of London Labour and Life, lending a hand to the dockers in their strike, organizing and leading Boys' Clubs. We did not pride ourselves that we were changing the social system, but we did make a great many friends among working-people, and they on their side taught us a good many things which it was useful for us to know.

In what way useful I may perhaps illustrate from my own experience, egotistical as it may seem. After a certain apprenticeship of the kind described, I went to Hull as the editor of a morning paper. My first thought was to get knowledge of the condition of the working-people in that city, and, following my Toynbee Hall preceptors, I got hold of the recent annual reports of the Medical Officer of Health. I found that in these, the Medical Officer, an excellent and courageous man, had year by year for several years past reported that 10,000 houses were "unfit for human habitation." The next step, following the same guides, was to discover where these houses were and to focus public opinion upon them. I found two other helpers, a clergyman and a doctor, and between us we visited and took notes of about half the numb⸱⸱, fair samples in every district. This took us most of our spare time during the next two years. But at the end of it we were so well primed that I was able to make a frontal attack on the slum-owners, without fear of the law of libel. In this way we got a very considerable slum demolished and a good many other of the meaner houses reconditioned.

The problems of the fishing industry and the conditions of seamen were treated in the same way; and thinking the live cattle trade, as conducted in those days, to be an abomination, I made nasty excursions in the Port Sanitary Authority's launches to meet the in-coming cattle-boats. To know the facts about everything was our ambition.

A little later another group of us started on research work for a rural policy. Charles Booth subscribed handsomely to the expenses, Arthur Acland helped us to map out the ground. We took typical villages in all parts of the country and found correspondents in each who sent us careful accounts of wages and conditions of work, differences of land-tenure, small-holdings (if any), etc. Part of this inquiry was historical, and one of our number (Dr. Slater) examined all the Enclosure Acts that we could discover, and subsequently wrote what is, I believe, still the standard work on this subject. I was the head-centre for the village correspondents and was to have written a book on the modern conditions to follow the historical part. Here disaster befell me. . . . I did write between fifty and sixty thousand words, but lost the MS. in moving house. However, the material survived, and was carefully summarized and much of it subsequently used in the Land Reports of the Liberal party.

By this time I had moved to London and become editor of the *Westminster Gazette*. I now had at my disposal a body of writers, some of them living in East London, who were able to deal from first-hand knowledge with the whole group of subjects commonly called social. Massingham, as editor of the *Daily Chronicle*, and A. G. Gardiner, as editor of the *Daily News*, were in the same position, and together we brought a steady stream of criticism to bear on existing conditions, accompanied by proposals for their amendment. I do not think I am making any immodest claim for these writers and students if I say that between them they contributed materially to the measures of social reform introduced by the Campbell-Bannerman and Asquith Governments between 1906 and 1913. From that time to this there has been no moment when my wife and I have not been responsible for some practical piece of work which has kept us in touch with working-people, and often the very poorest.

The young men of the left-wing tell me that most of this was waste labour. At the best it was "philanthropy," at the worst it was positively mischievous, since it was bolstering up a social system which was past mending. They have no patience with anyone who is patient with "capitalism." They say that we achieved nothing of importance in our time, that we did but skim and film the ulcerous place. They paint a picture of the proletariat—a word which we should never have ventured to apply to our working friends—under the heel of capitalist oppressors, living a miserable existence as wage-slaves; they will have no light and shade in it; they see nothing but an abomination ripe for destruction.

Now it is impossible for any of us who have been brought up in the way I have described to think of human society in these terms. We too have denounced all sorts of evils and written scathingly about the sins of an acquisitive society, but we know that in the working-class life, which is that of the great majority of human beings, there is a great deal of cheerfulness, happiness·and jollity as well as trouble, sorrow and squalor. We believe it to be capable of great improvement, and we know that it has very substantially improved in our lifetime. In the last forty years the wages of agricultural labour have about doubled and all other wages greatly advanced in real as well as nominal value. Owing to the better earnings of women and boys, aggregate family incomes show an even greater increase. Fifty years ago the fully employed unskilled labourer was receiving substantially less than is now paid to the unemployed, who in those days had no refuge but the Poor Law. Free education, sickness insurance, old age pensions, unemployment insurance have added substantially to higher wages, and through the radio and the cinema, science has brought to the humblest homes pleasures and opportunities of culture undreamt of in former times. At the same time sanitation and medicine have greatly prolonged life and abolished many abominations that were tolerated fifty years ago. All this may be nothing to a revolutionary writer who judges by some romantic standard of his own, but to deny that it has brought a substantial increase of comfort and pleasure to the working-people is to fly in the face of facts, as we of the former generation know them. Nevertheless, it must be denied, if our social system is to be condemned as fit for nothing but the scrap-heap, as our left-wing young men wish us to believe.

2

Holding this opinion they are naturally obsessed with the idea of destroying the things which we hoped to amend and improve. I am almost ashamed to say that over the mantel-piece of the big room at Toynbee Hall were inscribed such simple and homely mottoes as "One by One" and "Fear not to sow because of the birds." Not many of us were orthodox church-goers, and our moderns would, I suppose, call it atavism if I said that Christian ideas were pretty strong within us. The class-war was to us a repulsive thought. We believed in bridging the gulf between classes, not in fomenting strife between them. We wanted the general level of comfort raised to the point at which there would be a fair minimum for all, and we wanted the rich to make all necessary sacrifices for this, but we did not much care if above this minimum there were many degrees of wealth. We were unashamedly gradualists; we thought of society as a growth in which sudden upheavals were, if possible, to be avoided.

There is only one justification for destroying things, and that is to clear the ground in preparation for a new building which shall be nearer to the heart's desire. If they are not insane, those who wish to destroy a given state of society must be extraordinarily confident of their capacity to rebuild. They must be optimists beyond all other optimists. My difficulty with the destructionists is to discover how they intend to rebuild. The Webbs say casu-

E   65

ally in their book on Russia that Marx, the acknowledged master in the art of destruction, neglected to provide the "blue print of reconstruction." For lack of it his leading disciples in Russia plunged that country into a furnace of affliction, while they passed from experiment to experiment. In twenty years they have killed millions and all but exterminated one another in their deadly quarrels about the true revolutionary method. Enormously interesting, say our moderns, and so it is if one can regard Russia as a human laboratory, in which vivisection is legitimate for the advancement of political science. By all means let us learn what we can from the Russian experiment and hope that after twenty years it is beginning to take on the qualities of a peaceful and progressive civilization. But can anyone wish or think it necessary that this country should pass through the same affliction to reach the conclusion that Russia has now reached?

That conclusion is described as a "class-less society," and our moderns habitually speak of this kind of society as the goal of their dreams. If that means getting rid of social snobbery and other false valuations of human worth, it is of course to be desired, but in all other respects it is a tame and insipid ideal which could only be realized if human beings resembled one another as closely as ants and bees. In Russia, which is supposed to be the nearest approximation to this ideal, the grading of classes appears, according to the latest accounts, to be hard and steep. A large and well-paid class of bureaucrats takes the place of capitalists and aristocrats in the old societies; with them or just beneath them are officers in the army, engineers, managers, professional men drawing three and four times the pay of workmen; and skilled workmen twice the pay of unskilled. There are also favoured members of the ruling party enjoying privileges and advantages denied to the great majority who are not members of the party. Among all these, housing, dress and ways of life appear to correspond more or less to the differences of pay and income. Finally, on the other side of a hard line drawn between those who are supposed to belong to the proletariat and those who have not this congenital advantage, are to be found the surviving "bourgeois," all watched by the police and some outside the pale and in very much the same position as the "untouchables" in India.

Bar the intolerance which outlaws the bourgeois, I am not criticizing these arrangements. In fact I do not think it possible for any community to keep alive, let alone progress, unless it recognizes the necessity of different rewards for different services, and accepts the consequences in the social structure of this recognition. But it seems to me that my left-wing friends are under an illusion when they think of a society thus organized as "class-less." The classification may be better or worse, but it is even more intricate and in some respects more rigid, than ours.

As a Liberal, our moderns shock me with the light-heartedness with which they condone and excuse what I call atrocities, if only they are practised in the service of something that they think to be the truth. What they recognize as atrocious when practised by Nazis and Fascists they speak of as regrettable necessities when practised by Communists. In passing to the "class-less" society there must, they say, be a transition stage, when bourgeois opposition and heresy must be stamped out with an iron hand. Dogmatic creeds, whether political or theological, seem to have a peculiarly sadistic effect upon the human mind, but it is surely to be regretted that advanced modern thinkers should be infected by this intolerant cruelty about three centuries after ecclesiastics have been cured of it.

"Class-less" is only one among a multitude of words and phrases which our advanced thinkers employ as if they had fixed and generally accepted meanings, whereas nearly all of them have relative and variable meanings. "Capitalism," for example, is supposed to have a fixed meaning universally understood, whereas the thing indicated is all the time changing its character and in seventy years has so changed that the classical attack on it is largely obsolete. Socialism has never had a precise meaning and is habitually used to cover a great variety of opinions and practices. Communism, so far as it can be distinguished from Socialism, signifies a preference for sudden and violent methods to get rid of the existing order, but its adherents fall into deadly feuds with one another as soon as they seek to give it meaning in a new order. The only thing that Communists seem to have in common is hatred of Fascism, but these two "isms" are so much alike in their methods and even in their results that the differences between them seem more and more to be questions of terminology. On all vital questions relating to the organization of society—on the submission of all to one party, one doctrine, one leader—they are absolutely agreed, and the actual measures they adopt have often a singular resemblance. None of these "totalitarian" states appear to have any political principles. They improvise and invent as they go along, and except that they label their expedients Communist or Fascist, as the case may be, there seems to be no reason why they should be called by these names. A Liberal watches them all with varying emotions. If he must choose, his inclination is to give his vote in favour of the Russian against the German and the Italian experiments, for there are moments when Moscow seems at length to be blazing a new trail towards humanity and civilized progress. But it is generally just at such a moment that Moscow plunges back into some peculiarly odious manifestation of tyranny, as if to keep us reminded that Communism as understood in that country is Tsarism upside down.

I do not wish to dogmatize; I would only ask our advanced young men to think twice before they embrace any of these sects on the supposition that the claims which they make and the phrases they use correctly describe the realities in their respective countries or anything that could be realized in other countries. The old saying that Revolutions devour their children is still dreadfully true, and it seems also to be true that they devour the ideals with which their children started. We may hope that the countries which have been subjected to these ordeals will find salvation in their own way, but it is a puzzle to me that young Englishmen, with all the other alternatives open to them, should go searching for ideals in the dusty soil of revolutionary Russia, or (as another group of young men do) in Nazi Germany or Fascist Italy. The ruthless masters of Russia may yet beat capitalism at its own game of industrializing a peasant people, but if so, it will be by enforcing a discipline beyond anything dreamt of by capitalists upon a people with a serf tradition.

3

Two things specially pull me up in the propaganda of the left-wing parties. One is the disparagement of civil and political liberty which runs through it all. The other is the acceptance, as if it were a proved fact, of the popular slogan "poverty in plenty." Let me take these things in order.

First the disparagement of civil and political liberty. I read the other day an address delivered to a congress of foreign authors by a distinguished novelist and essayist, whom, if he would stick to his last, I should sincerely admire. His theme is freedom, and he begins by telling his audience that "freedom in England is only enjoyed by people who are fairly well off." "For the down and out it does not signify a plate of fish and chips." English freedom, he would have his foreign audience believe, is a branch of English hypocrisy. It is apparently nothing to him that the British workman is secured against arbitrary arrest and concentration camp; that he can form his own Trade Unions and strike against his employers; that he can join any party he chooses, organize and agitate to obtain a change of government; that no government can compel him to work or prescribe his hours and wages, that the provision of a minimum subsistence, if he is out of work, enables him in England, as in no other country, to resist the pressure of employers or of economic circumstances which would otherwise lower his standard of living. Not being a workman, this writer knows nothing of the part which free political activities play in the English worker's life. Never having lived in countries where these

liberties are extinguished, he has no idea of what they mean—
above all, to the down and out—or of the cruel persecutions
which follow when they are suspended or extinguished. I
wish all literary men and left-wing politicians who talk in
this strain could be transported for a time to the countries of
the Dictators and discover what would happen to them if they
permitted themselves to speak, act and write with the freedom
which they exercise as a matter of course in this country.

But what is the "economic freedom" which writers of
this school have in mind—the supposed reality for which,
according to their theory, the workman is offered the fraudu-
lent substitute of political liberty? So far as I understand it,
it is freedom to live without working. Only so can a man
do what he likes and go where he will, choose the ways of
spending time that he finds agreeable and reject those that he
does not. But this free man must be supported by other
people, and he is free only in so far as he is able to command
their services. Others, therefore, must be unfree in order
that he may be free. There are a few rich people at one end
of the scale, and a few tramps, vagrants and beggars at the
other end of the scale, who approximate to this ideal. The
first are usually denounced as parasites by the advocates of
"economic freedom" and figure as the "idle rich" in de-
nunciations from the pulpit and the platform. All the
religions agree that they have the greatest difficulty in getting
into the Kingdom of Heaven. The others—the tramps and
the vagabonds—purchase their freedom by reducing their
wants to a minimum. On this condition they enjoy the
wind on the heath and the open spaces. In so far as they
fail to supply their minimum wants, they too become parasites
and have recourse to workhouses and casual wards for food
and shelter.

The vast majority of mankind are between these two
extremes. They have to earn what they and their families
consume, and are therefore according to the definition
"unfree." They have to attend workshops, offices, shops,
at regular hours, be limited to short holidays at fixed times,

and are chained to certain employments at certain places. The "free time" in which they are their own masters is very short. Nearly all of them at different times—the doctor, the lawyer and the man of business no less than the wage-earner—may be heard complaining that they are "slaves," *i.e.* chained to the necessity of supporting themselves and their families, and sometimes to the self-imposed slavery of making money.

This is life for the vast majority—hard stuff, no doubt, which it is the proper object of politics to make less hard. A better distribution of wealth which may enlarge the spaces of leisure and freedom, the provision of a minimum of subsistence and security which may make it easier for the wage-earner to choose between different kinds of employment, and of pensions which may enable him to retire when he is past work, are the aims of a good social policy. We are as yet, let us hope, only at the beginning of these things. But when we are at the end of them, man will still, according to the definition, be "unfree" and will remain so until he is relieved of the primeval curse of having to work to keep himself alive. If he works for the State instead of for a private employer, he will still in this sense be a slave.

To confuse this kind of necessity with political tyranny is a wilful sophistication. In the mouths of Communists it is generally an excuse for the behaviour of the Russian dictators, whose suppression of civil and political liberty is thus presented as the sacrifice of a worthless imposture for the priceless benefits supposed to be conferred by the new order. If the British workman were foolish enough to yield to this argument, he would find that the "economic freedom" promised him in exchange for civil and political liberty consisted in placing his whole life under the control of dictators, who, since he had no civil rights, would be in a position to compel him to do any work which they prescribed on terms which they laid down, and, if he objected, to consign him to prison, exile or concentration camp, if they were merciful enough to spare his life.

4

A word now about the slogan "poverty in plenty." The acceptance of this as based on proved fact leads to the sweeping simplifications of left-wing doctrine. The world is supposed to be overflowing with good things which it is only prevented from enjoying by the wickedness of the small minority who are called "capitalists." They are the hidden hands, the sinister forces of evil, which create poverty and misery. Abolish them, get rid of the capitalist system, and all will be well. Those who believe this are relieved of the necessity of studying political economy; it is enough for them to denounce the existing social system.

The truth is, as every economic analysis shows, that the world is far short of the things that would be necessary to provide the mass of people with what these writers think of as the good life, and that an immense part, if not the whole of the problem, is to increase the product. To approach this in the rhetorical and sentimental terms which so many of our younger writers employ seems to me worse than useless. It calls for careful and patient analysis of a great many different factors, scientific, political and psychological. There is a rough but adequate test of the state of production in the figures of unemployment. The world lives on what it produces from week to week and day to day, and the maximum of "plenty" at any given moment is what it could produce, if the whole of its working population were employed. In recent years from 8 to 10 per cent. of this population has been unemployed. If all were employed and—a rather doubtful supposition—if the unemployed were capable of producing as much in proportion as those in employment, the output would not be increased by more than this percentage, which would be totally inadequate to provide the desired "good life." If we want practical proof of this proposition we may find it in the recent report of the Brookings Institute of America on "America's capacity for consumption." In this it is stated that it is "far beyond the capacity of the American economic system," working at its maximum, to bring the standard of living for all American families up to what would admit of a "liberal diet"—this according to its definition being what is normally enjoyed by English families of five with incomes of about £400 a year or a little over; and that in 1929, when American industry was working near its maximum, 19,000,000 or 90 per cent. of the whole were short of this standard, and 74 per cent. short of the income necessary to obtain what the investigators define as an "adequate diet."

Modern machinery and mass production have beyond doubt greatly improved the prospect, but they have not yet brought us within sight of satisfying the demands of modern men and women. These demands, it needs to be remembered, are constantly rising. With every advance of education a new idea of well-being is born. With every satisfaction of a want, a new want is created. What the great majority would have accepted as "plenty" sixty years ago is condemned as "poverty" by the great majority today. "Poverty" and "plenty" are not fixed and static, but relative and constantly changing ideas. It is, I think, true to say that the idea of well-being has had an enlargement in our time which is without parallel in any previous period, and that with it has come an awareness of the disabilities of poverty, which is also without parallel. Education and the spread of popular culture have led the mass of people to demand more of life than the producers of commodities are able to supply.

Further, "plenty" under modern conditions is not a simple but an extremely complicated idea. A few countries may be self-sufficing at the sacrifice of certain luxuries, but for the great majority a rising standard of comfort depends on assembling a multitude of products from all over the world, procuring them in their due proportion by the joint effort of producers, merchants, brokers and bankers, and distributing them in such a way that they shall not be deficient in one place and redundant in another.

73

5

Now, if this, or something like it, is the nature of modern economic society, all the simplifications which assume that we shall reach ideal conditions by destroying something called Capitalism and substituting something called Socialism go by the board. We must now return to the patient analysis of the very complicated problem of finding the system which best promotes the production of wealth and its fair distribution. There is a mass of experience, Russian, American, German, Italian, which ought to be examined dispassionately with a view to ascertaining how much of it we could absorb with profit in this country. And since first principles are challenged, these too should be examined impartially in the light of recent facts.

Let me indicate briefly certain things which seem to me to need exploring in this impartial way.

1. The various meanings of the word "property," and the extensions and modifications of it in modern times. How much of it is capable of being redistributed? How much would survive the abolition of the capitalist system and the destruction of the values that it creates? How far is the desire to possess property a necessary incentive to its production?

2. What is the meaning of the supposed distinction between production for profit and production for use, and what justification is there for the relegation of the former to an inferior moral status? Since profit can only be made by supplying people with what they want, is there any moral evil in doing this or any moral advantage when the State supplies what it thinks they want? What substitute can the State provide for the price mechanism of competitive industry as the measure of wants? How could this "free plébiscite of the market" be abolished without a serious curtailment of liberty?

3. As regards wages and conditions of work, is it certain or probable that State monopolies armed with power to

enforce their own conditions will do better for workmen than Trade Unions bargaining with private employers? Do the results in Russia, Germany and Italy, where effective trade-unionism has been abolished, encourage that belief?

4. As regards cheapness, is it certain or probable that a State monopoly, subject to political influences, will produce and be able to sell more cheaply than private industries in competition with one another?

5. As regards regularity of employment, is there anything short of forced labour that the State can do as the sole employer which could not be done equally well by the State in co-operation with private employers through unemployment insurance, etc.? What is the right definition of "unemployment"? Is the Communist or Fascist State entitled to say that it has "abolished unemployment" when it compels men and women to work at tasks and on conditions prescribed by itself, who in non-Communist countries receive unemployment allowances or public assistance without work? From the workman's point of view is there any gain in substituting the former system for the latter?

6. How far can any country obtain abundance for its own people without the co-operation of its neighbours? Can any State, acting by itself, surmount or neutralize the obstacles which tariffs, quotas and currency difficulties place in the way of the exchange of goods?

7. The relation between population and wealth-production. How far is Malthus's law still true? Can production keep pace with an increasing population on a rising standard of comfort? To what extent has the increase of wealth been neutralized by an increase of population or can a rising standard be secured by birth-control? Will there be more to divide between a smaller population, or will a diminishing population check the production of wealth? How far can "planning" proceed in the present state of doubt about the future of population?

8. A "fractional error in planning food-supplies for a whole country starves a multitude who would somehow remain

alive if they were left to fend for themselves." Is this true?
Is it borne out by the experience of Russia?

9. "The Communist State submits to a period of absolutism
as the necessary preliminary to the winning of liberty and
democracy." Is there any reason to believe that liberty and
democracy can be won or regained without the abandonment
of Communism? Is any reconciliation possible between free
institutions and the Communist (and Socialist) idea that
government is a science of which the laws have been discovered
by experts and must be administered by officials?

Such are a few of the questions which need to be explored
before prudent people commit themselves to sweeping changes
in the social system. I believe that a careful exploration of
them would yield positive as well as negative results, and
show us not only what to avoid but what we may with profit
adopt among the new ideas. But rhetoric and sentiment and
the bandying of abstract terms and superficial slogans are no
substitutes for economic thinking. Nor is it any use to be
very angry about everything every day. The great company
of modest hard-working bread-winners, who are the back-
bone of capitalism, are not the thugs and thieves that the
denouncers of the system appear to suppose. Nor is the
workman the sinless victim of their depredations that the
literary Communist imagines him to be. There are sinister
forms of exploitation and sweating which good politics under
any system must endeavour to eliminate. But to ask us to
believe that there is nothing of virtue or value in the method
of producing and distributing, which has been evolved through
centuries of human experience and which, incidentally, has
brought this country to the position of relative prosperity
which it now occupies, is to fly in the face of all probability.

6

The last thing any older man could wish in these days is
to quench the generous emotions of young men. It is to
their credit that they feel strongly about things which are

just causes of indignation. But it cannot be necessary that so much useful energy should be running to waste and even playing into the hands of reactionaries. If one asks why so many European Parliaments have made shipwreck in Europe in recent years, the answer is nearly always the same. It is because the sober Liberal elements in them have been swamped by left-wing politicians who have differed so much among themselves that they have been unable to keep any government in existence for more than a few troubled weeks. In their preoccupation with their ideologies and their differences about their millennial doctrines they have omitted to see that a certain competence in the art of administering and keeping order is the essential preliminary to trying experiments on the social system. When Parliaments fail to keep order, reactionaries walk in and take away the bauble. The reaction to tyranny from an incompetent Communism has been the great calamity of western Europe in recent years.

The British people are too old and too steady to be in any serious risk of this calamity. The worst that is likely to happen to us in this country is that our left-wing politicians may so frighten the electors as to doom us to a long period of "safety first" government, when we greatly need enterprising radical politics. Europe in the last twenty years has offered us terrible examples of the folly of plunging into revolution without any clear ideas about reconstruction. It seems wise to postpone talk about revolution until we are reasonably sure about reconstruction. When we have got to that point, we shall probably have found that revolutions are unnecessary. In the meantime let us beware of idealogues, by whatever name they call themselves. When they are on the warpath they are the most dangerous of human kind.

POSTSCRIPT

An article on this theme published in a newspaper brought me a little avalanche of letters from my juniors, most of them in very unflattering terms. They did not argue with me; they told me—told me what they thought of me, my antiquity, my lack of understanding, my ignorance of the true faith and doctrine. They said that I and my generation either wilfully or ignorantly made ourselves the agents of "capitalist exploitation," and charged us with a "complacent tolerance" of evils to which their eyes have been opened.

Since it is Liberals—"bourgeois Liberals"—and not Conservatives who are supposed to have been the sinners in chief, I am tempted as one of them to "put in," as lawyers say, a brief statement of facts.

Our juniors habitually speak as if the whole of the nineteenth century and the years up to the War were "the Liberal period." The truth is that in the fifty-two years of my working life, the Liberal party was only in power for eleven years, three very troubled years from 1892 to 1895, eight years from 1906 to 1914, when the War extinguished our efforts. If ever a political party "filled the unforgiving minute with sixty seconds' worth of distance run," it was the Liberal party in these years. Fighting every inch of the ground with the House of Lords and the powerful Conservative Opposition it laid the foundations of the democratic finance, graduated income-tax, surtax and death-duties, which now takes more than half the biggest fortunes, and established old-age pensions and the social services. We did not think there was anything servile or unholy in the relations between employers and employed, or that State monopolies administered by officials were likely to give more freedom to the workers; but we did our utmost to guard the legal rights of Trade Unions and to further their efforts to equalize the conditions between the worker and his employer.

When the War ended our place was taken by Socialists, who have broken the continuity of Liberal and Radical politics and called for fundamental and revolutionary changes in the whole social and economic order. So far they have succeeded only in frightening the country and driving it back on "safety first" politics. I would suggest to my juniors that instead of railing at the old Liberal party, they study its history and acquire a little of its competence in the arts of government and administration. If the next time they have the chance of office, they do as much as Liberal Governments did between 1906 and 1914, they will have deserved well of the country.

In the meantime, if I should venture to offer advice to my juniors, the first thing I would say would be that exaggeration defeats itself, if carried beyond the point of a picturesque enlargement of truth. There are, of course, very serious problems of poverty, but to speak as if the British workers, who are four-fifths of the population, are slaves living in slums, exploited by wicked men who cheat them of the wealth that belongs to them, is very unflattering to these workers, or would be, if they were not aware that it is un-true. It is, I believe, the fundamental falsity of these ideas which has doomed the Socialist party to sterility. The great majority of the British workers are not living in slums and are not slaves. A large number of them are owners of property and do not desire a revolution which would abolish property. Looking at revolutions and their results in other countries, the last thing they desire is that this country should be made the subject of similar experiments.

What they do desire is that there should be more property and that it should be better distributed. And what is being brought home to them and to all of us is that in spite of all recent advances, modern production is still far short of satisfying the reasonable demands of modern men and women. When the revolutionary steam and froth has been blown off, we shall return to that problem and seek to dis-cover the social policy which will ensure the best distribution of property and the largest production of things to distribute.

HISTORY AND PROPAGANDA

ALL over Europe today there is a persistent demand by different sects and schools that history shall be turned into propaganda for the theories that they favour. In Germany it has to be rewritten to support the idea of the totalitarian state, and its doctrine of blood and race; in Russia and in Italy it must be subdued to the official creed, Communist or Fascist, as the case may be. In this country Socialist critics dismiss as shallow and superficial all historical writing which fails to confirm their interpretation of events. This in itself is a small matter, but it tends to set a fashion which, I think, ought to be resisted. For if we let it go far, history, or what passes for it, will be cluttered up with a mass of speculation, much of it pretentious and premature, and nearly all colouring and distorting the statement of fact which, when the time comes for it, must be the basis of any sober and useful speculation.

When the time comes for it. These critics do not perceive that for the writer who is dealing with contemporary history, this time cannot be now, or only to a very limited extent. And for a very simple reason. In order to generalize to any purpose he must know the sequels and consequences as well as the antecedents of events, and these are necessarily hidden from him. A certain space before and after the events that are being recorded, a space in which it is possible to see them rising and falling in a certain rhythm, and to make an effort to plot their curve is essential to all theorizing about history. Here a distinction must be made between moralizing and theorizing. The clumsiest of historical writers can moralize—

stop, like a Victorian novelist at the end of a paragraph or a chapter, to improve the occasion—but theorizing in the sense of discovering the master-key to a period is quite a different matter. At the best it is a tricky business. After nearly 2000 years we find historians of the highest competence debating with one another about the causes of the decline and fall of the Roman Empire, and every other year some new theorist appearing on the scene, who claims to have discovered an unsuspected historic or physiographical process which throws all previous theories out of date. This chase after theories is an attractive game which kindles thought and sharpens wit, but it should not be confused with history, even ancient history. What, then, did actually happen is the question to which one returns at the end of all theorizing, and to keep the answer to it clear from generalizers and speculators, and even, I would add, from the distorting medium of genius, is more and more important as the story becomes more complicated. There is compensation here, for events have a mysterious power of telling their own story, if left alone. They even gather a certain volume and majesty which makes it presumptuous to chatter about them.

2

But what are these theories which the historian must convey through his narrative on pain of being dismissed as shallow or superficial? I pick up a review by an advanced thinker of a book of memoirs, and have the good fortune to stumble on one of them at first dip. "Doesn't it occur to him" (*i.e.* the author) says the advanced thinker, "that the War was a direct expression of the effort of world capitalism to transcend the contradictions in which it has become involved?" Why should so extraordinary an idea have occurred to any human being? Being of necessity somewhat familiar with the left-wing literature, I recognize it as a fragment of the liturgy which a neophyte has to recite on being received into the Marxian Church. All the members of this sect are taught to believe that the appearance of things belies their reality. For this purpose they have two principal teachers, Freud and Marx: Freud, who is brought in, often against his will, to show them that the simplest behaviour as they might suppose it to be, is the result of a complex of sinister and generally sexual impulses; and Marx, who proves to them that historical events, however remote they may seem, are manifestations of the evil complex which is called "capitalism." This they proceed to personify and endow with human attributes. They see it fighting with itself, getting tangled up in its own arms and legs and trying to "transcend" them, *i.e.* I suppose to disentangle itself or cut its way out.

Now this thought, whatever it may be worth, is not founded on fact or experience; it is deduced from a supposed historical necessity which requires the institution of capitalism to commit suicide, whatever capitalists may do to keep it alive. As Marx, and still more, as his disciples, have developed this doctrine, it appears to be a compound of Hegel and Calvin, the former contributing the metaphysical idea that positives are dogged by their negatives; the latter the idea of a moral doom which neither prayers nor vows nor any virtue on the part of the unregenerate will enable them to evade. The capitalist in this scheme plays the same part as the sinner in the theological scheme; he is the vessel of wrath, the author of all mischief, public enemy No. 1. His machinations must be unveiled, and even though according to the theory he is the helpless victim of powers beyond his control, no mercy must be shown him.

To minds which accept this teaching there can, of course, be only one explanation of an event like the Great War. It is the fulfilment of the prophecy of their founder and teacher, and if you or I stumble at this idea, so much the worse for you and me. The reviewer I have quoted is so carried away by this thought that he goes the whole length of asserting that the War was—not the metaphorical or symbolical—but the direct expression of the struggles of his monster to "transcend" its contradictions. Where other people see emperors, kings, statesmen, generals and armies, he sees embattled capitalists rushing to the fray in August, 1914, rushing to "transcend their contradictions."

Am I wrong in saying that this is about as meaningless a piece of jargon as was ever packed into the same number of words? There is not a scintilla of evidence to prove that there was any crisis of capitalism in 1914, or that the capitalist had anything to do with the War. If there is anything conclusively proved, it is Norman Angell's thesis that war is ruinous to the capitalist. So far as he operates in other countries than his own, he moves along the lines of least resistance, seeking his profit wherever he can find it. *Qua* capitalist, he prefers co-operation to competition, and would always rather sit down and share any available spoils than fight over them. If he and his kind were left in possession, and economic advantage were the sole or even the dominant human motive, we should be well on the way to making of the world a federal unity overriding national sovereignties and tariff boundaries, employing one currency and living and trading in peace. One of our chief troubles is precisely that when war comes in sight, the capitalist puts off his capitalist character and becomes the same kind of fiercely patriotic citizen as his neighbours. In July, 1914, the capitalists of all countries were imploring their Governments to keep the peace and predicting wholesale ruin if it was broken; at the beginning of August nearly all were shouting for war.

But if I say this or anything like it to an advanced thinker he will be ready for me. He will say that I am merely skimming over the surface of things and showing my ignorance of the profound truth which requires facts and events to be interpreted by contraries. Thus when I speak of capitalists imploring their Governments to keep the peace, I am really supplying proof that they were being driven by an inner libido which had to be satisfied by war. For some minds this idea of a hidden hand, turning things upside down, working impish mischief behind the scenes, unravelling by night what deluded mortals spin by day, has an extraordinary

83

fascination. It gives them an exciting sense of living in a half-magical world in which nothing is what it seems to be, in which dark forces are as actively at work in both the collective and the individual soul as devils and demons were supposed to be in ancient and mediaeval times. In this way modern materialism has come greatly to resemble mediaeval demonology, and its votaries are as angry as the priests of former times if one questions the existence of the demons or devils, with which they have peopled the modern under-world. If we deny them, we only prove our ignorance and superficiality, our failure to dig deep enough into the nature of things.

3

I was once witness of the performance of a water-diviner who was employed to find water on a friend's estate. The rod in his hands made convulsive movements which raised our hopes. But these were damped when he told us that the same result on the rod was produced by a little water near the surface and a great deal of water a long way down. When the rod jerked downwards, it might indicate a brook six feet below the surface or a subterranean river in the bowels of the earth. The only thing certain was that the diviner could never be proved wrong. If you dug a hundred feet or two hundred and failed to find the river, he would still assure you that it was there, though your shallow excavation had failed to reach it.

So it is with these subterranean theories of history. You can never prove them wrong, for however deep you go, most of them, like the miller's daughter in the song, will be deeper still. But in the meantime, while you are tunnelling in these murky depths, you will be very likely to miss the clues and pointers which history offers to the ordinary mind. Take this business of the economic interpretation of history. Why treat it as a disreputable secret lurking behind events, why not approach it simply? From the point of view of history the distinction between politics and economics is

84

quite artificial. The urge for wealth and for territory as a means to wealth, the instinct for defending possessions or acquiring new possessions, the desire to command trade routes and to obtain trade monopolies—these are motives which have been at the back of war and policy from the dawn of history. There is nothing specifically modern about them, and to attribute them to something called "capitalism"— supposed to have come into existence in the last part of the eighteenth century—is manifestly absurd. But undoubtedly the old motives have taken new forms in this industrial age; all through the nineteenth century we may trace a growing sense of urgency and pressure in the competition of governments for "places in the sun." The increase of population was stupendous; the number of available places in the sun was rapidly shrinking; the new nations which had come late on the scene felt that they must be up and doing or for ever be shut out. At the same time, the growth of the Protectionist system in the latter half of the nineteenth century led to the belief that Colonies, which the mother-country could exploit exclusively, were necessary to provide it with food and raw material. The international trader meanwhile was developing a system of world-wide trade which largely offset these exclusive tendencies and provided the world with an extremely efficient self-adjusting mechanism for the exchange of goods. When the Great War broke out, this system was working about as smoothly and efficiently as any human system will, and to restore its structure, shattered by the War, has been the professed object of all the nations since the War, whatever their internal method of government may be.

Again, when we come to the internal economics of a nation and trace the late and gradual emergence of the idea that poverty is a curable evil, new lines of inquiry open up. What are the conditions of wealth and population which promise the largest amount of well-being to the greatest number? How far is private property a necessary condition of efficient production? How far short is the total production

of a country or what it can purchase with its products, of
providing the mass of its citizens with the ingredients of the
good life? Is it probable that the aggregate of wealth would
be increased if the favoured minority of well-to-do people
were dispossessed? What are the different kinds of property
in the modern world and to what extent can they be redistributed without destroying the values attaching to them
under the existing system? What are the causes of booms
and slumps? What part is played by gold and currency?
I do no more than suggest a few chapter-headings. But
merely to set them out is to raise a strong presumption that
they are complex and difficult questions which are very
unlikely to be solved by formulas and theories detached from
knowledge and experience. Least of all are we likely to be
helped if we begin by supposing that all the difficulties inherent in the subject are due to supposititious devils working
behind the scene. Much of what is called advanced thought
is nothing more than intellectual laziness, which falls back
on abstractions to save itself the trouble of thinking things
out. It is so much easier to murmur "public ownership and
control" than to sit down to the problems of banking and
coal-producing; so tempting a short-cut to talk of "capitalism
transcending its contradictions" when the historical causes of
war are in question.

4

All this may be said without in the least disparaging the
contributions to knowledge and opinion which have been
made by the theorists or denying them their place in the
history of modern thought. Marx, in spite of all the violence
and suffering which may be laid to his account, has profoundly stirred consciences about the evils of poverty; Freud
has made real and important contributions to psychology;
Spengler is an occasional illuminant of high value; even
the racial theorists, Gobineau, Lothrop Stoddart, Houston
Chamberlain, have something to tell us, if we read them

with composure. But many of these writers have the peculiar quality of lighting fires in the brains of those who read them uncritically. To these they become masters whose voices proclaim indisputable truth which at all costs must be guarded against error. It is the invasion of government and politics by this kind of "truth" and its apostles which has brought the storms of persecution and intolerance that have raged over Europe in recent years. To keep historical and political writing clear of this infection seems to me a special duty in countries where writing is still free.

It is monism gone mad. There is as little probability of discovering one key to the problems of human society as there is of finding one remedy for the ills of the human body. We may even go most astray when we look for this key in what is called the economic interpretation of history. If there is anything that history teaches it is that man does not live by bread alone. There is a psychological, even a pathological side to the story. There are moments when the world seems to be swept by waves of religious or anti-religious fanaticism, or when some Berserker rage possesses a whole race; other moments when a sudden uprush of Quixotic irrationalism defies all analysis and sends a multitude crusading to some heavenly city. By what external standards shall we explain or justify these movements? I know of none. They belong to the inner nature of man, man the incurable mystic who soars to the heights and falls to the depths and seems perpetually to be in doubt whether he was intended to be God or brute. We are never farther from understanding his history than when we try to reduce it to a bloodless dance of isms and tendencies. Whatever it is, it has all the dynamic, unpredictable and infinitely various qualities of warm-blooded living creatures.

At every turn it presents us with a paradox. To make sense of his political institutions it must be presumed that man believes human life to be of supreme value, and that to protect it and enlarge its possibilities is the aim of the Government. Yet this evidently is the last thing which he

87

does believe. He gives his life without a thought, for a cause or a flag; he judges death to be preferable to even a slight breach of his code of loyalty and honour; he will die a thousand deaths rather than be branded as a coward. He plunges into icy waters to save a drowning child, courts destruction to beat a record in aeroplane or motor-car, or to scale some untrodden peak. Scarcely a day's paper comes without its tale of fantastic chivalry in contempt of death. And equally when his blood is up or his brain on fire, he will kill without mercy and hold life to be of no account in the pursuit of some cause which may be a compound of ignorance and illusion. Of all the intimations of immortality or eternity, none is quite so eloquent or mysterious as this inner witness to values beyond earthly values. It is apparently independent of religious belief. The anti-God crusader is as willing to die for his cause as the Christian missionary. The Madrid anarchist adjures his comrades to "take a pride in death"—which would seem to be the final reduction to absurdity of the creed which holds that life is all. If only he and his kind did believe in this creed, or if mankind in general could be induced to regard human life as sacred, nine-tenths of the problems of government would be solved at a stroke, and the remaining tenth be only the subject of amiable debate. But by the same token something tells us that the world would be spiritually dead.

We pause here on the threshold of the unknown. Except with the eye of faith we have no measure either of life or of death. Life is the subject of history, and immense numbers seem uncertain whether it is better to live or to die. Our inferences from the few little drops of time known to history throw only the dimmest light on the interminable future which science bids us expect for the human race. Let us make the best of it, but those who have lived long enough to see the new creeds going the way of the old, and the up-to-date vanishing with even greater rapidity than the out-of-date will be careful about flattering themselves that they have discovered the truth about history and humanity.

There are, nevertheless, certain things which history does seem to show us: especially it shows us in all ages man trying to stamp his pattern on the indifferent nature of things, man insisting that his ideas of right and wrong, justice and injustice, progress and backsliding have a real existence and an imperative claim on his loyalty and allegiance. Any attempt to tell his story which derides or despises this inner witness reduces it to nonsense. Permeating all history is the exciting sense of something at the heart of things which must be sought, though it is never found, and though the pursuit of it keeps men and nations in the seeths of unrest.

> All experience is an arch where thro'
> Gleams that untravelled world whose margin fades
> For ever and for ever as we move.

Nothing in the light of history seems less likely than that man will find rest in some classless equilibrium or Arcadian Utopia. The trouble with these ideas is not that they exceed but that they fall far short of the hopes and dreams of humankind and the rich variety of human nature.

III

A CERTAIN MODERATION

I

To commend moderation in these days is to write oneself down an incurable antique. Our moderns have no use for moderation. Not for them the golden mean so foolishly belauded by the Greeks. Moderation is mediocrity, and that is all there is to it.

There is a certain confusion here between thought and action. The thinker may, indeed must, go the whole way with his thought; he can shock or scare, wander at large in the free world of his imagination, and be hailed as seer and prophet. Now and again "the live coal behind the thought bursts into flame and the war of tongue and pen learns with what deadly import it was fraught." Or it suddenly becomes dynamite and blasts away obstructions that have defeated the pick and shovel of the patient worker. But these have been very rare incidents in the history of the world. The minor prophets, who are the immense majority, can go all lengths and do no more than provide a benevolent corrective to conventional thought. If they are in advance of their times, that is their métier.

But these, being of a literary disposition, have generally kept within their territory—the territory in which opposition can be removed with a wave of the pen and the perfect state inaugurated with a blare of assenting eloquence. Thus conducted, the criticism of practical politics from the points of view of the higher thought is an excellent thing, and the more we have of it the better. But if the higher thinker descends into the arena and puts a veto on the give and take, the compromises, the adjustments to opposing facts, the consideration for minorities which must be practised by politicians who desire peaceful government, he very soon becomes a public nuisance. All my life I have delighted in the brilliant raillery which Shaw and Wells have brought to bear on practical politics, while feeling warmly grateful to them for keeping out of the actual business of governing or trying to govern the country. Their relations with me and the likes of me who have been engaged in this humdrum business are just what they ought to be. They think me a very dull dog; I am grateful for any crumbs that fall from their table, which I can use in my plain cookery. The last thing I desire is to moderate their thoughts. But I have to remember that there is a difference between the things which they can say and I can say. There are all sorts of things which Shaw can say and be thought very bright and amusing; whereas if I were to say them, I should lose any little reputation I might have as a man of common sense engaged in practical affairs.

2

If anything has been brought home to the watcher on the political scene since the beginning of the century, it is that a certain moderation in the sphere of practical politics is the condition of keeping liberty and democracy in existence. Parliament, through which alone democracy functions, is the instrument of suasion and reason. It rests ultimately on the willingness of minorities to submit for the term of the Parliament, while they endeavour to persuade the electors to return them to power in the next Parliament. It is and must be persuasion all the way; the moment a party dreams of using force against its opponents, it throws a challenge to the entire system. We learnt that earlier than most people over the Ulster business in 1913 and 1914, when what would now be called a Fascist movement all but landed us in civil war. That experience so burnt into the memory of the British people that it has, I believe, greatly helped to save them from toying with any similar experiments in the years after the War. It was an inoculation which so far has rendered them comparatively immune from Fascism, Nazism and Sovietism.

We learnt also in those years that blind reliance on the sovereignty of Parliament would not save us if we passed the boundary between the things that can and the things that cannot be settled by argument and reason. To keep within this boundary is undoubtedly a delicate and difficult art, but it is the whole art of Parliamentary Government, and those who fail in it pass rapidly to dictatorship whatever principles they may profess. There are certain spheres in which the Parliamentary writ will not run. It is generally powerless against raging nationalist passions and deeply felt religious convictions; it cannot make revolutionary upheavals in the customary life of family and property; the inevitability of gradualness is its first law. At each step minorities have to be persuaded to submit and wait. If the state of Denmark has become too rotten or its controversies are too fierce for this treatment, it will not be mended by Parliament; it will fall into the hands of absolutists and terrorists who will extinguish its liberties.

3

At the back of all democratic theory is one fundamental assumption—that government is an art and not a science, an art of infinite variety and fallibility going forward by trial and error to conclusions which are never concluded and can only be dimly apprehended by the living generation. If we depart from this and begin to think of government as a science, of which the laws have been discovered by experts or revealed to prophets—a science directed to the building of a society of which they have the perfect plan—we have turned our faces away from democracy and are on the high road to dictatorship. If there is such a science and its laws have been discovered, it is absurd that they should be debated by inexpert parliamentarians. If there is such a society, it is criminal to permit it to be thwarted by a selfish or ignorant minority. The Stalins, Hitlers and Mussolinis who are in possession of this science do not argue with us, they tell us, and necessarily and rightly from their point of view. Dissent from them is not a difference of opinion; it is heresy, wickedness, malevolence, which must be stamped out.

I frankly own to a prejudice against all men of science who bring these ideas from the laboratory into politics. They take a cool interest in experiments on humanity, which to me are terrible. Their mental attitude is that of theology upside down. They are as certain that they hold the keys to the terrestrial heaven or hell foreordained for humanity by science, as the Church was that it controlled the gates of the celestial heaven or hell. It is these dreadful certitudes about the uncertain and unknowable which have worked such havoc in human history. The modern dictators with their "scientific" advisers behave exactly like mediaeval Popes, employing their secret police, as the Church did the Holy Office, to scent out heretics and deliver them over to the scaffold and the stake. I have taken some pains in recent years to follow the disputes between different schools of Marxists, and have been struck by the atmosphere of mediaeval ecclesiasticism which pervades them. Each is persuaded that something called the truth has been revealed exclusively to itself; none of them can bear that the shade of a shadow of doubt should be cast on their interpretations; they are as merciless to those who stray an inch from the path which they think to be the one and only right one, as to the heathen who dwell in the outer darkness of capitalism. Stalin treats Trotsky as Calvin treated Servetus, or would if he could get at him. The claim to infallibility is even a little more drastic in the political than in the ecclesiastical sphere, since the infallible Church could afford to let you go your own way when you had made submission to it, whereas the infallible totalitarian dictator claims your allegiance in the whole of your activities.

93

Mediaeval and modern history alike warn us that there is no ferocity comparable to that of the dogmatist let loose upon his fellow-beings. He kills without scruple and seems to revel in practising what other people call "atrocities" upon those who oppose him. The most hard-bitten militarist would shrink in war from the wholesale slaughter which the Bolshevist inflicts upon the Kulaks in his determination to "collectivize" them, or which marks the progress of Fascist, anarchist and syndicalist in their conflicts in Spain. The most violent of professional criminals would think himself disgraced if he were convicted of the disgusting sadism which the German race-theorist practises upon the Jew. There is nothing in the world of physical conflict to compare with the remorseless passions of the intellect or the tigerish zeal with which it will both inflict and court death when on the war-path.

4

The belief that human life can be laid out with the exactitude and precision of engineers and quantity surveyors planning a railway or a reservoir finds its most benevolent expression in the Webbs' book on Soviet Russia, and it is interesting to see where it leads. Where, asked the Webbs of their Russian friends, may freedom of discussion be permitted in a State organized on this assumption? The answer was, not at all among the "mass of unthinking men," and only up to a certain point among "intellectual colleagues and equals." These may debate among themselves and even be allowed to express their opinions in the form of "proceedings" or "transactions" of a learned society, provided they are not circulated to the vulgar or expressed in language which the vulgar will understand. But when once a decision is arrived at, even this discussion must cease.

"It is held that the success of the enterprise will be jeopardized, and may easily be brought to naught, if all those concerned in the work from the manual labourers and the skilled mechanics, the foremen and the assistant managers, up to the highest technicians and the director himself, do not whole-heartedly co-operate, with complete assurance and entire devotion in the execution of the particular plan that has been decided upon. Whilst the work is in progress any public expression of doubt, or even of fear that the plan will not be successful, is an act of disloyalty, and even of treachery, because of its possible effect on the wills and on the efforts of the rest of the staff. A grumbling sceptic or public 'grouser,' however able and conscientious he may be, may by his creation of a 'defeatist' atmosphere, actually bring about the fulfilment of his own prophecies of failure. . . . In any corporate action, a loyal unity of thought is so important that, if anything is to be achieved, public discussion must be suspended between the promulgation of the decision and the accomplishment of the task." (*Soviet Communism*, II. 1038-9.)

Exactly in this way did the infallible Church proceed in promulgating its doctrines. The dogmatic experts assembled in Ecumenical Council might speak freely among themselves up to the point when the decision was taken, but after that the dissentient must submit, or for ever be silent. No shadow of doubt must be thrown upon infallibility lest the multitude should be shaken in the faith. The analogy is curiously exact even on small points. The "transactions" of the experts in the political community are to be circulated only to the few, and to be in scientific language which the vulgar will not understand. Latin served the same purpose in the ecclesiastical community.

But in neither the one sphere nor the other was this, or could it be, the end of the matter. The dissentients, being intellectual men, were perhaps not silent, or if they were, the ruling infallible feared that they might not be. He had them followed up with his spies and informers, and presently had evidence that they were conspiring against him and his Church or State. Then he "purged" them, or brought them to trial in his own court according to his own rules, and presently had them making abject confessions on which he shot them or sent them to the stake. These are mediaeval memories in the case of the Church, but they are modern instances in the case of the totalitarian States. In pursuance of the method described by the Webbs—the method which regards criticism or opposition as "defeatism"—the Communist experts have slaughtered each other so ruthlessly in Russia that scarcely one of the old guard survives. In Germany the would-be critic walks in memory of the purge of June 30, 1934, and in Italy of other red-letter days.

5

Every country, it has been said, deserves the Government that it has, and it may be that the subjects of the totalitarian States have both deserved and will profit by the discipline imposed on them by their dictators. History will judge. But let us in the meantime be clear that if any party believes government to be a science of which it possesses the secret, it is set on the road which these countries have followed. On that hypothesis opposition is treason and the despotism of experts is the scientific way of life to which we must submit in mind, body and estate. Plato may be quoted for that idea, but he presumed the existence of a highly trained and deeply bred caste of supermen, whose superiority would be so evident to their fellow-beings that the latter would gladly give over to them the difficult business of government and remain cheerfully within the stations and pursue the occupations to which they were born and bred. And Plato in the end said that this pattern was more likely to be laid up in heaven than realized upon earth. Upon earth it leads to obscurantism and terrorism; the obscurantism which forbids thinking to the mass of men and women; the terrorism which compels their submission to a few well-appointed rulers. It means also in practice that the mass, being precluded from thinking, must be kept in a perpetual state of emotional ferment by propaganda, which more and more tends to take blatant and militarist forms.

It is difficult to believe that the political revivalism which has swept millions of young people off their feet in Russia, Italy and Germany can be more than a passing phase. There are, no doubt, people so constituted that they take the same mystical pleasure in bowing low before monarch or dictator as the devout do in prostrating themselves before the shrines of saints. But for the majority of reasonably educated people, this is the kind of fervour which quickly evaporates. It may be great arrogance to say so, but I cannot think of myself making the submissions required by the dictators without a total loss of self-respect. Is it possible that those crowds photographed with outstretched arms and rapt faces as they listen to Hitler or Mussolini could be composed of Englishmen ? Could the average kindly, tolerant English yield to this intoxication ? Can one see them shouting with the Moscow crowd when Stalin puts his enemies against the wall, returning thanks for Hitler's " purge," joining in the Jew-hunt, taking their daily dope from the censored press, reduced to whispers when politics are mentioned, picking their way between the traps laid by spies and informers, disbanding their trade unions, accepting any wages or conditions that authority prescribes for them and going obediently to labour camps, if it so determines ?

I like to think it impossible, and I do not believe that either Fascism or Communism would take exactly those forms if it got established in England. But Englishmen too need to be on their guard against this fanaticism which has ruined politics and extinguished freedom in so many countries. If eternal vigilance is, as Burke said, the price of liberty, a certain moderation is its essential condition. Parliamentarians must equally forswear revolution and counter-revolution and be content with the changes that can be grafted on to the existing parent stems. Those spread over a period of time may be so radical as completely to alter the character of the tree and its fruit, but those who want a new tree by the middle of next week must not talk about liberty or democracy or pretend to be parliamentarians. They must be ready to stamp out opposition and kill their opponents.

I believe liberty of thought and expression, freedom from arbitrary arrest and forced labour, to be ingredients of civilization for which there is no compensation in any

G   97

material prosperity or mechanical efficiency. It may be that the European dictators are right in thinking that the peoples who accept, or upon whom they have imposed, their rule have not reached the stage at which they can safely be entrusted with this liberty. Herein they throw a challenge to democracy which it must take seriously. A minimum of competence in the art of administration is the first condition of any system whatsoever. Men and women will rush to any shelter if they are threatened with disorder. If we look to the States in which Parliaments have been superseded by dictatorship we find that, generally speaking, they are States in which democratic Governments have failed to solve elementary problems of law and order. And the reason they have failed to solve them is again, generally speaking, because the left-wing parties scoff at moderation in dealing with their opponents and refuse even to sink their differences with one another in the interests of this minimum of administrative good government. Socialists, Communists, syndicalists, anarchists, wage an incessant war with each other about their theories and continue to wage it in the unsuitable arena of public administration. A very small infusion of Marxian theory in the British Labour party was sufficient to prevent the co-operation with Liberals and Radicals which was essential to ensure its competence as an alternative Government, and might well have saved it from such catastrophes as befell it in 1924 and 1931. The British in such circumstances save their Parliamentary system by reverting to Conservative or "National Government"; other countries in which Parliamentarism has much shallower roots chase the democrats off the scene and call a dictator to their aid. In both the moral is the same. It is useless to have plans for the regeneration of human society unless the regenerators understand the elementary business of holding it together in a framework of law and order, and will compose their differences sufficiently for that purpose. If liberty and democracy are to be safe, business must be carried on as usual, while the structure is being repaired.

IV

THE ORIGINS OF THE WAR [1]

I

THE origins of the Great War may be traced backwards for generations, perhaps for centuries. But for practical purposes the student must plant his boundary within hailing distance, and an obviously convenient place for our present purpose is the year 1871 in which the Franco-Prussian War was wound up with the Treaty of Frankfurt. This year saw the inauguration of the German Empire, the great new factor which for good or ill was to play the central part in the rivalries and contentions that culminated in the Great War forty-three years later, and the adjustment of which to the European system is still one of our major problems today.

In dealing with this period the student has before him a mass of official documents far exceeding any that are available for any comparable period of history. To name the chief of them, there are the forty volumes of the German *Grosse Politik*; the official German report of the 1919 inquiry after the War (a most valuable source which is too often overlooked); the twelve volumes of the Austrian documents; the twelve volumes of the British, so admirably selected and edited by Dr. Gooch and Prof. Temperley; the Russian *Livre Noir* and the many Russian documents published in De Siebert and Schreiner's *Entente Diplomacy and the World War*; the six volumes of the French documents and other French documents to be found in Bourgeois and Pagès's *Origins and Responsibilities* of the Great War. And then if

[1] A lecture delivered to the Schools of Modern History and Modern Greats, at Oxford, January 18, 1937.

you set aside the museums full of perishable and rapidly perishing newspapers, you have mountains of biography, autobiography, memoirs and reminiscences, in which the writers give their version of the parts which they played; some of them with a passion of self-justification which greatly complicates the task of the student. Never was the would-be historian so richly provided with material, and it is possible that he never will be again. For the peculiar circumstances which led the Revolutionary Governments after the War to make a clean breast of the equivocal proceedings of their predecessors are not very likely to be repeated.

But as is the bulk of this material so is the difficulty of dealing with it. How shall we thread our way through this labyrinth; how distinguish, if they are to be distinguished, between economic and political causes; what value shall we assign to the contributions of individuals, how far explain them or excuse them by supposing them to be in the grip of forces beyond their control? I do not suppose any other comparable period can be found which raises so intensively all the problems which attend the writing of history, political, psychological, economic, philosophical. There has been a tendency in recent years to attribute events to subterranean forces working to predetermined conclusions. Just as in the new psychology the individual is supposed to be in the grip of complexes and inhibitions of which he is unaware, so, in this new interpretation of history are the nations supposed to be the unconscious agents or victims of tendencies moving in cycles to their own frustration, of positives dogged by negatives in an unending dance of things contradicting themselves. I will only say, in general, that it is impossible for the *contemporary* historian to pass any judgment worth recording on these supposed subterranean causes. He knows the antecedents, but not the sequels and consequences of the events he is recording. His period is far too short for him to plot the curve of great secular and cyclical movements, if there are such. He has constantly to beware lest he make recourse to unverifiable hypothesis an excuse for neglecting the study of hard facts which is the first of his duties. All I can do in the short time at my disposal today is to deal with events as they seemed to a contemporary to happen, and to suggest to you certain milestones or landmarks which may help you to find your way along this steep and winding road.

2

To bring the subject within my limits, I must leap the Bismarckian period and plant my first milestone at the year 1891, the year of the preliminary Franco-Russian agreement which led, three years later, to the Treaty of Alliance between these two Powers. That marks the breakdown, twenty years after the Treaty of Frankfurt, of the Bismarckian policy of isolating France and keeping her in subjection. Bismarck had played his game with extraordinary skill, if with entire lack of scruple, and at one time he had contrived to keep Austria, Russia, Britain and Italy, and any minor Power that counted, in tow of Berlin. But this required a virtuosity not possessed by his successors, and on his departure from the scene we see the break-up of his combinations and the division of Europe into the two great camps which came to their clash twenty-four years later in the Great War. The German Emperor, William II, is now embarked on what he calls his "new course."

The next phase, spread over ten years, is the departure of Great Britain from her policy of isolation, marked first by her alliance with Japan in 1902, and finally by her Entente with France in 1904. These are my two next milestones.

Then follows the period of German reprisals which welded Britain and France together, and greatly contributed to make the Entente the anti-German instrument which the Germans alleged it to be. The Algeciras crisis of 1905-6, the Casablanca crisis of 1908, the Agadir crisis of 1911, are all stages in what the Editors of the British Documents call "the Testing of the Entente." This period figures in German history as that of the encirclement of Germany, for when in 1907 we added an Entente with Russia to our Entente with France, the Germans became convinced, or professed to be, that we were definitely trying to hem them in—to do to them what they had done to France in the years after the Franco-Prussian War. King Edward was supposed to be the author of this policy, and to be pursuing it as part of his quarrel with his nephew, the Kaiser.

A new chapter partly overlapping the previous one opened in 1908 with the annexation of Bosnia-Herzegovina by Austria-Hungary. The road now turns sharply to the East. From this point we are started on the chain of events which came to their climax in August, 1914. Two great Empires, the Austro-Hungarian and the Turkish, were now in process of dissolution, and all the expectant heirs were rushing to their death-beds. It was now highly probable that whichever of the two dominant groups prevailed in this great liquidation would for the time being be master of Europe east and west.

There was a period after the War when there was a disposition to interpret these events as due to petty causes—secret diplomacy, the incompetence of this statesman or that, the lack of foresight which caused certain Governments, especially our own, to get entangled in commitments and engagements which they had not understood, and so forth. I would ask you, if not entirely to dismiss this kind of interpretation, at least to put it into a secondary place. The more one studies this period the more one is impressed with the tremendous volume of the events which were rushing to the catastrophe of 1914. They were events which in the normal course of history might well have been spread over a whole century, perhaps several centuries; they were bound to shake the world to its foundations, and the supposition that any great Power could have remained a disinterested spectator seems, as one looks back on them, extremely remote from reality. Even the United States found it impossible to remain in this position.

3

With some such general outline in mind I would suggest for closer study certain questions which specially concern us as Englishmen. First, how did we come to abandon the policy of non-intervention—the "splendid isolation"—which for the earlier years of this period was the British attitude towards the European groups?

This isolation was never quite so complete as is sometimes supposed. Lord Salisbury's general line, which lasted till near the end of the nineteenth century, was one of leaning upon Germany and the Triple Alliance in his difficulties with France, especially his difficulties about Egypt. In 1887 he even let himself be persuaded by Bismarck into concluding the secret Mediterranean Agreement which made Great Britain for a time a naval partner of the Triple Alliance. But he seems to have been half-hearted about this, and in the subsequent years when certain of his colleagues, and especially Chamberlain, were pressing for an alliance with Germany, he steadily refused to go with them. In 1901 he gave the quietus to the final effort to draft an Anglo-German Treaty in a memorandum (British Documents, ii. No. 86) which ranks as one of the central documents of this period. You will find in it nearly every argument that was in debate up to the Great War. Could we rely on our fleet alone to save us from invasion or attack by our Continental neighbours? Could we, with our Parliamentary system, and our stubborn national tradition that Parliament should decide the issue of peace and war, enter into engagements which might very well take the decision out of our hands? Should we incur novel and most onerous obligations in order to guard against the dangers of invasion in the existence of which we had no sufficient reason for believing? On the strength of this document Lord Salisbury has been claimed as an unrepentant isolationist, who would have placed a similar veto on the French Entente if he had lived and been in office in the year 1904. Yet you

will observe that the major premise of his argument is that
the British fleet will be equal to defending Great Britain
and the British Empire even against a combination of
foreign fleets.

It was doubts on this subject which now cast their shadow
on British policy, and in the end decreed that whatever
partnership we entered into, it would not be with Germany.
As her commerce expanded and her Colonial ambitions
increased she began more and more to chafe under British
sea-power. Her experience in the Boer War had made her
angrily aware that all her plans for striking back at Great
Britain—flying squadrons, Continental Leagues, landings in
Delagoa Bay—were doomed to futility, so long as Britain
held the command of the sea. To get even with Britain by
building a fleet which would threaten her command of the
sea was now the dream of the Kaiser and the group of young
naval officers whom he had gathered about him. From this
time onwards you will find that every attempt to come to
terms with Germany broke down against the Kaiser's stubborn
refusal to abate this threat to British sea-power. The Kaiser
perceived, with perfect clarity from his own point of view,
that with his growing fleet and great army, Britain and
Britain alone, stood between him and the satisfaction of his
dreams, whether in Europe or oversea.

The contention between Britain and Germany on sea-power
thus became one of the great sundering issues—in some ways
the deepest and least susceptible of compromise in European
politics—from the year 1900, the year of the first great
German Navy Bill, up to the War. The Bill was frankly
aimed at Great Britain, for in the memorandum attached to
it, its authors explained that their object was to provide a
fleet of such strength that even the strongest naval Power
could not attack it without endangering its own supremacy.
With the growth of this rival fleet, isolation looked every
year more dangerous to British Governments, and in 1902
Lord Salisbury himself consented to the Japanese Alliance,
which sprang from a serious doubt whether the British fleet

would be equal to maintaining our position in the Far East against a possible combination of Russia, Germany and France, all of whom seemed equally hostile, if Japan remained free to join up with them.

If we judge by its results, the ironic spirit seems to have been at work in this treaty, for there is no evidence that its far-reaching consequences were at all in the minds of its authors. It is possible that if there had been no Anglo-Japanese Treaty, Russia would have been exploiting Manchuria in 1914 instead of taking part in the Great War. By guaranteeing Japan against the intervention of any third Power, this treaty enabled her to attack and defeat Russia, and, as its further consequence, drove Russia back to Europe from the Far East where the Kaiser had confidently hoped that she would be occupied for generations to come. In the meantime the crippling of Russia created a period of great peril for France who, with her partner out of action, found herself once again isolated and in serious danger of being attacked by Germany. In 1904 Count Schlieffen, the German Chief of Staff, the famous author of the Schlieffen plan for the invasion of Belgium, proclaimed that Germany's hour had come, the hour for a "thorough clearing up with France at arms. No waiting ten or twenty years for a world war, but so thorough a settlement that thereafter there should be no fear of a world war." France, he said, should be provoked until she had no course left but to take up arms.

4

Finding herself in this plight France forgot her grievances and approached England with the offer of an all-round settlement embracing Egypt and the many tiresome Colonial questions which had troubled the peace of the two countries in the previous years. To heal these old quarrels and place the peace on a firm footing seemed unqualified gain to all parties in England, and the Convention of 1904—known as the Entente—concluded by Lord Lansdowne and M. Delcassé, received the all but unanimous approval of all parties and both Houses of Parliament. I saw it in the making and can bear witness that it was considered by its authors and accepted by the public as being no more than what it ostensibly was, an amicable settlement of these oversea questions without bearing on the politics of Europe. If you look at the documents in the British series, which tell the story of the negotiations, you will scarcely find a hint of any other interpretation.[1] The British people, and the Liberals and pacifists not least, congratulated themselves on having taken a substantial step towards peace and set a good example to their neighbours. We had been on the verge of war with France over Siam in 1893, over Fashoda in 1898, and in angry mood over the Boer War and the Dreyfus case in 1899 and 1900. To get rid at a stroke of all these causes of quarrel seemed an unqualified blessing.

The view of the Germans and of the power politicians of Europe was far otherwise. These judged that the casting vote of Britain—the one remaining great prize in the game of power politics—had been given to the Dual as against the Triple Alliance. From the first, Bülow and Holstein, who between them controlled German policy at this moment, declared it to be incredible that British statesmen could be so naïf as to be unaware that in signing this convention they had deliberately broken with isolation and plunged into the heart of the European contention. To the last Holstein had believed that Germany had only to bide her time to buy British support on her own terms, and the sudden appearance of Britain arm in arm with France was a rude awakening from this dream.

From this time onwards we see Germany and Britain involved in a double misunderstanding. The British, who had given little or no thought to the European balance of power, could not believe the Germans honest in regarding the Entente as aimed at themselves, and considered their

[1] Sir Eyre Crowe in a Memorandum written some years later maintained that it had no anti-German edge to it.

resentment unreasonable and unfriendly. The Germans could not understand that the building of the great fleet upon which they were now bent, though entirely within their rights, was bound to be regarded by the British as a threat to their security and even to their existence. Yet both these interpretations were strictly in line with the logical processes of the two peoples, with the logic of power politics as understood in Germany, with the logic of sea-power as understood in England. So much must be granted, if we are to understand the sequel. Yet I think it is fair to say that the Germans so acted as to make the Entente fulfil their own predictions, *i.e.* to convert it from the friendly agreement on Colonial and oversea questions which the great majority of Englishmen wished it to be, into the fighting alliance with France which it eventually became.

The story is told quite frankly in the German documents. Within a few months of the conclusion of the Entente, Bülow and Holstein were planning reprisals against France on ground specially chosen to test the meaning and value of the "diplomatic support" promised by Britain to France in the new Convention. The spectacular landing of the Kaiser at Tangier, the peremptory demand that the Moroccan question should be submitted to a conference, the dead-set against the French Foreign Minister, Delcassé, filled Europe with alarm during the next twelve months, and in December, 1905, war seemed to be imminent. It was just then that the long reign of the Unionist party was ended by the resignation of the Balfour Government, and a Liberal Government took office with Campbell-Bannerman as its Prime Minister, and Grey as its Foreign Secretary. What would the new Government do, a Government presumably pacifist and anti-militarist? Would it turn its back on the Entente or stand strictly to the letter of the law, which promised nothing more than "diplomatic support"? Europe held its breath and waited.

The French view was that "diplomatic support" was worthless unless behind it there was at least a presumption that it would be backed by military action, if provocation went too far. That and that alone in their view would deter the Germans, as circumstances then were. Early in January, 1906, M. Cambon, the French Ambassador in London, was instructed to put the question to Grey. The French Government were persuaded that the Germans intended to break up the impending Conference at Algeciras on the Morocco question by making impossible demands, and then to declare war on France. Would the British Government contemplate the possibility of supporting France in arms in such an emergency, and, if so, would they consent to place on a regular footing the military and naval conversations which had begun informally under their predecessors?

It was an awkward moment, for the British elections were in full swing and Ministers were scattered in all parts of the country. But the four Ministers to whom the question was submitted—Campbell-Bannerman, Grey, Haldane and the veteran Ripon—were agreed about the answer. With whatever reluctance the conversations must be permitted. If war had even to be contemplated as a possibility, it would be folly to go forward without having any concerted plan of action between the two nations who, on that hypothesis, would be fighting together as allies. There were to be careful reservations. The French were to be warned that military plans did not commit us to action, unless Parliament so decided; military hypotheses were to be carefully distinguished from realities, yet if there was even a possibility of war, some plan for concerted action was an elementary precaution which in like circumstances would be taken by any Government in the world. There was much controversy in after years about the omission to consult the Cabinet; but no one ever suggested that the Cabinet, if consulted, would, or could, have given a different answer than that which was given by the four Ministers.

This was enough for the French, and enough for the Germans. The news spread that Great Britain contemplated action; the Germans began to say that they had never thought of pressing the Moroccan question to the point of war, and when the Algeciras Conference came, submitted to a settlement which, judged by their previous demands, looked like a serious diplomatic defeat. So ended the first round, but only the first round. Again and again—at Casablanca in 1908, at Agadir in 1911—we see the testing operation renewed on the same ground—by no means, it must in fairness be said, without provocation from the French, whose policy seemed at times to an English onlooker a rather gratuitous renewal of the quarrel. Every diplomatic battle, meanwhile, had its reflex in the competition in armaments. In proportion as they seemed to be foiled by Great Britain in their Colonial ambitions, the Germans became more determined to be even with her at sea. There followed in quick succession the German Navy Bills of 1906 and 1908, leading up to the great naval agitation of 1909—the year of the eight Dreadnoughts in Great Britain.

5

I would suggest to students of these years that they should read with special care the documents relating to the military conversations, as they are presented by Lord Grey in his memoirs, *Twenty-five Years*. They will discover here the germ of almost everything that followed, the doubts and hesitations attending British policy—doubts and hesitations surviving to this day—the endeavour to be fair to a European partner, and yet to reserve freedom to decide for ourselves whether we will act or not, when the time comes; the desire not to be entangled in the complicated and seemingly remote quarrels of our European neighbours; the feeling that we are an island, whose power is on the sea, and who should not be lured into militarism as practised in Europe by nations with conscript armies. In all this chapter of our history you will find material which may help you to answer the still unanswered questions of British policy. The questions which European nations asked us in 1906—are we a Continental Power in the sense that they construe this expression, and if so, how do we define our policy, and on what provocation will we intervene? are questions which they are asking today under a somewhat different terminology.

Then I would suggest that you study with some care Vol. vi. of the British Documents, the volume entitled *The Anglo-German Tension*, 1907-12, and side by side with it read Vol. xxviii. of the German documents. Let me just put in here that you will find Mr. Woodward's admirable book, *Great Britain and the German Navy*, of the greatest use in this connection. In the two volumes of the German and British documents you will find all the fears, ambitions, jealousies and suspicions on one side and the other that were driving the two nations apart—all these reflected in the dispatches of Ministers and Ambassadors, and the comments on them of the able permanent officials in the Foreign Offices of the two countries. At times you come upon passages of almost Thucydidean irony, as in the report of the Conference on the naval question held in Berlin on June 3, 1909, when the Germans seemed almost to have relented about pursuing the naval competition. This report fades out with Tirpitz assuring the assembled Ministers that "the danger zone in our relations with England will be passed in from five to six years, say in 1915," and the Chancellor, Bülow, saying sharply, "that is all very fine, but the question is still how are we to get over the dangers of that period?" The question seems to have been left unanswered.

If we turn now to the Austrian documents we shall find the far-reaching effects of the British-German naval competition where we should least expect it. On August 11, 1908, when King Edward was spending a day with the German Kaiser at Cronberg, Sir Charles Hardinge, who accompanied the King, had a conversation with the Kaiser on the naval question. Immediately afterwards the latter sent a cipher telegram to Bülow, in which he boasted of having threatened war if the subject were pursued. That, he said, had an immediate and salutary effect. "Hardinge was ready to eat out of my hand." "You must always," he added, "treat an Englishman thus."

The immediate sequel will be found in Vol. i. (p. 156) of the Austrian documents. Eleven days later, August 19, Aehrenthal, the Austro-Hungarian Foreign Secretary, presided over a Council of Austrian and Hungarian Ministers called to consider the plan for the annexation of Bosnia-Herzegovina which was to surprise the world in the following October. When asked about the probable attitude of Germany, he said they could be "absolutely sure of her, since she was now thrown back on Austria alone, especially after Kaiser William's rejection at Cronberg of King Edward's proposal to limit the German naval programme." So sure was he, that he did not consult or even take the trouble to inform the Kaiser before announcing the annexation. We have Bülow's account of the state of wrath into which the Kaiser was thrown by this treatment of him, but he had brought it on himself when he boasted openly of his triumph over Hardinge to his friends in Vienna. Aehrenthal was perfectly right in his estimate of the forces at work. The refusal to come to terms with Britain threw Germany into greater and greater dependence on Austria, until finally it was Germany who became the horse and Austria the rider.

6

If you will go back to the beginning of this period, you will find that Bismarck had certain rules which made the practice of power-politics in his hands relatively safe. One was to leave France free to satisfy her ambitions outside Europe; another was not to quarrel with Russia, unless he was on good terms with England, or with England unless he was on good terms with Russia; a third to beware of challenging England at sea; a fourth to keep German policy in German hands, and never to let Austria take it out of her hands. By the year 1914 Germany had violated every one of these rules; she had blocked French ambitions in Africa, she was challenging England at sea, she had come to the support of Austria against Russia in the annexation of

Bosnia-Herzegovina, and was being compelled by Austria to follow her lead in the bitter conflict which that stroke had precipitated in the Balkans. She had a far-reaching policy of commercial expansion through the Near East and Turkey to the Persian Gulf, which increased her dependence on Austria and even on Turkey. All this time the war on two fronts was an ever-present nightmare to her, and she complained bitterly of the policy of encirclement which she believed was being pursued by Great Britain, for it does not seem to have occurred to her that a policy which threatened the surrounding nations at so many points was bound to create the corresponding reactions.

After the conclusion of the Anglo-Russian Convention in 1907, the two alliances with their subsidiaries covered all Europe, and had long projecting spear-heads into Asia and Africa. The storm centre now began to shift to the Near East, where the annexation of Bosnia-Herzegovina had plunged the Hapsburg monarchy into a dangerous conflict with the Slavs of the Peninsula and its own Slav subjects. By this time peace and war were indivisible, and everything was at stake for everybody in any collision between the great Alliances, wherever it might take place. If Russia were beaten, France would be at the mercy of Germany, which would then have the whip-hand of Great Britain and the British Empire. If Austria went down, she would drag Germany with her. It was the sub-conscious perception of these consequences which set the pace of the arms competition. As war began to seem inevitable, all said with perfect honesty that they wanted armaments, as Bethmann-Hollweg put it, not because they wished for war, but because they wished to be sure of winning a war if it came. Victory might, as Norman Angell so cogently argued, be unprofitable, but defeat, it was felt, would be an immeasurable calamity. Under this impulse power was always being balanced, unbalanced and rebalanced at a higher level. When the clash came the balance was so nearly true on the highest level of which the nations were then capable that it took the terrible four years of the War of attrition to tip it against the Central Powers.

Where in all this was British policy? Prince Bülow, the consummate tight-rope performer, repeatedly uses one word about British statesmanship. He calls it naïf. And from his point of view he was right. Grey saw the European situation in the simplest terms and declined to be lured into any of the by-paths in which the European experts spent so much of their time and thoughts. He set no traps, he drove no wedges; he said what he meant without rhetoric or finesse. The great series of his dispatches published in the British documents shine out among the records for their truth and candour. Through all the eleven years in which he was responsible for British policy he had one predominant thought—that to let Germany conquer France would be disastrous for Europe, and eventually for Great Britain. To this he brought un-ashamedly what our moderns are apt to deride as the public-school spirit. He thought it intolerable that France should be bullied by Germany because she had made friends with us. Ready as he was to make friends with Germany, he would not let her make mischief between us and our other friends. If any-thing was needed to confirm him in the French—and later in the Russian—Entente, it was the browbeating of the Germans and their evident intention to make trouble for any nation that could not be brought within their orbit. There were divisions in the British Cabinet, but on one point they were unanimous. They would not give the pledge of neutrality in a war between France and Germany, which Germany demanded as the price of abating the naval competition. Russia had refused it in the old days; Great Britain was firm in refusing it in these later days. We can see Grey's ideas coming to their climax in his angry rejection of the final German bid for our neutrality on the eve of the War. Could not the Germans perceive, he asked, that it would be disgraceful for us to enter into this bargain at the sacrifice of our friends? Bethmann-Hollweg who, according to his lights, was an honourable man, could not perceive it. According to German ideas there was

nothing disgraceful in striking a favourable bargain if opportunity offered. These moral sentiments were out of place in
the world of real politics.

I have been over the ground with Grey many times in the
subsequent years, both when I was helping him with the
documentary part of his own memoirs, and afterwards when
I was writing my own book on the documents. He weighed
very dispassionately the various criticisms of his policy after
the event, such as that the Entente should have been an
Alliance; that we should have warned the Germans that we
should be found on the side of France if she was attacked,
that we should have raised a conscript army, and so forth.
In general, his view as I recall it was that in the existing
conditions of Europe, it was always doubtful whether any
such action would have encouraged the militarists of one
group or discouraged the militarists of the other, whether,
for example, any sudden increase of our land forces would
not have tempted the Germans to strike before we could be
ready. Especially he regarded the freedom which we reserved
for ourselves as a guarantee that our friends in Europe would
not pursue a policy which was unlikely to obtain the support
of the British Parliament and people. But all these questions
he regarded as academic. He, the British Foreign Secretary,
had in his time and generation to work within limits which
made the military alliance and the conscript army impossible.
No Government at that time would have consented to them,
no Parliament would have accepted them. It was in his view
the chief part of his duty so to steer his course as to carry
Cabinet, Parliament and people with him, for otherwise he
risked the greatest of all calamities—national disunity in, or on
the verge of, war. Belgium comes into the picture at the
last moment to heal the division between British parties.
No one would deny that indignation at the violation of
Belgium was an honest and honourable emotion. But that
also was a challenge thrown to one of the few settled traditions
of British policy, namely that the occupation of Belgium by
a hostile Power would be a pistol aimed at the heart of

England. It needed just this last stroke, combining sentiment and policy, to bring the British people into action.

7

The events of these years bring home to us the great difficulties of historical judgments. The student being well provided with wisdom after the event is apt to forget the limitations of public opinion, the darkness shrouding the future through which the statesman has to pick his way. For him the visibility is always bad. Few mistakes would have been made and few battles would have been lost, if statesmen and generals had shared the knowledge possessed by their critics. Had the men of this period been aware that war was to break out on August 4, 1914, no sooner and no later, they would no doubt have done a great many things which they omitted to do, or which in the then state of knowledge and opinion they were unable to do. We are confronted today with many of the same questions as in the years before the War, and with all the experience gained in the subsequent years we have very much the same difficulty in answering them.

Grey's own chief criticism of his diplomacy was that he had too easily taken for granted in the last years before the War that Austria-Hungary would follow where Germany led. At the London Conference on the Balkan question in 1912-13 he had seen Germany apply the brake to Austria, and he assumed that she would continue to do so. Therefore, to improve relations with Germany and trust her to control Austria-Hungary seemed to him the right line for the British Foreign Secretary.

He did sensibly improve relations with Germany through the Colonial agreement which was brought to a successful conclusion a few weeks before the outbreak of the War, but that had no effect upon the great play of forces in which all the nations were now involved. Grey had spoken better than he knew when he predicted that if the annexation of

Bosnia-Herzegovina by Austria-Hungary were condoned by the signatories of the Treaty of Berlin a train of events would be started which might be fatal to the whole Treaty structure. He was right; the annexation set in motion the fatal sequence which brought down the Hapsburg and Ottoman Empires in the ruin of the Great War. The Austrian documents, running parallel with the last volumes of the *Grosse Politik*, enable us to trace in detail the various stages—the Italian seizure of Tripoli, the Balkan wars, the results in Austria and Russia of the triumph of the Serbs, the conclusion of the Austrian and German General Staffs that the situation would rapidly grow worse for their two countries against Russia, France and Britain, if time were allowed for it to develop; above all, if Russia were given time to build the strategic railways she was contemplating and to develop her enormous man-power. In this last feverish period Great Britain appears only as spectator and observer. She might have said then, as Mr. Baldwin said three years ago, that her frontier was the Rhine, and her efforts were directed to clearing up her own special relations with Germany as the best contribution she could make to peace.

Suppose Great Britain had asserted herself in these remoter affairs, suppose she had insisted on keeping the London Conference in active being instead of letting it fade out of the picture in August, 1913, could she have stayed the course of events? It was the question that Grey asked himself more anxiously than any other in the last years of his life. The answer seems to me very doubtful, but there is no question which deserves closer study, for it is alive and important today. You heard Mr. Lloyd George say the other day that it would be impossible to mobilize a British battalion for an Austrian quarrel. That certainly would have been said with even greater emphasis in 1914 than in 1936, if the Government had shown any sign of involving us in the obscure quarrels—as they seemed to be—of Austrians and Serbs. Yet in 1914 they did mobilize all their forces in what seemed superficially to be just this kind of quarrel. Very few

Englishmen in those days were aware of the logic of the Alliance system which was to involve all the partners of both groups in any quarrel on any issue. Very few Germans and no Austrians had even a faint idea of the part which British sea-power—let alone a British army—would play in a war between the Alliances. You may read the Memoirs of Conrad von Hötzendorff, the Austrian Chief of Staff, and find scarcely a mention of Great Britain. He talks with Moltke, the Chief of the German Staff, who assures him that the Schlieffen plan will effect the conquest of France in six weeks, and again seems to have not the slightest premonition of any part that Britain may play. Great Britain was, in fact, the x of their equation, but none of them seems to have realized it.

8

The period is rightly described as that of the balance of power. Its general presupposition was that possession should be in proportion to power. Like blockade in war, possession had to be effective. *Beati possidentes*, but only if they had the power necessary to defend what they possessed. A nation which considered itself to have less territory than was warranted by its power was justified in seeking more; a nation which had more territory than its neighbours thought to be warranted by its power was open to attack by them. Policy and armaments were supposed to go hand in hand. Diplomacy consisted in drawing cheques on power, and required an unceasing but doubtful and hazardous estimate of an immense debtor and creditor account.

Bismarck, after the Franco-Prussian War, divided the nations into the sated and the unsated—those who desired only to keep what they had, and those who wished either to add to what they had or to recover what they had lost. He placed Germany and Austria-Hungary in the first, and France and Russia in the second of these categories. But these definitions were always changing. Before he left the scene, Germany had definitely joined the unsated, and was loudly demanding a place in the sun, and complaining that her late start had placed her at a disadvantage in the race for desirable colonies and spheres of interest. At the same time Russia steadily pursued a policy of expansion both in the Near East and in the Far East, and France made a bold bid for an African Empire without abandoning her desire to recover the territory which Germany had taken from her in Europe. Great Britain, though supposed to be the most sated of all the Powers, yet continued to add to her possessions, and her neighbours complained that her sea-power enabled her to outdistance them all and throw them back on her leavings. Let me repeat that there is no need to think of economic forces as secret and subterranean in these years. They were open and manifest in the conflicts of the Powers which, under one guise or another, were bids for wealth, territory and commercial advantage. The sense which seemed suddenly to possess all the great nations in the last years of the nineteenth century that the world was shrinking and time was short quickened the pace and gave a feverish energy to their competition. By drawing tariff boundaries round their Colonies most of them provided their opponents with an economic motive for conquest.

To isolate a dangerous neighbour and to prevent themselves from being isolated became for all the nations desirable, even necessary, objects of policy. All lived in fear, and sought safety by joining with the nations whose fears and antipathies most nearly corresponded with their own. In the forty years before the War we see the grouping of the nations constantly changing under the influence of this dominant motive. Tsarist Russia quits the Three-Emperors' League and joins hands with Republican France. Britain drops her quarrels with France and her supposed secular rivalry with Russia and joins forces with both against Germany and Austria. Italy wavers between the two camps, but when the crisis comes refuses to fight with her allies, and finally joins their enemy. The smaller nations are in the same unstable relations. Bulgaria, which owed everything to Russia, joined the Central Powers against her in the Great War; Serbia, which was the protégée of Austria at the beginning of the period, is her mortal enemy at the end. Throughout the period we look in vain for any sign that the great Powers are capable of working together for their mutual benefit on positive lines. It is always the negative motives, the common antipathies, the fears that they have in common which seem to prevail.

These words seem to imply moral judgments, yet before we pass them certain other aspects of the situation need to be borne in mind. I believe it to be broadly true that the structure raised in Europe in the generation before the War had a German and Bismarckian foundation. At all events it most nearly corresponded to the German idea of power politics (machtpolitik), to the idea of Clausewitz that war was a continuation of policy. Whatever its moral bearings may be, this idea is by no means to be dismissed as an illusion. Bismarck had shown how by careful preparation and fore-sight national unity could be obtained and national policies promoted by brief and successful wars which inflicted com-paratively small loss on either belligerent. The Bismarckian idea of short and successful war dominated the whole period and was only dispelled by the experience of the Great War, which revealed to all the Governments that science had substituted an altogether different idea of war. When the German Kaiser said he had not willed the War, he spoke truly. Neither he nor his military advisers willed the Great War. The war which they had in mind was the war of the Schlieffen plan, the war which was to be fought to a successful conclusion between August and December. Similarly it may be said that no one willed the political structure—that enormous and complicated parallelogram of forces—which crashed upon the heads of its engineers and artificers in 1914. At no moment had any Government or statesman the same sense of responsibility towards it as a man may have for his own handiwork. As the years went on it became more and more a collective product to which scores of Governments and thousands of individuals had contributed their quotas, and nearly all something which could justly be arraigned as aggravating the mischief. Further, when we speak of fears and antipathies we must think of them not as fictitious emotions, but as genuine and well-justified anxieties. Britain and France had good reason for fearing Germany; Germany had good reason for fearing the combination of France, Britain and Russia; Austria the best reason of all for thinking that a combination of Russia and Serbia would be ruinous to her loose-jointed Empire. If we are thinking in terms of war-guilt or war-innocence the account is an extremely complicated one, in which the final reckoning may wisely be left to Divine Providence, or that handiest of refuges for a historical writer, the historian of the future. It would be too crude to speak of the Great War as a preventive war, yet in the last months before it broke out we see the military leaders of the Central Powers confiding to each other that time is running against their group, and evidently thinking it to be a positive advantage of the ultimatum to Serbia that it will bring Russia in and enable her to be fought before she has built her strategic railways and speeded up her mobilization.

It seems to me of great importance that this period should be studied *sine ira ac studio*, and that we should put out of our minds the short and angry view which imputes all the responsibilities to one generation, to one set of statesmen, to one country. It is natural and tempting to think of the War as a great gulf or watershed dividing past and present; it is more important to see the present, if we can, in the light of the past, and to clear our minds about the continuous stream of unsolved problems which still trouble our peace. There is only one moral which is quite certain—namely, that the old kind of foreign politics will not go with the new kind of war.

V

BRITISH "HYPOCRISY"

I

No one can have studied European affairs without becoming aware of a chronic, if subconscious, irritation with Great Britain even among her best friends. "British Pharisaism," "British hypocrisy," are expressions which have too wide a vogue not to have some meaning, however much Englishmen may protest that they are undeserved. I have visited Clemenceau in Paris at a time when the British-French Entente was supposed to be at its closest and warmest, and have found him in much the same state of grumbling annoyance at British characteristics as in the same year I had found the redoubtable Baron Holstein in Berlin.

The root of the trouble was a sense of the inequality of the conditions between them and us. *We* could talk from the highest moral altitude, use the most improving and reproving language, and then, when our advice was not taken, pull up our drawbridge and retire behind our moat. *They* could not talk to one another in this way without risking wars in which their countries would be invaded and their young men killed by the scores of thousands. To them the diplomatic structure of Europe was a delicate balance of forces requiring the utmost discretion and reserve on the part of those who handled it; to us, or at all events to the British Liberal, it was Satan's invisible kingdom, inviting the rebukes of all honest men. To Bismarck statesmanship was expertise in the handling of forces for the benefit of his own country; to Gladstone it was hot-gospelling in which the iniquities of the great offenders were exposed and the opinion of the civilized world set in motion against them.

I think it may be argued that if Gladstone had been listened to in 1878 and the nations induced to take his view of the ultimate consequences of Turkish rule in Europe, there would have been no Great War in 1914. His appeals to divine Providence in his Midlothian speeches have an uncannily prophetic ring. Yet when I have read in the German documents the story of Bismarck's laborious and persevering efforts in the early months of 1878 to effect the compromise which prevented the Russo-Turkish War from spreading over all Europe, I can understand, if not sympathize with, his impatience when Gladstone rushed in upon this scene—Gladstone with his long-term morality and his total incomprehension of German and Austrian liabilities in these affairs, if they could not be composed. How could it be explained to Gladstone that it was a prime necessity of German policy at this moment to keep Germany, Austria and Russia together and that any forcing of the issue which compelled Germany to give her casting vote for Austria against Russia, or Russia against Austria, would be ruin to the Three-Emperors' League and the entire scheme of policy which Bismarck had built up since the war with France? Such things might be communicated in confidence to the "Old Jew" who, alone of English statesmen, had the European mind, and would be greatly flattered by being taken behind the scenes in the high diplomatic world. But if confided to Gladstone, they would be proclaimed to the world from a platform on Greenwich Common, with accompanying anathemas on the German and Austrian selfishness which prevented divine Providence from working its will on the outrageous Turk.

That he had saved the peace of Europe by bolstering up the Turk, and that Gladstone would have destroyed it by his bag and baggage policy was Bismarck's claim, and on the short view of the case it was difficult to gainsay him. The sufferings of the Christian subjects of the Turk were no doubt, as he admitted, very regrettable; but, if the choice had to be made, it was better in his view that the Turk should kill Serbs and Bulgars than that Germans, Austrian, British and

Russians should kill one another. Seventeen years later Gladstone had his last fling against the Turk, who was now massacring Armenians. Once more British opinion was greatly stirred, and Salisbury, the Conservative Prime Minister, used language which was scarcely, if at all, less reproving than Gladstone's. By this time Bismarck had ceased to control German policy, but the European judgment of the British attitude was substantially what his had been of Gladstone's remonstrances in 1878. It was all very well, said the other Powers, for Great Britain to take this high Quixotic line, but they all had important reasons for not wishing the Balkan question stirred up: Germany far-reaching commercial schemes which required the friendship of Turkey; Russia and Austria a joint arrangement for dividing the Turkish inheritance, when the time came, which was not yet; France her newly-formed alliance with Russia which required her to keep step with her partner. The Ambassadors met in Constantinople in the autumn of 1895, and in conformity with his instructions the British Ambassador expostulated and pleaded only to meet with a polite obduracy from his colleagues. Sitting there the great Powers decided, through their representatives, as the British Ambassador reported to his Government, that the "endless misery" should go on, while that "subtle observer," Sultan Abdul Hamid, played them off one against another. Go on it did until twenty-three years later the downfall of the Turkish Empire involved most of them in its ruin.

Lord Salisbury explained to a disappointed public that the British fleet could not cross the Taurus mountains, and there he had to leave it. The foreigner commented that it was precisely this fact which made British humanitarianism so untimely. Great Britain could stir up a righteous wrath, and then in a stately way move her fleet and, if it came to war, vent her indignation in a perfectly safe action at sea, whereas they would have to move vast armies and be launched on a devastating struggle, if they began quarrelling about Turkish reforms. Moral indignation was a luxury in which Great

Britain could safely indulge, but a most dangerous emotion for other people. The famous German Under-Secretary Holstein was persuaded that, whenever she mentioned the subject of Turkish reforms, Britain was laying a trap for her neighbours. She wished to involve them in a war in which she would take little or no part herself, but benefit, as the *tertius gaudens*, from the weakening of her neighbours and competitors. Never for one moment could Holstein be brought to admit the possibility that Great Britain, or indeed any nation, could be honest when it professed to be pursuing a disinterested or ideal policy.

2

Bismarck said, with obvious reference to Gladstone, that whenever he heard a statesman talking of "his duty to Europe" he knew him to be up to mischief. Grey had a taste of this judgment in 1908, when he protested in the name of international law against the annexation of Bosnia-Herzegovina by Austria-Hungary in defiance of the Treaty of Berlin. "International law?" said the Powers in unison. "Where have we heard that phrase? Who in the world, except this strange Englishman, ever dreamt of attaching a serious meaning to it?" Grey, like Gladstone before him, was prophetic of evil to come, if Europe stood by and allowed solemn treaties to be broken with impunity, and every word that he said was justified by the events of the next six years. But this was an abstract and remote idea to the practical politicians, who wanted only to turn the immediate corner. Russia, who had been cheated of her share in the rather disreputable bargain which her Foreign Minister Isvolsky had struck with the Austrian Minister Aehrenthal behind the backs of the other Powers, desired only that England should compensate her by consenting to the "opening of the Straits"; France desired nothing except that the whole tiresome business should be wound up by giving Russia what she wanted, and both Germany and Austria would have been glad to be quit

of it on the same terms. But there stood Britain blocking
the way to a sensible settlement which would have satisfied
both Austria and Russia, and doing it in the name of a high
morality which no one could believe to be her genuine
motive.

What could she be after? Aehrenthal confided to Tittoni,
the Italian Foreign Secretary, that he found Grey's policy
"totally unintelligible," and Tittoni cordially agreed with
him. Clemenceau, who should have been Grey's best friend
in Europe, went to visit King Edward at Carlsbad, and spoke
angrily about the imprudence of English public men, and the
untimely movements of English public opinion. It was all
very well for Britain to mount this high horse and throw
her challenge to Germany and Austria; if it came to war
she could make a nice hole in the sea by sinking the German
fleet. But what would happen to France, upon whom the
German wrath would fall, and what could Britain, who
had no army, do to help her? Either Britain must provide
herself with a conscript army and accept the same liabilities
as her friends in Europe, or she must keep to her insular
affairs and refrain from plunging about in these high matters.
Clemenceau's strictures, repeated with embellishments in Berlin
and Vienna, led to the belief, which is seriously repeated by
the editors of the Austrian documents, that Great Britain was
deliberately inciting her neighbours to a war from which she
would benefit as spectator and *tertius gaudens*.

It did not need Grey's denial to show the absurdity of this
belief. All through these months, as the British documents
show, he was working honestly and laboriously for a settlement which would satisfy his own sense of legality and
prevent a collision between Austria and Russia. But scarcely
anyone outside the British Isles appeared to think it possible
that he could seriously put himself to this trouble for so
elusive an object as the sanctity of a twenty-year-old treaty,
and when presently it turned out that neither he nor his
Government was prepared to go to war to undo the accomplished fact of the annexation of Bosnia-Herzegovina, there

was much sarcasm at the ineffective meddling of Great Britain. She lectured and scolded and gave herself great airs over her less scrupulous neighbours, but when it came to action, she left it to them, and retired behind her moat. Russia, who in the end was compelled to give way before a German ultimatum, felt deeply aggrieved, and for a time toyed with the idea of leaving the Triple Alliance and crossing over to the German combination. British ideals, said the others, were all very well, but they could not be pursued on the cherished British principle of limited liability in Europe. What Britain would do, not what she said, was what concerned them. To suppose that they would give way when she shook a minatory finger or read a reproving lecture was a *naïveté* of which only the islanders could be capable.

That there was a point at which she would act, and do so formidably on the continent of Europe, was brought home to her neighbours six years later. But it would be a mistake to suppose that suspicion of British idealism or the belief that it is a form of British hypocrisy has ceased to exist in Europe. The League of Nations has been haunted by it from the beginning. All through the years following the peace we may trace the passions and emotions of the old Europe breaking through the new writing on the much-worn palimpsest. The British complained that France conceived the League merely as the guardian of her own interests embodied in the Treaty of Versailles; the French that the British looked indulgently on every breach of Covenant or Treaty which chimed in with their commercial interests. The French pointed to their devastated areas and claimed passionately that payment from the Germans was necessary and just; the British presented an economic argument to prove that making Germany pay would be ruinous to European trade, which meant—said the French—to the profits of British merchants and shipowners. When France decided to march into the Ruhr and take what Germany declined to give, Britain again became the villain of the piece; the villain who, by encouraging German resistance, brought ruin on that

effort. On the other side the British complained that the lack
of economic sense in the French and their ruthless determination to stamp on their former enemy were blasting the hope
of pacification through the League and postponing indefinitely
the return of prosperity to the world.

Memories of debates with French friends and politicians
come back to me from these years. They were quite amicable,
but it was evident that the French had no greater belief in
British idealism than Bismarck or Clemenceau in the former
days. The argument came to its climax in the autumn of 1935,
when the Abyssinian affair was boiling up to its crisis. It was
1908 over again, with Mr. Eden and Sir Samuel Hoare
playing the same parts as Grey and Asquith in the affair of
Bosnia-Herzegovina. The old hands in France were as frank
about British policy in these months as Aehrenthal and Tittoni
had been about Grey's proceedings in 1908. Once more I
heard the words "totally unintelligible." Could I seriously
maintain that Great Britain, who had consented to German
repudiation of just debts, who had looked on while Germany
rearmed and committed other flagrant violations of the
Treaty of Versailles, had suddenly developed a Quixotic
zeal for the Abyssinian victims of Italian aggression? Was
it not patent to everybody that we saw in the Italian case a
threat to British imperial interests, to our position in Egypt
and the Sudan, and were doing ourselves exactly what we
reproached them with doing—using the League of Nations
for our own convenience and according to our own con-
ceptions of policy? If we would only confess it, no one
would mind, but this pretence of a loftier morality than was
practised by our neighbours was what irritated and exasperated.

As an Englishman I know that this reading of our motive
was untrue and unjust. I know that the British people were
moved by a deep and generous emotion. But we deceive
ourselves if we suppose that this was at all widely believed
outside the British Isles. To the French realist a total commit-
ment of British and French forces to the vindication of the
Covenant against Italy, while Hitler was evidently waiting to

improve the occasion, was an act of political unwisdom which could only have been contemplated by insular politicians who were in a position to hedge their liabilities. All through these months an argument went on behind the scenes which curiously recalled the debate of 1908-9. Were we prepared to go all lengths in defence of law and treaty? Would we guarantee France against the consequences of breaking with Italy, be prepared to mobilize an army if Hitler broke through into Austria, or committed acts of aggression against Poland or the little Entente? Were we, in fact, prepared to act, as well as denounce, whenever a breach of Treaty or Covenant was established, or would we pick and choose according to our own judgment of our interests, or according as the emotions of our people might be kindled to the boiling-point on one issue but not another?

It was the failure to answer these questions in the explicit manner which French logic required that, more than anything else, brought an impotent conclusion to the policy of sanctions against Italy. As the lesser evil to a breach with us, France consented to a half-hearted *démarche* against Italy, but when talk of war began, the inequality of our respective liabilities again leapt to the minds of Frenchmen. The whole of the beautiful Riviera exposed to Italian bombs, Paris so much nearer than London to Italian air-bases! Great Britain comparatively safe, perhaps compelled to evacuate Malta, but using French ports and harbours, and bringing them into the front line of attack! Reprisals no doubt, but upon the ancient and beautiful cities of Italy amid the execration of the world—and all this for the sake of Abyssinia! These horrible results might be risked on stern necessity for the sake of vital interests or national honour, but could Great Britain possibly be serious in expecting France to risk them in order to keep Mussolini out of Abyssinia, Great Britain, who carefully hedged her own liabilities and would not even commit herself to come to the support of France outside the area of Western Europe, which she considered to be her own sphere of interest?

Again in the following months there was laughter in the world when the question of restoring German Colonies came up, and British statesmen and newspapers began to argue as if to be deprived of Colonies was a blessing in disguise, which Great Britain in pure benevolence was anxious to confer in perpetuity on the German people. Still more when they solemnly convened a Conference on Raw Materials with the air of offering a far preferable alternative. No one, it was said, would have behaved in exactly this way except the British.

It would be no bad exercise for the British to consider why this comment is so often heard.

VI

REFORMERS AND DICTATORS

I HAVE never ceased to think of Erasmus, whose quater-centenary was celebrated on July 11, 1936, as the most fascinating figure of sixteenth-century Europe. It is customary to contrast him with Martin Luther—the smooth, subtle, opportunist man of the world with the dynamic, fulminating reformer. Some slight equivocations when he was called upon to say "Yes" or "No" to Luther, and an engagingly candid confession that he was not the stuff of which martyrs are made, have exposed him to this construction, but it is, I think, essentially unfair.

Erasmus was a lion with his pen. To break out as he did against the corruptions of monks and priests, and to wage an almost single-handed battle—at all events in the early years—against the most powerfully-massed vested interest of his time, was an act of the highest courage, which ought not to be in the least disparaged because his weapons were wit, skill and scholarship, instead of thunderbolt and tomahawk. Erasmus was most deadly when he was suavest and most moderate.

Then consider what a tremendous business he did when he disinterred the Gospels from the mould and dust of the monastery libraries and launched them on the world in his new Latin translation, with "notes" skilfully and daringly constructed to bring out the contrast between the precepts of the Master and the practice of so many of His disciples. Or consider again the brilliant raillery of the *Praise of Folly*, poured out impartially upon laymen and ecclesiastics, and wringing withers over a wider area than almost any other satire in literature.

The unceasing peregrinations of this man, his indefatigable writing and lecturing, his enormous and inexhaustibly interesting correspondence, his friendships alike with men of action and men of learning, with emperors, kings, popes and scholars, seem when recorded sufficient to fill the lives of half a dozen men. When it is added that he suffered from chronic and painful ill-health, we have the measure of his indomitable spirit. He was often faint, but always pursuing. He loved learning and scholarship, and could no doubt have found happiness in the quiet life of the gentleman and scholar, but what spurred him on was an unsleeping hatred of fraud and imposture, leading him to act as under the pressure of some inner necessity to expose it.

His relations with Luther raise the eternal question of revolution and evolution. Erasmus believed that the Church could be reformed from within. But this meant tolerating and temporizing, keeping in with pope and cardinals, inducing them to take a step here and a step there—things hateful to Luther, who was for ever banging doors, defying authority, and setting the veto of conscience upon all compromises and middle courses. The portraits of the two men may be painted so as to make the one seem the flincher and the other the hero, but those who remember the horror and cruelty of the struggle which followed, and the competition in persecution and intolerance which it inflicted on religion for the next hundred years, may think twice before putting Erasmus into the pillory. The objection to reform from within was not that it was intrinsically a meaner idea than blasting from without, but that in the case of an infallible Church it was almost a contradiction in terms. Certain corruptions might no doubt be cut away without touching faith and doctrine, but the reforms which Luther directly, and Erasmus implicitly, desired undoubtedly required changes in the dogmatic structure which the Church regarded as beyond challenge.

Lecturing seventy years ago on Erasmus, Froude told his audience that it needed a great effort of imagination to realize the intolerance of the European world in the early sixteenth century. I wish it could be said that any such effort was necessary in these days. The effort needed nowadays is rather to suppose that any comparable modern man could have the same influence or be allowed to spread his doctrine to so many countries.

Erasmus was an international figure, so much so indeed that one hardly remembers that he was a native of Antwerp and that his birth-name was Gierard. He was equally at home in the great cities of Europe and in London, Oxford and Cambridge. His voice carried from Rome to the cities of the North; his writings, being in the Latin which they all understood, were read by the educated everywhere and appealed to a common culture which they were proud to share. A modern Erasmus, if such a one can be imagined, would find his writings banned in at least half the countries of Europe, and if he travelled and lectured and talked with the freedom that the sixteenth-century Erasmus did, he would be fortunate if no worse fate befell him than to be deported.

This is a gloomy thought for the quater-centenary, but it cannot be shirked. There is nothing Europe needs more today than the recovery of a European culture to which powerful and freedom-loving Europeans may appeal over the heads of censors and dictators. With all our modern apparatus of Press and wireless we are worse off in that respect than in the sixteenth century. A modern Erasmus working in the political sphere as he did in the ecclesiastical, and bringing to bear on it the same incomparable gifts of wit and irony, would be of inestimable value in these days, but to drown his voice and blot him out would be the instant resolve of the rulers of at least half Europe today.

·　　·　　·　　·　　·　　·

I have been reading in the *Hibbert Journal* (January, 1937) a learned and interesting article in which Dr. Nicklem endeavours, as the modern phrase is, to "restate" Calvinism in terms which may make it conform to modern religious ideas. The effort requires a certain mysticism which seems to me foreign to the hard clean determinism of the Calvinistic doctrine. That can only be explained away by suggesting that Calvin did not understand the implications of his own doctrine. However, Dr. Nicklem has stirred my interest to the point of making me resolve to get "the Institutes" and read them if I can. It would, I suppose, be impossible to make a list of the twenty books which have most influenced the world without including it, and I feel a certain shame in having to confess that I never till now thought of looking at it.

Yet behind his doctrine looms the figure of the man himself, and no modernizing of the doctrine can make me think of him as other than one of the world's great terrorists. Herr Stefan Zweig's portrait of him in the book translated and published last year under the title of *The Right to Heresy*, has the obvious political motive of presenting him as the prototype of the modern dictator and is somewhat painted up for that purpose. Yet the parallel is just. Calvin's government of Geneva was a tyranny in which theology played the part played by "ideology" in the modern dictatorships, and it needs only a slight stretch to see in Calvinism on the one side and the Inquisition on the other the sixteenth-century counterparts of Communism and Fascism. Calvin himself is an apt illustration, for while he was a stern guardian of the faith, he was also a capable administrator and earned just credit for cleaning up the city of Geneva and providing it with what the modern world calls social services. His apologists speak of him in much the same terms as Communists and Fascists do of Stalin and Mussolini. He cleansed the streets, he restored discipline and, if he killed and persecuted, it was from grim necessity. Whether in the nameless horrors of the modern revolutions a parallel can be found for the atrocious cruelty of Calvin's method of doing Servetus to death is more than I know, but the apologists of either make one feel that theology and ideology may be equally fatal to humanity.

133

What one waits for in vain in the countries of the dictators is the appearance of some hero of liberty who will stand up to them as Sebastian Castellio did to Calvin. Herr Zweig says truly that Castellio's "Manifesto on behalf of toleration" is one of the great original documents in the history of free thought. It is time we had another.

PART III

THINGS SEEN

I

THE GREAT DURBAR

I

DELHI, *November*, 1911.

As you walk along the Ridge at Delhi—that central and most sacred spot in British Indian history—you look down on a sea of tents. Take a few steps downwards and it is half-screened by green trees in the foreground, but from the higher levels it stretches away unbroken for two miles across the plain. From above it seems to be a confusion of all sizes and shapes, but descend into it, and you find it to be a cunningly designed canvas town, intersected by roads, varied by gardens, and polo grounds, provided with post offices, telegraph and telephone stations, and possessing a ceinture railway of its own to take you from camp to camp or into Delhi city. The roads have familiar names, Mall and Kingsway, and, though creations of yesterday, they are broad and smooth and excellently designed for pageants. Just under the Ridge, on the eastern boundary of the area, is the King-Emperor's camp, with the old Durbar house in its grounds. It is neat but not gaudy, and is sufficiently impressive without challenging the Eastern gaieties and splendours of the Indian Princes' camps. Two miles away, at the northern end, is the Amphitheatre, which is the scene of the principal outdoor ceremonials. The Processional route between the Royal camp and this Amphitheatre is lined with innumerable camps of all sizes and kinds, and in them are gathered all the principalities and powers of India—the Viceroy and his Council, Governors, Lieutenant-Governors, and Chief Commissioners, great and wealthy Princes, petty chiefs, men from the plains, men from the mountains, men from across the border, Sultans from Arabia and the regions about Aden. Each has his own camp and his retinue, but to enumerate them would be to write a Homeric catalogue, a task to which I am wholly unequal and which would not enlighten the reader.

The great Durbar camp is thus a collection of smaller camps, each of which has its own garden and enclosure, with entrance gates and semicircular drive. Many are surrounded with hedges of " morning glory " in full flower ; there are chrysanthemums and palms in the gardens, and heroic efforts have been made to make the ground look green. Where grass has failed, mustard and cress or some other low-growing green vegetable makes a cunning substitute. The commonest type of camp consists of large square tents in pairs, one behind the other, on two sides of an oblong on the far side of which is a group of large marquees or roofed tents, connected by canvas passages with each other. In these are drawing-room, dining-room and smoking-room, and concealed behind them are the kitchens and service-rooms. All these big tents are elaborately carpeted and furnished, warmed with stoves and lit with electric light. They make luxurious club-rooms for the colony, which has its bedrooms in the smaller tents grouped round the square.

The idea that you rough it or suffer any hardships from camp life in the Coronation Camp is a delusion—at all events if you are fortunate enough to be entertained, as we are, by a hospitable high official. Your tent is charmingly furnished, warmed with a stove and lit with electric light. You sleep in a comfortable bed with spring mattresses, and have a Persian carpet to your feet. Your servants have their tents outside, and are always within call. The bathroom is thrown out behind and makes a separate room. You will hear the jackals by night, and may be woke in the morning by a scuffle of crows tobogganing down your canvas roof—a game they play incessantly—but these are the only touches of wild nature in your smooth and pleasant existence. To be quite truthful I ought perhaps to add that a jackal walked into one of the military camps and bit a colonel in the chest. But this was a solitary incident. The jackal was said to be mad, and the colonel was sent to the Pasteur Institute.

2

The ruling Princes have let their fancy loose and spent riotously on their camps. Kashmir with its elaborately carved wooden enclosure wall (since presented to the King), and Hyderabad with its more austere but stately and dignified expanse of garden and tented space, are specially admired. But half a dozen others barely fall short of these, and a score more are on the scale befitting the ruling Prince. Some have triumphal arches—one, I specially noticed, is adorned throughout with a very chaste design in silver-gilt spoons—and some substitute ornate little buildings in concrete of the White City type for the big central tents or shamianahs. Most of them are gay with bunting and illuminated at night with a profusion of electric lights, which entirely outshines the modest display of the Government of India and Provincial camps. There is probably within the camps of the Native Princes the finest collection of Oriental rugs, carpets, embroideries and hangings in the whole world, and a fire in this area would destroy a vast number of priceless and irreplaceable things. Jewellery and state robes of gold and silver tissue are on the most extravagant scale. In the processions the Maharajahs wear their jewels as horses wear harness, and you look on miles of glittering fabrics until your eye is wearied with the dazzle of them. Many of the Princes have brought their regalia, which vary from gold and silver maces and big symbolic objects, for which I have no name, but which appear to be of solid precious metal, to the painted fans and tinselled horse-trappings of the petty chiefs. Here, as elsewhere, India gives you every variety. This group might come from Central Africa; that one might be dressed for a state ball at Windsor Castle. I hear Western people around me laughing at the absurd get-up of a chief from Bhutan, but some of them, I will swear, went to the Coronation at Westminster last year in costumes which would look quite as outlandish to his eyes, and which have nothing but custom to make them less ridiculous.

It is not, however, the grandees or their fine clothes and sumptuous shamianahs that make the chief interest of this place, but the vast number of different sorts of men that are gathered together in it. The intelligent traveller goes about like a tiresome child, asking endless questions which no one can answer. Where does that brown man come from, why does he carry that thing on his back, why aren't his servants the same colour as himself; why does this man stain his beard pink and dress in silver tissue, while that one dyes his beard black and dresses in white cotton? Where are Bhor, Sachin, Rajpipla, Chamba, Bamra, Chatarpur and a dozen other names that one reads on the gateposts of different camps? It comforts one a little to hear hardened old Anglo-Indians asking each other the same questions and failing to get answers. My ignorance is abysmal, but who is there that knows or ever can know the whole of this country?

The Durbar is a vast animated museum of all the human specimens that India provides, and there is an inexhaustible interest in just walking about and looking at it. Ethnology is veiled in the West; here it is sharply defined in face, form, dress and colour of skin. As you walk about London you may conjecture that this or that man may have French or Italian blood in him; here the people are unmitigated Punjabis, Madrassis, Bengalis, Rajputs, Pathans, Baluchis. They are divided by race, united loosely by religion, which again divides them. Such unity as there is is imposed on them by the Central Government, and, as one looks upon this scene, it is impossible at present to think of them as united in any other way.

I have just returned from a drive through the camp and into the city of Delhi. The road is thronged all the way with smart English folk in motors, innumerable ekkas—small native carriages with little square canopies stretched above tiny platforms, on which four people will squat, with two on the box in addition—ruling Princes in four-horse landaus swarming with retainers, and escort in front and behind, all ablaze with blue, scarlet, purple and gold; carriages that look like meat-safes on wheels; every shape and size of buggy and cart, scandalously overloaded, according to our Western notions; and occasionally camel carriages, and even carriages drawn by six camels.

Inside the Kashmir Gate we came upon a Jain procession—elephants smothered in tinsel, with canopied images on their backs, priests on other elephants, and apparently the entire contents of several temples carried by bearers in a procession which would far outshine the gaudiest that could be seen in Spain or Southern Italy. Though it occupied the whole of a long street, and came within hailing distance of the great mosque, it appeared to be treated with tolerant good-humour by the sightseers, the vast majority of whom were Mohammedans.

I am told that while the Durbar lasts Mohammedan and Hindu will be careful to avoid the scandal of communal quarrels.

The narrow streets of Delhi are a mass of decorations, not planned on a uniform design as we saw in Bombay, but to all appearances the free manifestations of the lively fancy of the separate householders. Since there are no two houses of the same shape and size in the whole city, this is a good scheme, and the result is an Eastern blaze, which is only spoilt when some more ambitious shopkeeper decides to be European. The crowds are dense, and our carriage can only creep. After three hours spent in looking on this scene, I throw caution to the winds and come away entirely convinced that we are witnessing the most extraordinary demonstration ever made by this country to any of its rulers—a thing of deep, perhaps unfathomable, meaning for the King-Emperor and his Government.

3

Of all pageants and ceremonials the great Durbar itself was by far the most beautiful and wonderful I have ever seen.

It combined three things, each perfectly in its place—a great popular demonstration, an assembly of the richest and most powerful in the splendid Oriental manner, and a magnificent military display, with the King and Queen as centre and climax of all three. Imagine a vast amphitheatre, not less than half a mile in circumference, of which one half consists of a great covered structure, filled with the grandees, high officials, ruling Princes and their retinues, and visitors of honour; and the other half of great mounds of people in the open, under a brilliant, scorching sun. In the middle are two pavilions hung with red velvet embroidered with gold, one of which projects further into the centre, and has a gleaming gilt dome. In the first the King receives the homage of the high officials and Native Princes, and from that he advances with the Queen along a crimson-carpeted causeway to the second, where on high thrones they can see and be seen by the whole of the vast assembly. To right and left of them are the soldiers—horse, foot and artillery—in great masses, with the mounted heralds in their pantomime costumes, who execute charming manœuvres in the foreground. The military display is immensely enriched by the variety of the Indian regiments, and the Imperial Cadet Corps, sons of ruling Princes, in blue and silver, comes flashing by, superbly mounted.

But this is merely a bald inventory of the scene, and words can give no idea of its splendour and brilliancy under an Eastern sky. In London the word "crowd" suggests a dim, grey mass. Here it is incredibly gay and vivid. The tiers of spectators in the distance look like huge flower-beds, in which the blooms are green, yellow, pink and rose-coloured turbans. The children are so arranged that one mass of them wear blue turbans, the next yellow, the next pink, and all these make broad bands of colour—not dead, motionless colour, but moving, glittering, animated colour, which catches the sun at innumerable different angles, for every little head is wagging with excitement. There are none of the patches of black which mark the differences of sex in the Western crowd.

The men, of course, vastly preponderate, but their finery is gayer and simpler than any that Western women wear, and one sees the whole mass as a blaze of yellow, pink, scarlet and blue.

In the covered half of the amphitheatre the splendour is of a different kind. The whole of the lower tiers are occupied by the ruling Princes, Maharajahs, Nawabs, Sultans, with their sons and heirs, Ministers and retinues. These are dressed in velvets, brocades, cloth of gold and silver, and woven fabrics of extraordinary beauty. They are piled with jewels—diamonds, emeralds, sapphires and rubies of the size and brilliancy of Covent Garden "properties." For a display of the jeweller's art there could be nothing like it elsewhere in the world, and—what cannot be said of Western jewellery—the settings are worthy of the stones. For once the European ladies, with their smart toilettes from London and Paris, take second place. The finest of them are dim objects beside the meanest Rajah. I will not dwell on the ritual of the pageant, but I never saw anything in Europe more perfectly organized. From beginning to end there was no hitch. The King and Queen did their part to perfection, the Queen exciting universal admiration by the grace of her walk and carriage. One after another the high officials and ruling Princes go up to do their homage. It is no slight ordeal to advance across the causeway and to back from the presence and down the steps with all eyes upon them. The Princes salute according to the custom of their countries, and one splendid old fellow waves his arms and retires at a dance amid general applause. My Indian friends see differences of intention in some of these salutes, but my Western eye is not trained to catch these subtleties.

How shall the King-Emperor be arrayed so that he may be instantly recognized by his loyal subjects in India and strike their imagination? Manifestly he cannot outshine the potentates of this country. No conceivable confection of cloth of gold, encrusted with diamonds, rubies, sapphires and emeralds would enable him to do that. The most opulent imagination could not design a state carriage or a retinue which would eclipse in glory those which have been brought to Delhi by Princes of quite minor States. All solutions have their difficulties. The King in the uniform of a Field-Marshal or Admiral is only one of scores of people in uniform who press closely together at the central group in the processions; and when a helmet is added, recognition becomes complicated. One hears a dozen suggestions—that one elephant should be permitted in the camp and that the King should ride it; that he should wear the robe of the Garter—obviously inhuman under this scorching sun—that he should ride quite alone with the Royal Standards borne behind him, and long intervals in front and behind—which the policemen are supposed to veto. A popular solution has been a tweed suit, with sola topee and gilt pugaree. Thus garbed and riding beside the Queen in a simple state landau, with four horses and outriders and Indian servants behind holding a gold parasol and what appears to be a large gilt fan, he is universally recognized and acclaimed. I have been among a crowd of Indians on the polo ground this afternoon, and seen them dance with delight at the appearance of the King and Queen in this equipage. Whosoever invented it deserves a special decoration.

This question of costume is of high importance. At least a million and a half of people from all parts of India have been in and out of Delhi city and the Coronation Camp this week, and all of them want to be able to go back to their towns and villages and say they have seen the King. Whether they will cheer or not when he passes is a thing which no one can predict; but if they do not, nothing can be inferred from their silence. According to the ideas of some of them, it would be gross disrespect to make any noise while the King is passing. I stood the other day among a group of them and saw the King pass almost in silence. Then a strange thing happened. As soon as he had gone, they began shaking hands, congratulating each other with obvious delight at having done what they had come out to do—namely, *see* the King. If you walk about this camp, you will see dense throngs of people, among them are thousands of little children, decked out in their best—which is very fine indeed—all anxiously waiting to see the King, and running from point to point at any rumour of his coming.

Indeed, the main object of the Durbar is that this great multitude which is coming into Delhi shall have the simple pleasure that they desire, and that when they go back to their towns or villages, they shall be able to hold their heads a little higher because they have seen the King.

Our bearers went out on this quest yesterday and returned saying that they had "seen their God." The reception of the King-Emperor exceeds all the expectations of the official world and had no analogy in Western experience. One sees it as an uprush from the subconscious mind of India, the desire for a sovereign, slumbering for centuries but awakened to life by this event. Malcontents and critics are swept into line by it and give to the King-Emperor what they deny to his Government. For in his person India becomes one people under one lord and exalts itself while it deifies the King. The impulse is universal, and the people seem to be celebrating not a Royal visit but a Restoration, or the recovery of some ancient and long-lost symbol of religion. The thing pulls you up short if you have thought about the masses of India in terms of Western democracy; clearly these people are not parliamentarians or constitutionalists. Six weeks ago I heard people arguing apprehensively that the King's visit must be a failure, because he could give no largess and issue no proclamation which would be in keeping with the Eastern idea of monarchy. I feel convinced, after looking on at this scene, that it would have mattered not a straw if he had had no boons to offer and issued no proclamation. There would still have been the same mystical enthusiasm among the masses at the return of the King-Emperor. The King has filled his difficult rôle with dignity and affability, but while he is in India he can do no wrong. The Raj looks on and is pleased, but a little puzzled. It wonders how it can rise to the occasion, turn this sentiment to practical account, and avoid the possible reactions when the presence is withdrawn and there is a swing back to Congress politics.

.   .   .   .   .   .

This is a truthful record set down at the time, twenty-six years ago. Whether in the subsequent years there has been any change in the sentiment of the Indian masses is more than I can say. But I believe it would be a great mistake to underrate the part that falls to the King-Emperor in any constitution for India.

II

AN AMERICAN FRAGMENT

December, 1927.

AMONG the many places in different parts of the world which I have marked down as places of residence when I am finally retired, is a certain house above the Cheeseman Park in Denver, Colorado. It is a pillared Georgian structure, about 6000 ft. above sea-level, affluent and comfortable-looking, with a pleasant garden city all about it, and just across the road is a charming marble portico which a benevolent lady has erected as a memorial to her husband and an adornment to the park. These are incidentals; the main point is that almost every window in this house looks across the town and beyond it to the long sweeping line of the Rockies, from Pike's Peak on the east to the great snow-fields and summits which melt away into the sky on the north-west. This is how mountains should be seen—at least by those who have ceased to dream of climbing them—and, unless it be the view of the Himalayas from Mahatsu above Simla, I can think of no unbroken line along a great curve of the horizon which equals this one. The sunset on a November evening strikes near the middle of it, turning the whole range from pale amber to hazy blue, and then down the scale of amethyst and pink to the final velvety purple against an orange sky. Twilight is short in this region, and we watched it till darkness fell and the night-chill sent us back to our hotel, but envy filled us for the owner of the house, who looks on this scene from his windows morning, noon and night.

You have the same scene behind you when you depart westward from Denver to the coast, and as you climb up to the Colorado plateau the mountains slip down the horizon till you see only their white edges on the rim of the green and brown upland. In the morning you wake to find yourself approaching the causeway, which takes you forty miles through (not across) the shallow part of the Great Salt Lake. What it is exactly that makes these great salt inland seas a waking dream of desolation is more than I can say, but even in the glittering morning light which turned its waters into silver and clothed the surrounding mountains with a haze of tender blue, this lake seemed the solitude of solitudes, and if there could be water on the moon, one might think it a scene from moonland. Nothing lives in these dense salt waters; there is no sign of habitation on their shores; the wild duck which disport themselves in the brine and seem to like it are said to render themselves unfit for human company or consumption—which is perhaps why they do it. The scene is one of fantastic beauty, but it causes a slight shiver.

The train passes on into the Nevada desert, which to the English eye is a real novelty in landscape and a thing of rare beauty. Right and left are vast rolling expanses of sagebrush, grey-brown and spring-green on the sandy soil, and closing the horizon on either side jagged, deep blue mountains, with flashes of vermilion on their flanks. The scene changes incessantly as the sun rises and sinks, and new mountains come into view and are swept with waves of colour. It is not wholly desert; cattle, goats and even horses find a living on the sage-brush; and there are immense ranches where now and again one may see the steers being rounded up and get exciting glimpses of real cowboys doing their own business in the wild. Darkness comes on a winter evening long before you are tired of this desert.

Finding that if we kept to our plan we should make the descent into California in the dark—which is what most travellers do—we left our train and sleeping-car and, risking our reputation, found a lodging for the night at Reno, Nevada—the Mecca of those who have wearied of matrimony—and took train again the next morning. We were richly rewarded. If I had to choose the six most beautiful day's journeys that I have taken in my life, I should place the descent into California across the Sierra Nevadas very high among them. There are finer snow passes in Europe, and the Himalayan gorges and valleys are beyond compare, and the slopes of the Apennines and the Alpes Maritimes seem at times the loveliest things in the world, but this Californian journey takes you through snow passes into great forests, with lakes in the heart of them, and brings you out into peach-land and vine-land and apple-land, breaking down steeply into the great fertile plain under a brilliant sun. On the lower slopes olive and palm and all the sub-tropical tribe flourish abundantly, and added to them is the English walnut, now in favour with the fruit-growers, who report that it grows three times as fast as in England. Look back and you see all this against a background of immense Californian pines with the snows above, and now and again you catch a glimpse of the Sacramento River running swiftly through a wooded gorge.

Then leaving the mountains you run for an hour or so over the Californian plateau, where the fruit-growers are making their fortunes, and pass through Sacramento to the delta which lies between that city and the Bay of San Francisco. Part of that has been reclaimed and makes splendid wheatland, another part is reedy marsh into which the tide comes, and where snipe, quail and wild geese abound. Flocks of all kinds are feeding or wheeling in the air regardless apparently of the train and of the sportsmen who have built their clubhouses on piles in the marshes. As night falls, the mountains to the north become a deep violet, a faint pink mist comes up from the marsh, and the tidal waters flash between the reeds.

It is dark when we come to Oakland and take the ferry across the Bay to San Francisco. But the city is in the usual blaze of light, its vast sky-scrapers being illuminated from top to base, and the advertisements keeping up an incessant twinkle which is reflected in the waters of the Bay. We are aware of something gigantic, precipitous and entirely American which must be discovered by day.

III

FROM AN EGYPTIAN SCRAP BOOK

Cairo, *January*, 1931.

In Istambul today one asks in vain for the dancing dervishes of Theophile Gautier's Constantinople. If there are old inhabitants who remember them, they think it wiser not to say so. For under the Ghazi modernism is in power, and dervishes who dance are not in fashion. But the ancient Moslem world may still be found in Cairo, if you know where to look for it. Find your way, if you can, on a Friday afternoon to the Monastery of the Mevlevis, and there you may still see these holy men in their mystical ballet. I will not say where it is, for having seen them I feel half-ashamed of my intrusion on their privacy.

The core of the monastery is a very ancient tomb-mosque where four nameless saints have reposed for many centuries. The ground rises precipitously behind the tomb to a flat ledge on which is built the circular building that serves as a dancing hall. The two buildings are connected, and from the gallery above this hall you look down into the tomb. The penetrating smell of old mosque, which is the religious atmosphere of the Mohammedan East, comes up from below and keeps us reminded that we are on holy ground. The dancing floor is a circle with a diameter of about fifty feet, and an inner circle is marked within the outer circle. The spectators sit in an amphitheatre of wooden seats, very much as in an old-fashioned circus.

Precisely at the time fixed the dancers, fourteen in number, file in and walk slowly round the outer circle, bowing, as they pass their leader, who has seated himself on the ground just outside it. With the exception of two who have undergarments of blue and grey respectively, all wear long black robes over white tunics and flowing white skirts, and on their heads are tall cloth hats like inverted flower-pots.

After the first procession they seat themselves on the ground in an attitude of prayer. Six or seven of them are portly, grey-bearded men, who seem to be well advanced in years. Then begins the religious ceremony. The musicians in the gallery—a violin, two flutes and a drum—strike a long wailing note, which gradually develops into a sort of melody gliding through half-tones into a theme which is perpetually repeated. This lasts for five minutes, and then an Imam chants what I take to be passages from the Koran. He has a tenor voice of beautiful timbre, and an intonation not unlike that of a priest singing Mass. When he has done, the leader of the dancers offers a prayer.

The dancers are still sitting, but if you have been watching them, you will have seen them beginning to sway, as if under the influence of some secret emotion. A minute or two later they rise to their feet and once more begin to pace round the circle. Their movements are slow and stately, and they pause frequently to bow to one another and to their leader. Then suddenly they throw off their outer robes, and the next time they go round the leader breaks away and starts spinning with outstretched arms. The next follows, and the next, and in a moment all are spinning with their arms stretched out and their skirts whirling, until from above they look like so many spinning-tops.

Presently four, including the blue skirt and the grey skirt, occupy the inner circle and greatly accelerate their pace. These four are now revolving about twice as fast as those in the outer circle, and the variation in the pace between the inner and outer circle is an extremely subtle and effective piece of choreography. The arms of all fourteen are kept rigidly out-stretched, and it seems a miracle that in this small space they never touch or even brush against each other. A venerable old man walks about among them, apparently urging them to greater and greater effort, and he, too, is never once touched.

I have never seen a ballet dancer who equalled the speed of the blue skirt and the grey skirt in the inner circle. It seemed impossible that they should go on and not drop from giddiness and exhaustion. Yet on they went minute after minute, looking from above as still as sleeping tops; and when finally the leader called time by stamping his foot, retired with perfect composure to their seats on the ground.

Three minutes later they started again, and the whole process was repeated. After another short interval they were starting again, but by this time I was beginning to feel slightly sick and came rather hastily away.

Out in the open again one wondered a little how old gentlemen—six or seven of them looked at least seventy—could disport themselves in this way. But I am bound to say that while I watched I felt not the slightest inclination to laugh. They had on their faces the ecstatic expressions of men wrapt in devotion; beyond all doubt they believed themselves to be dancing before the Lord. From the beginning to the end the whole thing was utterly simple, and in its own singular way, impressive.

Certainly the manifestations of the religious spirit are many and strange, but so thinks the Moslem about much that passes for religion in the Western world.

．　　　．　　　．　　　．　　　．　　　．

I was in Cairo on the day in January, 1926, when the great gold coffin of Tutankhamen was brought down from Thebes, and was allowed to see it before it was exhibited in the museum. I have now (1931) seen it again with a thousand other objects from the same tomb provisionally arranged in the museum.

Something I wrote on the former occasion drew down on my head a rebuke from one of our advanced art critics. Piling on his adjectives, he wanted to know how I, who had presumably seen the great statues in the Cairo Museum and other symbolic works of what may be called the Epstein period of Egyptian art, could pretend to admire those imitative, representational, realistic, unimaginative products of an evidently debased period. A young digger, at work near the Great Pyramid, confirmed this critic to the extent of dismissing them as "vulgarly modern," and this I find is the general attitude of those who are working in the fourth millennium B.C. to those who are at work on the second.

I am unrepentant. I positively rejoice in the fact that for once we have a literal transcript of this ancient life without the intervention (if that must be conceded) of the too imaginative artist. We need not always see everything through the distorting medium of genius. As for age, the great Pyramid may be twice as old, but for me it is enough to have this sudden re-creation of a sumptuous kind of life lived 3200 years ago—before Jerusalem, Athens or Rome was dreamt of, and when all but one little corner of Europe was still in the Stone Age. To repeat my previous offence, I defy anyone of ordinary susceptibilities not to feel a thrill of awe and wonder as he looks at the belongings, precisely as they saw and handled them, of men and women who lived before Moses and Agamemnon, when Greece and Rome and the Christian era were undreamt of. If the modern art critic is above these thrills, he must be asked to step out of the way for this occasion, and let the rest of us find a simple pleasure in the fact that these are not battered relics of antiquity, but things new and bright, coming straight out of the tomb, just as they were laid there 3000 years ago. I say frankly that I even get a certain pleasure from seeing ancient thumb-marks on painted objects handled 3000 years before they were quite dry.

Viewing it thus, I find many of these objects to be exquisitely and touchingly beautiful. In a very moving and pathetic way they tell the story of the boy King, the Marcellus of ancient Egypt, who died before his time, and was passionately mourned by the whole country. There can, as one looks at these things, be no doubt of the depths of emotion with which artists and craftsmen set themselves to the making of beautiful things to surround him and comfort him and minister to his needs in the other world.

Again and again one comes upon his portrait—life-size statues, statuettes, the superb gold mask with the blue enamel now famous all over the world; graven stories of his life at home with his young wife, or hunting with friends and courtiers on the banks of the Nile. Now he is in delicate profile, now in full face with dreamy eyes, but always with the same dignity and gravity which is yet youthful and simple. One can trace the whole of his short life from the nursery to the grave. There is the little chair in which he sat as a child, the toys that he played with, his first writing-set, his dicing board, the beds on which he slept, the throne on which he sat as a king with his wife by his side, his attendants and courtiers presented in exquisite little statuettes; his shoes, his walking-sticks, his chariot, his State barge—and then finally, as a climax to the whole, that amazing gold coffin with the lovely figures of the two goddesses protecting him with their wings.

The glamour and glitter of these objects are indescribable. No photography can give any idea of their sumptuous colour or of the intricacy of the craftsmanship which is lavished upon them. Through it all one gets the sense of a scene thronged with human beings. Those who look for it will find a whole portrait gallery in this collection—ladies of the court, gentlemen of the court, soldiers, slaves, dwarfs, men and women of all complexions and races. There is scarcely one which does not convince you that it is the image of a living person, and the variety of types is extraordinary. The general picture presented is that of a highly cultivated, luxurious and artificial civilization, as it was no doubt for the few gathered about the court; but there are hints of the underworld, the slaves and captives who ministered to the lives of these few. The handle of one of Tutankhamen's walking-sticks is an ingenious design in which a Nubian slave is uncomfortably bound up with someone who looks like a modern Evangelical preacher, but who is probably a captive of some Semitic race.

Archaeologists conjecture that a great many objects which are not funerary—*i.e.* which were not constructed specially to minister to the dead—were placed in this tomb. Not a little seems to be just the furniture of the palace, but why it should have been entombed is a mystery. But the whole story is a mystery. The little that we know of Tutankhamen is that he was somehow made the instrument of undoing his father-in-law Ikhnaton's great religious reformation, and that he either came back voluntarily, or was brought back forcibly by the priestly faction, from his father-in-law's capital at Tel-el-Amarna to the old capital, Thebes. Whether he died a natural death, or his end was hastened by one or other of the factions, and whether his tomb may not have been made a cache of precious objects for fear of another revolution, can only be guessed.

The attendant calls time and the museum is closing. I must come again another day and yet another. As I go down the steps from the gallery, a serious elderly man picks me up and asks me whether I do not share his feelings that the rifling of this tomb is an act of sacrilege which should never have been permitted by the Egyptian authorities. I do not share it at all. On the contrary, the bringing of these things to light seems to me an act of justice to the boy-King and the nameless company of artists and artificers who joined to pay him this tribute. This streak of light on the misty twilight of ancient history stirs thought, and, whatever my artistic critic may say, kindles imagination all the world over.

. . . . . .

January, 1931.

For the ideal rest-cure I can imagine nothing better than a few weeks spent in going backwards and forwards along the stretch of Nile between Assuan and Wady Halfa (or Shellal as its up-river port is called). The little steamers are clean and comfortable, the food is good, you need do nothing but keep your eyes open.

The sky throbs with light and colour in infinite variety from dawn to dark; a cool breeze comes over the great expanse of water. There are temples and villages on either shore, and, when the steamer stops, a chattering crowd comes down to meet it. On the river itself the Nile boats with their swelling triangular sails and different kinds of human and other freight make busy streets of many of its reaches, and if there was nothing else to look for, there would be always the birds—flamingoes, geese, ducks, osprey, cranes, herons and the flocks of white pigeons which circle about the villages. Crocodiles may be seen lying on the little islands with crowds of birds apparently in attendance on them, as Herodotus observed. On the western shore the sands are bright yellow, and one peeps between the desert cliffs into the great Sahara, which stretches a thousand miles or more before a human dwelling is seen again. On the western or Red Sea side the sands are grey and the rocks nearly black, and here, too, there are three or four hundred miles of desolation before the sea is reached.

Sometimes the river narrows and runs under steep rock cliffs rising sheer out of the water, but more often there are fringes of cultivation on the shore and groves of palm, tamarisk, mimosa and acacia clustering about the villages. As you go along, you hear incessantly the whining sound of the water-wheels scooping water from the river in a chain of buckets, and pouring it into the little canals which irrigate the cultivated plots—the patient ox going round and round exactly as in the days of the Pharaohs.

Some moments dwell specially in memory. About six in the morning on the second day I was awakened by a light coming into my cabin which told me that something was happening. I stepped out and looked across the river to a flaming orange sky behind a wall of jagged cliff all violet shot with green. Below on the shore was a palm grove dimly made out against the background, and the whole was reflected in silver water which gave the dark masses the sheen of black satin. A moment later bright rays streamed up into the sky, and then the sun came suddenly over the ridge, extinguishing the whole scene and turning it into a grey dazzle. I have never seen so much happen in so short a time.

For years past I have longed to see the great Rock Temple of Abu Simbel, which is the glory of Upper Egypt, and one comes to it on the evening of the second day. It is indeed a stupendous affair. The mere mechanical feat of scooping a sort of cathedral 180 feet long and 60 feet broad and 50 feet high out of solid rock leaves one gaping. The word "cathedral" gives the best idea of it, for it has aisles and side chapels; it narrows towards the innermost sanctuary, and its roof is supported by enormous square pillars. But the total effect in the glare of the electric light provided for the benefit of the modern traveller is neither dim nor religious; it is grossly intimidating and barbaric.

All the monuments that Rameses II has left behind him in Egypt suggest that he was an insatiable egoist and self-advertiser. The great seated Colossi which flank the temple entrance are all portraits of Rameses, and there are at least a score of his portraits in the sculptures on the walls within. He is god and man alternately; Rameses the man is seen making offerings to Rameses the god. He stands thirty feet high against each of the pillars supporting the roof. He is doing heroic deeds in all postures—shooting arrows in his chariots, standing haughtily over prostrate captives, smiting his enemies with a club, hacking at them with a curved sword. Thus is he seen in the great series of sculptured pictures illustrating the war which he waged with the Hittites some 3200 years ago.

When the time comes to raise monuments to the modern dictators, the sculptors will surely come to Abu Simbel for their models. In the meantime, to see these piercingly vivid pictures coming out of the mists of time is to get another of the great thrills of Egyptian travel. Abu Simbel is certainly not a temple of peace. Any Nubian invader tempted to come this way would have looked up from the river to see these frowning figures keeping guard over its doors, and, if he had gone within, would have learnt of the terrible prowess and ruthless character of the great Sovereign who ruled all Egypt and had conquered the Hittites and brought Palestine under his sway. There are many more beautiful monuments in Egypt, but there is none which in the same way brings home to one the haughty pride and ruthlessness of the ancient conqueror, or his entire conviction that he was one with the gods, and that they were all in league with him. The whole company of heaven—Amon-Re, Mut, Re-Harakhte, Isis, Astarte—is depicted on these walls, and the King is familiarly at home with all of them.

We shall come back the same way, but I do not want to see it again.

IV

IN THE SUDAN

February, 1931.

I HAVE been over the field of Omdurman, traced the line of the British advance, seen where the 21st Lancers charged and were ambushed, and stood on the spot where a friend of my youth, the young Hubert Howard, was killed, just in the shadow of the Khalifa's house.

The battlefield is a vast sun-smitten yellow and brown desert with streaks of flashing light marking the course of the river on the north and great lumps of basaltic rocks rising steeply out of it on its western bank. Low on its southern rim is the town of Omdurman, and looking carefully you can make out the battered remains of the Mahdi's tomb, and behind it the long line of low mud houses on the northern limit of the town.

Today it is a solitude, but one thinks of the horde of dervishes—that "low white cloud" with their spears flashing in the morning sun—which rushed out of Omdurman on September 2, 1898, and were mowed down by the British guns. If ever bloodshed was justified by results it was the blood shed on that day. In the thirty-two years that have followed, the town of Omdurman has been converted from a filthy slave mart into a populous, thriving and cheerful native city; and Khartoum across the river, in the apex of the triangle between the Blue and the White Nile, is the centre of a peaceful and highly efficient administration which extends over a territory as big as Europe, bar Russia, and joins up with the Belgian Congo on one side and British East Africa on the other.

I am staying in the palace of the Governor-General, built·

on the ruins of the old palace in which Gordon stood his last siege, and a tablet in the entrance hall marks the spot where he fell. From my windows I look across the river towards the desert and the low mountains on its rim—the view which Gordon scanned day by day for signs of the relief which came too late. Moored on the opposite shore is his steamer, the *Bordein*, which looks much as he left it and as he used it to prospect down the river, with the wooden palisading and rough sheet-iron which served him for shelter against rifle-fire still on the decks. It is nothing but an old Thames steamboat of the type in use in the sixties, and its funnel has a scalloped top according to the fashion of that period.

All along the river front is a broad and shady avenue flanked on the landward side by the public offices, the head-quarters of the soldiers and the houses of the officials—spacious houses with deep verandas surrounding them. A little back from the river is the Anglican Cathedral, and close by it the bishop's house, which seems to be thronged at all hours by natives and English. I hardly know how to describe the radiating influence which Bishop Gwynne sheds over both communities. His "propaganda" is to be a standing example of the Christian life to both Mohammedan and Christian; and the love and affection that go out to him are among the memories of this country that I shall always cherish.

A bridge across the White Nile at the end of the avenue connects Khartoum with Omdurman. The latter consists mainly of mud houses, but they are modern mud houses, built on a careful plan and scrupulously clean. A few brick houses for offices, schools and the housing of officials give a European touch, but the whole is an example of how a native town may be kept native, constructed at small cost, and yet avoid the dirt, smells, overcrowding and accompanying diseases that afflict most Eastern cities. Doctors, school-masters and school-mistresses are the pioneers of progress in this city. At Gordon College, across the river in Khartoum, a few English teachers with a large native staff are turning out young Sudanese to man the Government Departments, and passing a good many on to the Kitchener School of Medicine, where presently they will be qualified to run the little hospitals and medical stations which are being multiplied under the control of the English medical staff.

Gordon College, with which the name of the late Sir James Currie will always be associated, has in front of it the eternal problem of education in the East—how to provide a sufficiency of literates for the needs of the country and its administration without creating a discontented intelligentsia, for whom no employment can be found. It seems easy to say draw the line at a given point, but with an effervescing zeal for education as the mark of progress running through the population, and parents demanding that their sons shall have the same rights and chances as other people's sons, the thing is, in practice, very difficult. Gordon College tries to divert the stream into science, agriculture and handicraft. Its laboratories are the centres of the special research work that the country needs—qualities of soil and seed, ways of combating insect pests, effects of irrigation, etc. A devoted man is on the way to rid the country of one of its worst afflictions, the swarms of locusts which come suddenly from East and South and devour the crops. He has made a profound study of the nature and life history of this creature, and discovered that it dotes on arsenic and dies almost immediately on eating it. So he prepares an enormous quantity of bran soused in arsenic, and when locusts are signalled distributes it to the cultivators by aeroplane. The destruction of locusts and the saving of crops by this means have been on an immense scale, and if French, Belgians and Italians could be persuaded to co-operate I am told that it might be almost a complete specific for Central and Northern Africa.

$\cdot \qquad \cdot \qquad \cdot \qquad \cdot \qquad \cdot \qquad \cdot$

The greater part of the Northern Sudan is a vast, flat plain, divided unequally into desert, irrigation lands and lands on which crops are grown during or after the rainy season. The desert extends 50 miles south of Khartoum into the great triangle between the Blue and the White Nile—a space roughly 160 miles by 120 in its broadest part—and then gradually gives way to the irrigated area, which stretches the whole way south to the Sennar or Makwar dam from the reservoir above which it is watered.

This is the territory of the Sudan Plantations Syndicate, which works on an ingenious partnership system with the cultivator and the Government, these two taking 40 and 35 per cent. respectively and the Syndicate 25 per cent. of the yield of the cotton when it is sold. This has avoided the evils and complications of landlordism, as seen in Egypt, and till now has given each of the partners livelihood, revenue and profit in fair proportions. A great main canal, fed from the reservoir, runs from south to north of this area, and hundreds of side canals branch out to right and left, carrying the water into the cultivated area, with yet smaller canals and channels to distribute it among the crops. The flow is regulated at all points by sluice gates, which enable the water to be turned on and cut off at the requisite intervals. The business requires constant watching and inspection, lest the land should be over-watered or under-watered, and complete confidence of all parties in its fairness and competence.

Syndicate and Government work together in a benevolent supervision of the tenants, who have the thriftlessness and light-heartedness of the Sudanese Arabs, and require some persuasion to work on their lands instead of amusing themselves in the villages and—when they have a little money on hand—hiring others to do the work. They have a great deal of mechanical ingenuity, and handle motors and tractors as if to the manner born. An irregular service of motor-buses—wooden boxes on wheels furnished with benches and a tarpaulin rigged up over them—carries tenants and labourers backwards and forwards between the villages and the lands. They are fearsomely overcrowded, and rock heavily in a sea of ruts and furrows. The whole of this country is literally a creation, and it has all been created in the few years since the

completion of the great Makwar dam provided the water
There is now water enough to carry the irrigation right up
to Khartoum, and the prosperity of the country and its
progress in the future depend on the area which can be profitably irrigated and cultivated.

I know nothing quite like the sensation of coming down
the desert from Khartoum and seeing the green gradually
coming up. In England green is a colour which one takes
for granted as the universal background. But here one learns
its virtue and value, its infinite variety, its deep refreshment,
the thrill of it as the sign of man and his work in the waste.
The wide expanses of the deep green cotton plants with their
yellow flowers and white tufts, the fields of flowering bean
with their delicious scent, and the sun flashing on it all, fill
one with a great content.

I took train at Wad Medani, the capital of the Province,
and came towards evening to the Sennar or Makwar
dam, the key to the whole scheme, and one of the great
triumphs of the late Lord Cowdray and his firm, S. Pearson
& Son. I knew it, so to speak, by heart, for in writing
Cowdray's Life I had described its construction from material
provided for me by the engineers. But that was writing;
this was seeing. There, in front of me, was the island in mid-
channel—now almost blasted away—which enabled the river
to be divided into two parts, and each separately "unwatered"
for work in successive seasons; there, just below me, the
deep channel where engineers worked breathlessly against
time to find and build on the rock foundations before the
flood returned; and above, stretching right across the river,
the whole massive structure with its sluices and spillways like
the arches of an immense viaduct. To take it all in and
realize the immensity of this work requires some knowledge
of what is below as well as what is visible to the eye above
water, but it is on all counts a most noble achievement.

Behind it, up the river, the reservoir stretches like a great
lake as far as the eye can see. Below, on the western bank,
engineers and officials have made themselves a charming little

cantonment, with gay gardens round every bungalow, and a little park with swimming pool and tennis courts, in a blaze of tropical plants and shrubs. The thermometer has been near 100° in the shade all day—and this is mid-winter—but the sluices are open on this side of the dam, and the rush of waters which come foaming and tumbling down-stream makes a refreshing sound.

As the sun sets the air rapidly cools, and a delicious breeze comes in from the desert.

.   .   .   .   .   .

From Makwar I travelled all night in a saloon carriage, most thoughtfully provided for me, across the great plain of the Sudan to El Obeid, the capital of Kordofan, the central and largest province and the southernmost point of the Sudan Government railways. It was easy going, for this railway is one of the most comfortable in the world. I have a bath in my saloon, an Arab to wait on me and cook for me, and the largest sleeping compartment I ever travelled in.

El Obeid is a town of about 20,000 inhabitants, with several thousands more drifting in and out of it. The native part of it consists of groups of mud huts, some square with windows, and even occasionally two storeys—indicating great pros-perity—but the majority of the familiar beehive pattern with round, thatched roofs. The centre is the market-place, thronged, when I saw it, with all the types of Sudanese Arabs, men and women, and quantities of children, also camels, donkeys, cows, goats, dogs, crows, vultures and hoopoes.

A flat, dusty space separates the native town from what in India would be called the cantonment, *i.e.* the European quarter. Here is the apparatus of government, the Governor's house, the houses of the District Commissioners and officials —neat bungalows with deep verandas, each with its own garden—the Government offices, the headquarters of the Camel Corps, the club and an excellent hospital in which the medical officer wages incessant war with the many and strange diseases that afflict the native population in this part of the world.

I cannot pretend to think this an enviable place of residence. There is a scorching sun even in mid-winter; except for the well-heads there is no sign of water, and most of the trees are leafless. Right to the horizon on every side stretches a dusty, featureless plain, covered with bleached grass, withered durra or scrub. Yet, if I may believe the officials who live in it, El Obeid is a charming station, and nothing could be more stimulating and interesting than the opportunities it offers for talents and intelligence. And quite seriously, after spending three days with Mr. Gillan, the Governor, I have come to think so. For this seemingly featureless country begins to give up a little of its secret as one looks at it. A vivid, chattering people pours out of villages which are almost invisible till you come up to them. The plan of cultivation begins to reveal itself; you distinguish the settled peoples from the nomads—the little parties with their camels, donkeys and goats, going, as they will tell you, to Mecca, but in all probability just yielding to the vagrant instinct which keeps the people from the West constantly on the move.

It was King's Day—the anniversary of the day in January, 1912, when King George and Queen Mary visited Port Sudan—the day after I came to El Obeid, and a brave show they made of it; in the morning horse races, camel races, donkey races for the men; in the afternoon sports and gymnastic displays for the schools. There were 120 entries for the horse races, with the police keeping or trying to keep the course. The riders were exuberant but erratic, and some of them took short cuts through the crowd. The camels also made wide detours from the prescribed course. But it was all immensely good-humoured, and a message from Buckingham Palace, read by the Governor, raised enthusiasm to a high pitch.

The sports in the afternoon were on the perfect public school model, and watched with the keenest interest by a great crowd of enthusiastic and admiring parents. I had the high privilege of presenting the prizes. The smart turn-out of the black Boy Scouts would have warmed the heart of the Chief Scout, and I promised to let him know about them when I got back.

After all, I begin to feel that I have painted the landscape in too dusty colours. Sunrise and sunset are an enchantment, and sleeping in the open under the stars one looks up into a heaven of indescribable splendour and beauty. Only in this latitude does one begin to know the glory of the heavens. Jeans and others may talk of the emptiness of space. Here at all events it is "thick inlaid with patines of bright gold." Indeed, the gold prevails and seems only to be punctured with little black peepholes into space.

And here, as everywhere, the Englishman plants his garden. In my Eastern travels, whether in India, Egypt, Palestine, the Sudan, I have come to think of the garden as the sign and symbol of his presence. Last week I asked a District Commissioner if he found life hard on the peculiarly barren waste on which his lot had fallen, and he answered that his only complaint was that the Public Works Department had refused to let him have water for a flower garden. In El Obeid there are lovely little gardens round every bungalow. I made an inventory of the flowers in one of them, and found oleanders, rose and white, "morning glory," bougainvillæas, bushes of yellow tecoma, frangipani, pink and sweet-scented, and beds of portulacas, nasturtium and petunias. To sit in one of these little gardens in the cool of the evening and drink in the scent of flowers as the twilight passes into night is one of the thrills of travel in the Tropics.

V

AMONG THE NUBAS

I

February, 1931.

IN the last weeks I have travelled many hours by car over deserts and have been pleasantly surprised at the comparatively smooth going over roadless, and, one would have thought, all but impassable ground. But the mirage has worried me. I have read many reassuring scientific explanations of its cause and origin, but none of them prepared me for its queer effect on eye and brain. At first I thought the vision of a shining river with palm-shaded villages on the brim to be a happy relief from the interminable brown waste through which I was passing. But no reminder that it was a freak of refraction could quench the sense of disappointment when it moved on. Again and again one seemed to be just reaching this delectable break in the interminable journey only to find it snatched away by an invisible hand. The heat, the dust in one's throat, nose and eyes all seemed to be aggravated by this ghost of cool clear water just out of reach. After a time disappointment becomes exasperation, and exasperation fades into something between dreaming and delirium, a semi-hypnotic state in which nothing seems real or substantial.

Yet if one can watch them composedly as in the train between Wady Halfa and Khartoum, which passes through one of the ugliest deserts in the world, these phantasmal landscapes are things of indescribable beauty. One sees them not moving on as one goes forward, but passing to the side of one as an ordinary landscape seen from a train. Heaven knows where they come from or what they reflect, but nothing could be more exquisite than the cool silver mountains reflected in crystal lakes which they so cunningly counterfeit. It is only when they move ahead that they have the touch of mockery which attends all deceptions.

Once again I have slept in the open and seen the miracle of the starry heavens in these latitudes. As I lay on my back and looked up, the dazzle was such that I had to cover my eyes before I could think of sleep. The nearest stars seemed to be falling on me, and looking up I saw rank behind rank of glittering jewels. Dante's lines thrummed in my head:

> O Settentrional vedovo sito
> Poiché privato sei di mirar quelle.

Of all the glories of the south, the sky at night is the greatest. If one came for this alone, it would be worth while.

.   .   .   .   .   .

2

I am off south again, accompanying the Governor of Kordofan and his wife in a fast car which takes us across a hundred miles of dusty plain to Dilling, the centre of the Nuba mountains district. Behind us is a lorry bringing our camp outfit and provisions for three days, for we are seriously on trek, and tonight we shall camp out at a rest-house in the heart of the Nuba mountains.

This hundred miles is the most interesting road I ever travelled, for along its space one sees the entire transition from clothes to no clothes—from Europe and Asia to the heart of Africa. At the north end of it is the Sudanese Arab, like all his tribe, one of the most abundantly clothed of human beings, who, if he is a self-respecting man, covers even his legs with his flowing gallibea. At the southern end is the stark-naked Nuba, who seriously thinks clothes to be nasty and unhygienic, harbourers of lice and other impurities which defile the human form divine.

All along this road you may, so to speak, see clothes coming off. The Nuba who comes up it concedes something to Arab prejudices by covering a part of him with a loin-cloth, but this grows scantier as you approach Dilling, and in Dilling itself a large number of the inhabitants of both sexes and all ages are completely without clothes. Correspondingly, the human types change. You leave behind the long-faced Arab and greet the round-headed, flat-nosed, full-lipped, woolly-haired negro. I cannot pretend to think their faces beautiful, but a large number of them are physically splendid. Where physical defects cannot be concealed, pride is enlisted against them. Men and women are tall, and most have perfectly straight backs, and beautifully shaped arms, hands and legs. They walk with a certain swagger and have a free swinging gait. The children are slim and lithe, and very active on their feet. They seem a jolly and cheerful people, and are laughing incessantly about something. To my companions all this is familiar, but it takes me some time to adjust myself to this very novel scene. Dilling is a little town of the ordinary Sudan type, with British offices and bungalows, Arab shops and houses, even a cotton market of its own. To see half the inhabitants going about naked and the other half taking it as a matter of course is even stranger than if all were naked.

But at Dilling we are only on the outskirts of this country, and we have another thirty miles to go to get into the heart of it. In front of us to the south lie the Nuba mountains, a vivid blue in the distance showing a sharp jagged edge against the sky. After twenty miles we begin climbing up a narrow valley with steep rocky hills rising seven or eight hundred feet on either side. They are fantastic hills formed of vast brown boulders, to all appearance thrown at random, as engineers say, and lying as they fall. Along the skyline little boulders are perched on the edge of big ones, like the rocking stones one sees in Cornwall, and so delicately poised that one might suppose a touch would throw them over. Everywhere in the interstices are Sunt trees—the dominant acacia of the Sudan—which perform extraordinary feats in finding footholds and filling spaces.

169

But the tree of trees in this district and in all this part of Africa is the Tebeldi, which stands monstrous and solitary on almost every piece of flattish land. I can never see it without being tempted to laugh at it. With its vast barrel-like trunk rising straight up two-thirds of its height, and short gesticulating arms, which sprout rather than branch from the top of this trunk, it is the sort of tree Mr. Arthur Rackham has drawn in his pictures of the bad parts of Fairyland. Yet it is a most serviceable creature and the positive salvation of some villages in the dry season. Its trunk may be hollowed out and converted into a water tank; its bark woven into fabric; its fruit, though nutty and tough, is full of nutriment. The Dassa stalks of which the Nubas build their beehive huts are tied together with rope made of its bark.

The Nubas of Solara, the village where we are to camp, have heard of our coming, and are swarming down the valley to meet us. Some have stopped by mud pools and are doing their toilets. There could be no greater mistake than to suppose that because they have no clothes they dispense with this part of the human routine. Far from it. Their hair is done in elaborate patterns picked out with safety-pins. Their bodies are washed and polished, oil rubbed in till they glisten like mahogany. Many of them are adorning themselves for the occasion with pale grey mud picked from the pools and worked into original designs on their black bodies. Some of these designs are obviously caricatures of clothes. One has got himself up like an Arab office-boy he has seen at Dilling, with short-sleeved tunic reaching to the knees rubbed in with mud, and black skin left about the waist to show where the boy wears a sash. Very effective. Another is similarly adorned with a mud jumper and shorts.

Nearly all wear necklaces, bangles, nose-rings or ear-rings, and the women have bead belts of various colours showing whether they are single, married or affianced. Newly initiated young men wear fur collars, and women who have recently had babies long strips of fur down their backs. As we came up to the village five or six hundred are gathered on the flat space in front of the rest-house in readiness for the dance which is to celebrate our visit. The women break into the ulalele—the shrill, burbling chorus which is the sign of welcome—and the elders advance offering both hands.

Follows a long pause in which certain young men prance about with enormous swagger, but nothing else happens. Then it is conveyed to us that something has gone wrong. The drum is broken and they cannot dance without it. We produce a tray and a stick to beat it with, but the idea is either not understood or summarily rejected. It takes half an hour to get another drum, and the time is filled with more prancings by the young men and incessant clapping of hands. At last the new drum arrives, and to its beating the whole crowd gets in motion. They go slowly round a circle in single file, young men, old men, girls, brides, married women, each in a separate formation, never touching or mingling with the others, but just walking round and round and stamping their feet. The children seem to go as they please, running about and dodging between the groups. A few of the men have spears which they brandish, but most are content with the strong straight poles which nearly everybody in this country seems to carry. They shout and laugh as they go round, and the general effect is that of a glistening mass of black humanity revolving in the sun.

There is a curious lack of finish about it all. You always think that something more is going to happen, but nothing more ever does happen. A young man starts to turn a somersault, but repents at the last moment. The dancing is varied by wrestling, but just as the wrestlers seem to be getting to grips someone rushes out from the crowd and parts them. It is the tribal rule in these days that no sport must be serious. There was a time in this village when wrestling went on to its conclusion, but the Nuba hates to be beaten, and the defeated wrestler was apt to go by night and stab the victor. So the elders decided that there must always be friends at hand to part them before their blood got up.

The District Commissioner shakes his head a little on

observing that certain braves have girdled themselves with a wisp of cotton for this occasion. These young modernists, he says, are by no means the best of the tribe, and they may need watching, as in Europe we watch Communists and Bolsheviks.

. . . . . .

As we sat at dinner on the evening after the dance in the mud-hut, which was our dining-room, this being lit by a few candles on the trestle table, we heard a little sobbing sound coming out of the darkness behind.

Turning round we saw a little black girl, about eight years old, with the tears pouring down her cheeks and evidently in great grief. An Arab who knows something of the strange language of this tribe was brought in to question her, and he presently made out that she had come to the dance in the afternoon and lost her bowl in the crowd and could not bear to go home without it, the bowl of painted gourd being one of the treasures of the household. So she had waited about till dark fell, and then slipped into our dining-room in the hope that the District Commissioner, who was there at dinner, would be able to find the missing bowl. He did not find it, but he did succeed miraculously in getting her another and better one, and she went away comforted and happy.

This little incident tells much more than anything I could write about the relations of the District Commissioner and the people in this region. He is a very young man, not long from Oxford and barely in his thirties, and he is often almost alone in these wild mountains where there are nearly half a million of the naked people. But he loves his job, and speaks with affection of the people, for whom he chiefly fears an intrusion of what is called civilization.

He looks with concern on the cotton planting which is creeping in to the south and bringing business men in its wake; he thinks a mistake was made when the Government recruited for the Sudanese battalions from this area. True, the ex-soldiers reverted quickly to the nudity and other tribal customs of their birth-land, but they brought with them an undesirable aptitude in rifle-shooting and certain modern ideas of a disturbing character.

This, however, he said had not gone far, and their primitive simplicity was almost unspoilt. They were, according to their own standard, an exceedingly moral people with a strict discipline, especially in sexual matters. Companionate marriages, which could be discontinued on repayment of dowries, were permitted, and divorce allowed on the same condition, but there was no promiscuity and the sexes treated each other with great respect. It seemed to my eye that the women did most of the heavy work, but they have a powerful physique and superb carriage which make it impossible to think them as put upon, and they seemed never happier than when carrying immense loads on their heads as well as children strapped to their backs.

The religion of these people is a rather vague belief in one god approached through ancestor worship and the mediation of witch-doctors. The witch-doctor is a very important person, and though he is supposed to be appointed by divine inspiration indicated by foaming at the mouth, I gathered that the tribes took discreet measures to secure that the divine choice was a sensible one.

Rules of conduct and etiquette are many and intricate. Smoking, for example, is permitted only to unmarried girls and old people. For grown men it is thought unmanly. The girls came up holding out their pipes for us to fill with our English tobacco, which they think a great luxury. I exhausted my pouch and went pipeless for two days in my desire to please them. The half-million Nubas have at least three languages between them, and one group of villages may be totally unable to understand the language of another group. All the languages are, so far, unintelligible to Europeans, but the District Commissioner is making a valiant effort to master one of them, and he conjectures that all of them are of Bantu stock.

Having still a vivid memory of the Indian North-West

frontier, I could not help thinking it great good fortune for the Province of Kordofan that the 500,000 Nubas who inhabit this region are not, as the Pathans, raiders by instinct and tradition who seek pastime and plunder on the plains. Their instinct is just the reverse. Having for generations been chased and raided by slave-hunters, they have learnt to stick to their mountains. Now and again they flare up amongst themselves, and fourteen years ago they flung into a rage and killed a District Commissioner—a crime which had to be punished by a regular expedition—but usually they are quiet and docile, and an occasional "punitive control" suffices to keep them in order.

To get on to one of the ridges in these mountains and look down on the vast rolling landscape fading to the distant blue of the southern horizon is to have the queer sense of looking over the edge of things into the heart of savage Africa. To the west lies French Equatorial Africa, to the south the Bahr-el-Ghazal and the Congo. Half a day's journey would bring one to the regions of big game and tropical forests. But this is my farthest point south, and from now my face is turned north.

VI

AN ADMINISTRATION

IT was past sunset when I got to Kosti on the White Nile and met the Governor, Mr. Pawson, on his steamer which was to take us by night downstream to his capital, Dueim. It was a disappointment to me that this part of the journey had to be done by night, for the steamer coming up had seen a good many hippos on this river, and I was denied that privilege. You really do seem in these parts to be in the middle of zoological nature. I heard at Kosti that lions were only twenty miles away, and becoming uncomfortably aggressive towards flocks and herds. The Governor was turning over in his mind whether he should accede to the petition of certain villagers to be permitted to carry sporting rifles to deal with this enemy. I said surely, but he observed that lions had a queer habit of multiplying so soon as it was known that their presence was recognized as a valid reason for carrying rifles. Nothing in this country is as simple as it seems.

At Dueim I was permitted to attend a native court, and heard a case tried, the Governor interpreting for my benefit. The courthouse was a small, whitewashed room with a thatched roof and no ceiling. All round it seated on the ground were the sheiks, who acted as magistrates. The case to be tried was that of a native policeman who charged his wife with improper conduct with another man in the police lines. He was brought in, and, seating himself on the ground in the middle of the circle, opened his own case with much vehemence, being occasionally stopped and questioned by members of the court.

After him came his principal witness, a woman, who was sharply cross-examined. Then the wife appeared, tearfully

175

denying the charge, but also closely cross-examined. Then her witness was similarly treated, and finally the co-respondent, also vehement in denial. After this the parties withdrew and there was a buzz of conversation round the circle, which ended in the policeman being recalled. The court was against him, but it was admitted that his wife had been indiscreet. He was told to be more careful in future about bringing charges without sufficient evidence, and admonished to live peaceably with his wife and forget this incident. Then she was brought in and received a little lecture about wifely behaviour, after which they both took an oath to respect the judgment of the court and live peaceably together in future. It was all conducted with the greatest gravity and dignity. I was assured that the judgment carried complete assent and that the parties would abide by it.

All over this territory the Administration has to be constantly on the alert to prevent the traffic in slaves which, but for this vigilance, would go on merrily between the west and the Abyssinian border. A round-up last year released a thousand slaves destined for Abyssinia, and landed some scores of slave-merchants, including one notorious old lady, in gaol for long periods. What to do with the released slaves is often a very perplexing question, and getting it into the minds of Sudanese Arabs that slave-holding is morally reprehensible is uphill work all the way.

The car which took me back from Dueim to Khartoum threaded its way through fields of durra and bean, and then for long stretches ran along the west bank of the White Nile. There was no visible road, but the Arab driver seemed to know every inch of the way and made clever little detours to avoid the worst bumps. The crossing of a wide reach of the river under a high wind in a small native felucca looked something of an adventure. The sail seemed enormous for the size of the craft, and its handling did not inspire confidence. Questioned by my companion, the chief navigator explained that he had come to oblige the real owner, who was ill; and, though he had never sailed a boat before, he had seen it done and thought he could do it. He was sternly enjoined to reef his sail and take to oars. And so we got safely across. When the water below you is full of crocodiles, it is better not to take chances.

.   .   .   .   .   .

I gather that the British officials who administer this country have become a little sensitive about the haloes which have been placed about their heads by certain writers and travellers. They have a thoroughly British objection to being presented as other than quite ordinary people engaged in quite commonplace work. To hear them talk one would suppose there was nothing in it.

I will endeavour to respect this feeling and to state in the most matter-of-fact terms what they are doing. There are about 200 officials, or, if one adds the inspectors and officials of the cotton syndicate, about 600 all told. The officials are mostly Oxford and Cambridge men, many of them quite young, and between them they administer an area nearly as large as Europe bar Russia. A large part of the country is sun-scorched, brown desert, and much of the rest—except in the rainy season—is only scantily covered with strands of dried-up grass, poisonous-looking bushes, or stunted and leafless trees. There seems to be no particular reason why human beings should live in one part of it rather than another. All the villages are much alike—clusters of round beehive-shaped thatched huts with mud walls, and scarcely any have greenery about them or shelter from the blistering sun. Yet large numbers of human beings do live and multiply in this region, and fifty years ago they were the helpless victims of plunderers and slave raiders. Being a physically splendid race, of great stature, they were in great demand in the slave marts of Africa and Asia. The 200 administrators have brought peace and security to these people, and by degrees are teaching them to manage their own affairs, to do justice among themselves, to improve their primitive agriculture and the breed of their camels, donkeys and cows. Also they are providing them with medical and sanitary services, and schools in which they learn to read and write in their own language and some of them are taught English. Under this treatment they have increased in thirty years from about two millions to nearly six, and they are becoming extremely zealous about getting themselves and their children educated.

The officials work, if one may so speak, by rule of thumb; that is to say, they are as little like officials and as much like benevolent squires in an old-time English village as climate and circumstances permit. Their ruling idea is to work upwards from existing tribal institutions, and to impose as little as possible of what is new and alien. Thus, for all minor offences and misdemeanours justice is done by village sheiks, and even in the graver cases the District Commissioner, who sits as judge, has sheiks for his assessors. Enormous pains are taken to prevent miscarriage of justice, and the very few capital sentences that are carried out are carefully scrutinized by the legal authorities and finally by the Governor-General. The basis of everything in this country is the sense that justice is done and that the poorest are sure of a fair deal. Soldiers are few and far apart, and a small native police force suffices for all the purposes of law and order.

The central Government is situated in Khartoum, where are the departments and their directors, corresponding to the Secretariat in India. For local administration the country is divided into provinces, each with its governor, and these again are sub-divided into districts, each with its district commissioner. I look down the list of these officials and find it scintillating with the names of famous athletes. My first host, when I left Khartoum for the south, was Mr. R. V. Bardsley, the Oxford and Lancashire cricketer, now transformed into Governor of the Blue Nile Province. He met me at breakfast on my first stoppage, sixty miles from Khartoum, and took me in his car to his capital at Wad Medani, giving me a fascinating account of the country as we travelled the next fifty miles. It is specially responsible work, since his province includes the great cotton district on which so much depends.

My next host, and an extraordinarily kind and hospitable one, was Mr. J. A. Gillan, a famous Oxford oar, now Governor of Kordofan, the largest of the Sudan provinces. Then, when I started north again I fell into the hands of Mr. A. G. Pawson, Winchester and Christchurch, a renowned double Blue (cricket and football), now Governor of the White Nile Province. The list shows a great many more, but these come within my own personal knowledge, and I can attest that the government of these African provinces by "old Blues" is a wise and benevolent rule. All speak with enthusiasm of their Chief, Sir John Maffey, and great as are the distances which separate them from Khartoum and from one another, one is conscious of an all-pervading team-work.

I have known far too many "Blues" in my time to share the common delusion of foreigners and others who write about our country that the Englishman who is good at games is necessarily or generally a mental deficient. If there are such the Sudan Government is wise enough not to choose them, but it is also wise enough to know that, added to other necessary qualifications, a proficiency in games, and still more the faculty of being good captains and leaders of their fellows, are a warrant of just the kind of efficiency that this country needs in its officials.

These men have good health, steady nerves and cheerful tempers; they take the rough with the smooth, and play fair with the natives and their fellow officials. Be it large or small, they take special pride in "running their own shows," and they speak with enthusiasm of the rare and special opportunities offered by some peculiarly forbidding patch of scorching desert or remote solitude among the savages of the mountains. And they bring their wives with them, who also seem to share this enthusiasm, though it is a little harder on women when the thermometer marks 118° in the shade, as it often does in summer.

I have tried to be matter of fact, as I was enjoined to be, but I find myself warming up a little as I go along. I really cannot help it. As one passes from district to district and sees the picture unfolding before one's eyes, the impression it makes is ineffaceable. As an example of quiet competence, entire absence of pomp, vanity or self-assertion, and loyalty to a common cause, there can be nothing better in the world today.

179

VII

IN PALESTINE

March, 1931.

I HAVE talked by the hour with Jews, Arabs and Christians, heard the views of officials, and faithfully written home my own views, for what they are worth, on the problem which confronts the Mandatory Power in its effort to carry out the "Balfour declaration." I sympathize with each in turn, and pray that the spirit of give and take which seems to have fled from the modern world—whether East or West—may some day descend on them and bring them a happy issue out of their numerous afflictions.

But in the meantime let me forget it for a space while I look at the scene before me in Jerusalem, which, though Jew and Arab may battle over it, is still for millions of Europeans the place of the Holy Sepulchre. A thousand pens have described it, and the details are familiar—so wrongly familiar that I find myself all the time correcting mental pictures and preconceived ideas which differ from what I see.

I knew, of course, that Jerusalem is a city set upon a hill, but, if I knew, I had not realized that it is nearly 3000 feet above sea-level. The little railway which brings you up from the coast winds steeply up a long valley, mounting by zigzags like a Swiss mountain railway. From the Mount of Olives which rises to the east of the city, you look down across the stony wilderness of Judaea to the Jordan Valley and the Dead Sea—1500 feet below sea-level, and over 4000 feet down. Beyond, closing the horizon to the south-east, is the long straight ridge of the mountains of Moab, rising some 4000 feet from the floor of the valley.

It was a new thought to me that Jesus and His disciples

had this vast prospect before them when they went up into the Mount of Olives.

With its great circuit of walls and gates—Crusaders' walls, Saracen walls, Turkish walls—Jerusalem has the outward aspect of a mediaeval place, a place of battle and strife, as indeed it has been through a large part of its history. I had supposed it to be more or less level, but in fact it is built on four hills, with its steep, narrow, cobbled streets running up and down the ravines between them and its houses piled on the hillsides. Within the circuit of its walls it is one of the most beautiful unspoilt Eastern cities. I have walked in it for hours to find endless fascination in its steep winding streets, its stairways with the houses overhanging, its bazaars with their vaulted roofs, the beautiful vistas, whether one looks up or down, the constant surprises as one turns a corner and sees an ancient church or mosque or a Crusader's arch. There is no wheeled traffic within the walls, but camels and donkeys and sheep thread their way through the human crowd. And what a crowd! Where else in so small a space can one see so many different kinds of human beings? Priests of all the Churches, Greek, Latin, Armenian, Copt, monks, nuns and friars, rub shoulders with bearded Rembrandtesque Jews, Arabs, Egyptians, veiled Moslem women, bold-eyed unveiled peasant women and a multitude of children. It is mediaeval Europe in an Eastern setting—but the dominant note is Eastern, Arab, Moslem.

The Christians are in their separate enclave in which Churches and nationalities fight incessant battles for their respective priorities. No sign here of Christian humility. All the last want to be first and to make the first last. The Protestants pursue their competition outside the walls and are rapidly defacing the landscape with new buildings of a modern type which shout at one another. The ex-Kaiser's church and hospice ruins the beautiful slope by the south-east corner of the walls with what looks like a monstrous railway station. Within the walls the Latin and the Orthodox conduct their warfare in the picturesque mediaeval manner. French,

German, Italian, Russian, Armenian, Copt, even Abyssinian,
all have their separate churches, monasteries, convents, hos-
pices, and all are mutely or aggressively asserting their claims
to the sacred sites. Their pressing and jostling are open and
flagrant in the Church of the Holy Sepulchre, where their
chapels and altars crowd in upon one another, and it is difficult to say which of them surpasses the others in the costliness
(and tawdriness) of its offerings. One's guide faithfully points
out that the jewels on the dreadful statues, all gold or all
silver, the gifts of great sovereigns, are worth millions; but
this undoubted fact merely starts the reflection that wealth,
piety and art go ill together.

Yet if one can suppress these details, the whole is impressive
and in its way beautiful. I had no idea of the size of the
great church, or rather the group of churches, which covers
the traditional sites of the Crucifixion and Entombment and
is called the Church of the Holy Sepulchre. They have
blocked each other's light so that you walk from one to the
other, or grope your way up the steps which lead to the
many different levels, in a spacious gloom which gives the
sense of being in a vast catacomb dimly lit with the lamps
and candles that hang before the numerous altars.

The whole is a growth of time, seemingly without order
or plan, but marking all the centuries of Christian history
and struggle. It has been shattered by earthquakes, ravaged
by Moslems, barbarously reconstructed, but you can look
nowhere without seeing lovely fragments of ancient building
—massive marble columns with Byzantine capitals, encrusted
mosaics, beautiful inlaid pavements, and wrought-iron screens.
Unfortunately the official guide whom you must have pushes
you on before you have time to take in a tithe of it.

But it is brought home to one in Jerusalem that this place
is not only the Holy City of Christendom, but one of the
holiest of Moslem holy places, ranking only after Mecca and
Medina. I am bound to say that in the great Dome of the
Rock (commonly called the Mosque of Omar) and the other
great mosque on the side of the ancient Jewish Temple, there

is a sense of peace, unity and dignity which is lacking in the Christian shrine. The Orthodox and Latin Churches have not been able to compose their differences sufficiently to bring the care and regulation of it under one control, whereas the Moslem sects have sunk their differences in a united effort to protect and restore these noble buildings and to rescue them from modern and tasteless accretions.

I think of the great Moslem sites I have seen—the great Mosque at Delhi, the Taj Mahal at Agra, Santa Sophia at Constantinople—and am tempted to say that the Dome of the Rock, with the adjacent buildings, is the most beautiful of them all. The site is superb, and the lay-out of the different levels, with the long terraces of steps, the arches above them, and the beautiful ancient cypresses flanking them, is a work of genius. Apart from the Dome, the Mosque of El Aksa, whatever its origin, is surely the finest basilica in the world.

Just down below is the Wailing Place of the Jews, and on the other side of the valley is the Garden of Gethsemane. If you remember that you are standing on Moslem ground and look on both sides, you will begin to understand the problem of Jerusalem and Palestine.

· · · · · ·

I have spoken of Jerusalem; let me now add a few glimpses of the country beyond, as one sees it today.

The road from Jerusalem to Nazareth takes one over a succession of mountain ridges, rising from two to three thousand feet above sea-level, and between them are spacious valleys, down which one looks to more mountains closing the western horizon. The uplands are bleak and stony, and almost the only trees are the olives and figs on the sheltered lower levels. There are a few Arab villages on the higher ground, and camels and goats seem to thrive on the scrub and coarse grass which they find there, but only in the valleys does it look a land of promise for the human settler.

The distant views are enchanting—fold upon fold of grey-blue hills, which now and again open out and show a broad belt of glistening sea. The shape and sweep of the hills remind one of the Yorkshire moors or Cumberland fells, but the road is alive with camels and donkeys and Palestine Arabs in the charming and many-coloured garments of the country. The valleys look prosperous and are closely cultivated, the vivid green of their rising crops intensifying by contrast the brown and grey bleakness of the higher ground.

Coming out of Samaria the road passes steeply down to the great plain of Esdraelon or Megiddo—scene and symbol of strife in Biblical history, but now a wide stretch of fertile and well-tilled land, with the Valley of Jezreel opening out of it to the south-east. Then it mounts by zigzags to Nazareth, a little town enfolded in hills and climbing steeply up the hillsides. With its olives and cypresses and yellow-washed houses it might be any little hill-town in Provence, and there is nothing to do in it except just to look at it and let the thought sink in that this was the home of Jesus. There is a large monastery up the hill to the west, and on the other side a beautiful old Turkish house with blue-black cypresses in its garden.

The road mounts again as it leaves Nazareth, and for the next nine miles passes along a high plateau with great views on either side. Then it begins to descend towards the Sea of Galilee, and, as it turns a bend, the snows of Mount Hermon glistening in the sun sixty miles away to the north come suddenly into view. It is mid-February, and the time of the lilies and tulips is not yet, but the hillsides are already a feast of flowers—big anemones, scarlet, pink, mauve; white violets; asphodel just beginning; clusters of pink cyclamen under bushes of rosemary and yellow broom; stone-crop, thyme, and all the little flowers that scent the mountain air as one treads on them. I can think of no scene more lovely than this descent to the Sea of Galilee with the flowers on the hillside.

The lake gradually reveals itself as one goes down—a gleaming steel-blue sheet of water, fourteen miles long and six miles broad, with stony, barren mountains to the east and stretches of green coming down to the water on the north and west. There is scarcely a tree in sight, and no signs of the towns, Bethsaida, Chorazin, and others which were thick on the shores in the time of Christ. Capernaum is little more than a site, though it contains one very interesting ruin, that of an ancient Jewish synagogue, possibly on the ground where Christ taught in the synagogue. There is only one considerable town remaining from ancient times, namely Tiberias, and that, though Eastern and picturesque, is dirty and ill-kept. The one road which goes down to the lake is all mud and broken pavement, a slippery trap for the feet; and the only space in which you can sit by the lake is occupied by a broken-down landing-stage and beer-garden.

Yet, sitting there as the sun goes down, one forgets all this in the enchantment of the scene. The afterglow in this country is a thing of indescribable beauty, and when the sun has gone the recesses of the barren mountains become a purple velvet against which their ridges and projections are softly outlined in a pale amber light. The snows of Hermon are rose-pink, but gradually fade into the sky as the twilight falls upon the lake. Watching here and listening to the Convent bells, one can easily believe this to be the Holy Land.

It took us five hours of leisurely motoring along (for the most part) excellent roads to get from Jerusalem to Tiberias. It must have taken Jesus and His disciples at least seven days to go up from Capernaum to Jerusalem, walking on foot on the stony paths up the mountain sides and down into the valleys, along the plain of Esdraelon, through Samaria and so on to the Mount of Olives, and into Jerusalem by the Valley of Jehoshaphat. Many of the villages still bear the familiar names, but reading the Gospel story one gets the impression that it must have been a vastly more populous country in the time of Christ. On that the hope is founded that it may still be restored, but no one who has seen this country as it is now, can underrate that task.

The Church of the Nativity at Bethlehem may or may not be, as it claims, the oldest Christian Church in the world, but it is certainly a very beautiful basilica, and in striking contrast to the debased Gothic nineteenth-century church which the Roman Catholics have built side by side with it. The grottoes containing the traditional sites of the Birth and the Manger extend under both churches, and their rivalry is punctuated by the precisely marked boundaries which divide their shrines and altars. The loud claims of both to know the exact truth about the smallest unverifiable detail do not conduce to a pious state of mind, and I own I was relieved to come out of this gloom and take my fill of the glorious landscape to be seen from the terrace outside.

A vast amphitheatre descends in sweeping curves to the Dead Sea, and beyond is the long blue line of the mountains of Moab. Anemones and cyclamen are thick upon the ground beneath one, and, as one looks down, masses of pink almond blossom sing out against a background of olives. A long vivid green slope in the middle distance marks the "fields of the shepherds," and fades away gradually into the stony wilderness by the Dead Sea. On these hills and overlooking this vast prospect is the traditional scene of the Nativity.

If it is cold and foggy in Jerusalem, as it may easily be in the winter months, you have a simple remedy—go to Jericho. Go down the steep zigzagging road between the stony mountains, past the Inn of the Good Samaritan, along the grey plain by the Dead Sea to the charming oasis of bananas, palms and orange trees, in the middle of which is the little town of modern Jericho. It is almost always sunshine there, and there is a nice clean little inn where you can get a good lunch or spend a night in comfort. The view over the town to the Dead Sea and the mountains beyond is superb, and to be there at sunset time is to enjoy one of the great moments of Eastern travel. The flashing greenery against the ash-grey plain, the deep-blue waters and the mountains beyond doing their daily transformation scene are things defying description but eternally fixed in memory.

I have in my pocket a little blackened grain of wheat taken with a thousand more like it from a newly excavated house on the walls of the old Jewish city, which Prof. Garstang and his little band of archaeological students are now bringing to light. The house was evidently burned over the heads of its occupants, and quite probably when Joshua took and destroyed the city. Somehow it thrills me a little to handle this tiny survivor from the city which Joshua so ruthlessly destroyed.

VIII

TOWARDS THE WEST INDIES

December, 1932.

I SHALL never see the Azores.

"*The Commander regrets that in consequence of the delay caused by bad weather the ship will be unable to stop at the Azores and will proceed direct to Bermuda.*"

Until I read that on the notice-board this morning I had never realized that I had within me a secret passion to visit the Azores. Now these Islands suddenly take on a golden glamour. I think of them as Islands of the Blest, objects of desire to go down with me to the grave with a thousand other thwarted hopes and dreams. I paint them as sunny, blue, serene, with calm waters in sheltered harbours, and look out in despair at the wild grey waste of driving rain and tumbling seas which is the actual prospect. What is worse, the intended subject of this chapter is slipping away to the east without my having got even a glimpse of it, and I am reduced to talking about the weather.

There is, however, something to be said about the weather when you are a thousand miles out on the North Atlantic in Christmas week. When my steward called me this morning I expressed a modest hope that it was getting better. He said there were certain good signs. The bell-boys had not been sick this morning, and only three of the stewardesses. There were a dozen of us at breakfast out of 300, and after it I foregathered with a little group of elderly gentlemen, with whom I compared notes.

We were all of us in the same plight. We had all of us with incredible rashness assured our wives and daughters that after "perhaps a little movement for a few hours or so crossing the top of the Bay" we should be sailing on sapphire seas with glassy surface. And now they lay groaning in their cabins and wanted to know what we had to say about it. We betook ourselves to the chart, staggering along the deck in full flight from a big sea which swept over the bows and pursued us with a drench of spray. The chart told us that we were in mid-ocean about the meridian of New York, with 2000 miles to go before we reached the sapphire seas. We decided hastily that that was a fact to be concealed at all costs.

We met again the next morning, and once more compared notes. The night had been one of crashings in all directions. Our experiences were many and varied. One said that a large flower in a pot—the parting gift of a devoted daughter—had leapt from its shelf in the night and all but demolished his wife. Bottles, glasses and jugs had made themselves merry, and the floors were strewn with their fragments. I myself had sat for an hour wedging with my foot a large wardrobe trunk which was itching to join the dance.

All the same, cheerfulness was breaking in. There were about fifty for the Christmas service in the dining-saloon, and it was well worth while. As we struck up "Christians, awake, salute the happy morn," a sudden but most appropriate pitch sent the stern flying into the air and took the whole congregation off its feet. The recovery of balance in the midst of Divine service is a thing which needs great discretion. A thoughtful wife ministered to a husband from a flask; a few ran and were seen no more that day.

I suppose that to the seasick this will seem a heartless narrative, but it is not really so. I know all about it, for up to the age of thirty I suffered every pang of that horrible malady, and thought myself an incurable victim. Then I began seriously thinking about it and came to certain conclusions, which the sight of so much unmerited suffering tempts me to repeat, though I can by no means guarantee that they will apply to others. The chief of these was that if I could get into my head that the ship was moving against the horizon instead of the horizon against the ship I should be cured of the giddiness which is the chief cause of sea-sickness, and automatically make the adjustments necessary to follow the motion of the ship instead of resisting it. A very little effort enabled me to do this, and I found to my great relief that I was cured.

So in future instead of yielding to the nauseous confusion, and lying in a heap in a cabin, I spent a few minutes at the beginning of a voyage, or whenever the sea became rough, in watching the movements of the ship and discovering exactly what she was doing, pitching, rolling and at what angles; and thus, in a few minutes I was able to do consciously what most people do subconsciously after three or four days of intense misery, *i.e.* adjust their internal mechanism to the moving platform of the ship. When you have done this you ride the ship as you would ride a horse; until you have done it, you resist its movements and go on behaving as if you were on dry land, and the ship of course takes its revenge.

I know of at least one man who has profited by my example, and he thanked me with tears in his eyes, saying that I had changed his whole outlook on life, since his business required him to cross and recross the Channel every week. So I write it down now in the hope that there may be at least one other—for if you cease to be sick at sea, a whole new world of enjoyment is opened up to you.

．　　．　　．　　．　　．　　．

We are at last on the sapphire seas, and the sufferers seem miraculously to have forgotten their woes. Sloping down south-east from the North Atlantic in mid-winter you savour to the full the change from winter to summer which is the delight of travel at this time of year. Day by day the grey waters have turned to blue, the sea has been spotted with the orange Saragossa weed, and those who have kept a look-out have seen spouting whales and flying fish. Last night gave us the first southern sunset with its luminous green space between the orange of the horizon and the deep blue of the zenith, and the new moon hanging on its back high up in the sky. One hails it again with an indescribable elation; it is something which no northern travel can give, something which lingers in the memory until one comes the same way again. With good luck we shall see many of these sunsets, for we have yet fifteen hundred miles to go before we reach our southernmost point.

Bermuda, where we have spent today, desires it to be known—desires it emphatically and indignantly—that it is not the West Indies. It is Bermuda, all by itself, a group of islands cunningly joined together by causeways and bridges, and asserting its own individuality by a steady refusal to permit motors in its territory. For half the day I explored it in the Governor's launch, which threaded its way in and out of bays and creeks; and for the other half I drove on land in a victoria drawn by a pair of piebald horses.

When you are on the sea in these regions, you look into the sea, for below you are lovely gardens of coral and anemone, with strange opalescent fish darting along their paths, and so clear are the waters that you can see every detail of the sea-floor forty or fifty feet down. Here is the true fairyland, and nothing could be more exquisite than its little forests of mauve coral with the paths of green seaweed running through them.

The land rises from the sea to an average of about 150 feet and is pleasantly wooded with pine and the local cedar. It is seldom more than a mile wide and often much less, and in its circuit of fourteen miles makes a great loop enclosing the sea, as is the way of coral islands. You drive in and out of a succession of little wooded bays, with rocky shores, meeting the sea first on one side and then on the other.

The place strikes one as exceedingly populous. All along the shores are white stone two-storeyed houses, most of them with gardens sloping down to their own bathing beach. The most imposing of these are the "cottages" of wealthy Americans who come here for three months in the year, and, together with a great crowd of American trippers, make the fortunes of this place. There are charming gardens and pretty little landscapes wherever you go. Bananas grow in the hollows sheltered by the pines and cedars on the hills above them. These and a few potatoes and vegetables are the sole edible products of the islands. But there are masses of hibiscus, scarlet, buff and yellow; great clumps of oleander, now just coming into blossom, bougainvillæa of the magenta kind in rather excessive quantities and many flowering trees and shrubs whose names I could not discover. In a few weeks' time the Bermuda or Harriside lilies will be all over the ground and a few of them were already on the market. In the garden of Government House scarlet cardinal birds and Bermuda blue-birds—gay little birds about the size of bull-finches—were taking a bath in a pool under the trees.

Except for the American villas, many of which are ingeniously planned and daintily constructed, there is nothing in the buildings to catch the eye. But the white stone of walls and roofs make an agreeable glisten in the sunlight, and Hamilton, the capital, is for that reason not unsightly. The population is "old Bermudan" of British stock with a negro proletariat, the descendants of the slaves of former days.

I asked what the white people did for a living and was told that they kept shops and had the oldest legislative Assembly in the Empire. They do one another's washing, depend for profit on American visitors and import four-fifths of their food from the United States. Food Imperialists are trying to persuade them to divert their orders to the Empire, but they don't see the fun of paying freights for a fourteen days' sea journey when they can get what they want from over the way.

The importance of this place for us is that it makes excellent headquarters for the North American and West Indies fleet, and if rich Americans choose to find their pleasure in it, that, too, is a convenience to the Bermudans, and helps to solve what would otherwise be an extremely difficult problem. It is undeniable that the Volstead Act has contributed to this result, and whether its repeal may have an adverse effect is a question I heard rather anxiously discussed.

IX

JAMAICA AND DOMINICA

January, 1933.

JAMAICA undoubtedly has a lurid past. It had been the scene of every sort of wickedness that was practised on the sea—piracy, buccaneering, filibustering, etc.—and, judging from its history, it seems to have had an irresistible lure for bad and violent men who slaked their thirst and warmed their cockles with its rum.

It has again and again been devastated by earthquake, fire, hurricane and pestilence; and its tombstones and the abundant funerary monuments in its older churches bear grim witness to the toll it has taken from those who have governed and administered it.

It remains, nevertheless, one of the loveliest spots on earth. I saw it first just after sunrise from the sea, and it is stamped on my memory in that aspect. There are certain great approaches from the sea which one never forgets—the approach to Naples, the approach to Constantinople, the approach to Smyrna—and the approach to Jamaica ranks with these. The Blue Mountains stand high on the sky-line and sweep down in splendid curves to the promontories which enclose the Bay of Kingston and Port Royal. The mountains seem to rise straight from the sea, but are in reality six or seven miles from it. As we come near, this space gradually reveals itself as a region of great trees and pleasant gardens studded with white houses which gleam in the morning sun. On the shore is a populous town with docks, wharves and deep water anchorages from one of which we presently walk ashore.

The port looks busy. There are a score of tramps and fruit-boats, one or two passenger ships at their berths; an

N   193

old-fashioned schooner is being towed in and a number of motor-boats and small sailing-yachts are fussing about the bay. The town is of the tropical colonial type, and makes a general impression of white paint, green shutters and deep verandas. All streets converge on a central square in the middle of which is a large fountain basin filled with the loveliest blue lotus I ever saw.

There are stores with many departments giving themselves the air of Selfridge's and Harrod's combined, and the side-walks in the chief streets are roofed over to keep out the sun. The people are nine-tenths black, and though they are tanned by the sun the white ones look conspicuously white against the dark background.

Even at 8.30 in the morning Kingston is undeniably hot and rapidly stoking up. We take car to the Constant Springs Hotel—about six miles away, and 600 feet above the sea, just under the Blue Mountains. A delectable spot and charming hotel. We want breakfast and have no doubt at all what it should be—lemon squash and a dish of iced Jamaica fruits, paw-paws (a kind of local melon), green oranges, pine-apples, fresh picked bananas, delicious and refreshing. Here we could stay for days just doing nothing but look up at the mountains, with their wooded gorges and sharp edges against the sky, or down across the cocoa and banana groves to the deep blue sea and jutting promontories across the bay. It is an enchanting scene with a magic light over it all, and the rich colour—flashing light and violet shadows—which comes only of heat and moisture. Up here there is a cool breeze, which in the afternoon may be a gusty wind, and the atmosphere is not only tolerable, but exceedingly pleasant. If you want exercise there is a golf course where you can play in the early morning or late afternoon without getting uncomfortably hot.

I shirk all sightseeing in these places, for what one wants to see in a short time is the normal country and the daily life. In Jamaica, take a car and drive anywhere, and stop anywhere and talk to anybody. Your drive will take you along roads bordered with banana and sugar plantations or through stretches of jungle, as one would call it in the East, with superb trees and flowering trees on either side. Always for a background you have the Blue Mountains, and when you ascend you look down on bowery hollows crowned by summer seas.

The Island grows everything that the tropics produce—cocoa, coconut, rubber, nutmeg, mango, coffee, pineapple, kola, cardamoms, and of course banana and sugar. The vast silk-cotton trees are among the biggest trees in the world, and second only to the Californian redwood in antiquity. They are superb creatures with an enormous girth of trunk, and in the span of their branches beyond all rivals.

It worries me a little to see so many living and growing things of which I do not know the names, and I protest when my driver tells me that a long-tailed very black bird with a face like a parrot is a nightingale. I say it is not, and he says it is, and there we have to leave it. I protest again when he calls a vulture-like bird as big as a guinea-fowl a crow. Whatever it is, it is not a crow, and it trills like an Indian kite. Humming-birds I concede. I have never seen them before, and they correspond to the pictures of them. Charming little creatures.

Jamaica is now 60 per cent banana, and in this way has somewhat insured against the adversity that has overtaken sugar. I spoke to a planter who grew all sorts of things, and he admitted that he "had not done so badly." But he was bitter about sugar. He spoke as if the extraction of sugar from beet was an impropriety—an outrage against nature which had provided the sugar-cane, and obviously intended it, and it alone, for the use of man. Else why should it have been called sugar, and what else, he wanted to know, was entitled to the name? He asserted positively that beet sugar could never have been grown profitably without bounties and subsidies, and he seemed to think the object of these was merely to spite the West Indies.

His utmost wrath was reserved for the British subsidies,

which he denounced as fantastic and absurd, the worst of all the subsidies. Half the money poured out on British beet would have equipped the West Indies with modern plant which would have enabled them to conquer the world and knock the bounty-fed European sugar out of the market. Preference was all very well in its way—except that there was nothing like enough of it—but the true Imperialists would have developed Imperial sugar, the real sugar, the only sugar, in its West Indian home.

.   .   .   .   .   .

Leaving Jamaica, we steamed for two days along the Caribbean Sea, in sight, for most of the time, of the southern coast of San Domingo. A stiff breeze keeps the air cool and whitens the crests of the deep-blue rollers, but the sun is tropical and it is pleasanter to sit on the shady side of the deck.

I can report nothing of San Domingo except that it looks mountainous and very green from the sea, and that those who profess to know talk gloomily of what is happening in its interior.

On the morning of the third day we anchored off Antigua, famous for the old dockyard in which Nelson refitted his ships in his chase of Villeneuve to the West Indies, and also for a literary association which has always lingered in my mind. For it was in Antigua that Jane Austen placed the West Indian estate of Sir Thomas Bertram, of Mansfield Park, and it was to and from this island that he was making his perilous voyages while his heartless family were rehearsing those lamentable private theatricals in his mansion at home. Unfortunately I could discover no one in Antigua who had ever heard of Sir Thomas Bertram, and inquiries about his estate proved fruitless.

It is a pleasant enough island, with a neat little town and a delightful bathing beach, but we are passing from island to island and the vision of them gets a little blurred, as one adds another and yet another to one's collection. As the absolute quintessence of tropical scenery I am inclined to put Dominica at the top of my list.

It is positively everything that a tropical island should be. Steep, volcanic mountains, with jagged edges and deeply wooded ravines, rise sheer from the sea; sugar-cane and banana make vivid green patches against the purple shadows of the woods; in the woods are vast deciduous trees, banyan, silk, cotton, mahogany, cocoa, almond, as well as tall tree-ferns and fan palms. By the shore are wooden houses veiled in greenery splashed with bougainvillæa and hibiscus. The sea is amethyst shot with pale green, and there is a long line of white surf on shore. Exactly so would a scene painter depict a tropical island as a back-cloth for a nautical opera.

When I go ashore on these islands I make a practice of choosing a little black boy among the dozen who are loitering on the jetty and telling him to be my guide. This immediately raises a chorus of remonstrances among the eleven who are unchosen. They dwell disparagingly on the past life of my boy, and his numerous disqualifications for the honourable office which I have assigned to him. I thereupon become his vehement champion and start on my way with the eleven trailing behind me and the argument continuing, until it drops from sheer exhaustion.

In Dominica—it being Sunday morning—my boy takes me at once to a central position in the little town of Roseau, where, as he points out, I can hear four services going on at the same time—a priest intoning mass in the Catholic cathedral, Anglican chants rising from the English church over the way, hymns issuing from the Presbyterian and Wesleyan churches, both within a stone's-throw. Since all doors and windows are open, the sacred strains mingle at this central point and make the island seem a very melodious and religious spot. I ask my boy which of the denominations has the largest number of adherents, and for answer he points to two cemeteries, Catholic and Protestant, and bids me observe that the Catholic has three times as many graves in it as the Protestant. Clearly an intelligent boy.

The boy next takes me up a very steep hill to a great view commanding two splendid bays and thence plunges into a deeply wooded gorge with a deliciously cool stream running through it. Here I insist on sitting down. The sun outside has been blisteringly hot; the boy goes at a tremendous pace, and I have been ashamed to lag behind. But there is a limit.

We now have a serious conversation. What language do the black people speak among themselves? French patois— give me a sample of it. A voluble stream in which words like *méchant, pas, bête*, come occasionally to the surface, but accent and intonation undeniably French. I asked what the people lived on and what work they did, but got only the vague answer that there were plenty fish, bananas, sugar, coffee.

He now said I must go to the museum and see the biggest beetle in the world (the so-called Sawyer Beetle). I certainly hope it is the biggest, for it is as large as a small bat, has a body encased in armour, four large wings, and fierce mandibles more than two inches long with which it saws wood and inflicts painful gashes on human flesh. I expressed a hope that it was not very common on the island, but the boy said it was quite common and seemed to be proud of it. I drew its portrait, but the only specimen I could get to sit to me was (fortunately) dead, but (unfortunately) had its wings folded under its casing.

The boy took me finally to the botanic gardens, a place of rare beauty and most beautifully kept by its English curator, an old soldier who is also a scientific botanist. He told me something of his problems and his life on the island. Less than four years ago the entire garden was laid flat and his work ruined by one of the fearful hurricanes which periodically visit these islands. He told me a grim story of that visitation—how he had been deputed to take charge of the women whose husbands were away, how they just held on hour after hour in the shuttered house, uncertain whether it would stand another blast, and when it finally passed, how they broke out simultaneously into screams of laughter, like shellshocked men he had known in the War. His cheerful reflection was, nevertheless, that there might not be another for fifty years, and in that faith he had started to replant and build up his beautiful garden.

The little handful of white folk who live in these tropical paradises have to pay for their privileges. The planters' bungalows, with their wide verandas, look cool and comfortable, and some of them have charming gardens, but steaming heat is the portion of their occupants for a large part of the year, and there is a constant battle to be waged against mosquitoes and the diseases they carry. One could not live many months in the most beautiful of them without developing a positive craving for the cool, clean climates of the north, but in these winter months they are ideal for the traveller who seeks the sun.

Every hour or so a cooling shower sweeps across them, veiling the hills in a grey-blue mist and making the loveliest rainbows over the sea. You may get wet, but it is no matter, for in ten minutes the sun will have dried and warmed you all through.

X

ST. VINCENT AND TRINIDAD

January, 1933.

WE are passing through an archipelago with islands in front of us and islands to right and left of us, and all are beautiful with their volcanic formations and jagged mountains rising out of the sea. Santa Lucia and Saint Vincent, which we visit on consecutive days, are like little sections of the greener parts of Switzerland coming down to the sea, except that the greens are greener than the greenest Swiss. Coming closer, one sees the tropical detail, the palms, the sugar-cane, the great forest trees, the little wooden towns spreading along the shore and the towers and high roofs marking the churches, chapels and cathedrals, which are an invariable feature of the West Indian town. Nearly all seem to have cathedrals, and some of these are quite interesting eighteenth-century buildings, abounding in monuments and tablets, from which it would appear that the former inhabitants and administrators of these regions outshone all ordinary mortals in piety and exemplary living.

The black boy I chose to take me round the capital of St. Vincent more than justified my choice. He was a boy scout, one of a large company which had been drilled and trained by an admirable man, who, finding himself temporarily deprived of his occupation by the burning of the radio station which he was appointed to control, turned himself to this work.

I told the boy I wanted flowers and he took me at once to the only place where I could get them, and I came away with an armful of tuberose and giant maidenhair. I told him I wanted to see nutmegs growing and he took me to the botanical gardens—a lovely spot with cool streams running through it—where a gardener very obligingly cut me a large branch with the fruit hanging on it like large round plums.

The boy next took me to the religious centre of the town, and, pointing to a pleasant-looking square house, said that it was the abode of a "Reverend Wesleyan," who had had thirty of his churches blown down and had built them all up again. This admirable man was unfortunately absent, but the boy introduced me to a young coloured minister who talked very earnestly about the politics of the islands.

The boy took me next to a large arrowroot field and bade me observe that the work of harvesting and planting was going on at the same time. What I chiefly observed here, as elsewhere in the islands, was that nearly all the hard work was being done by women, while the men looked on. I was assured that the women prefer it so, and both sexes are said to be well satisfied.

The boy then desired me to inspect a ginning factory for the sea-island cotton, but I am tired of ginning factories, having seen a large number of them in Egypt, and instead I induced him to sit down and tell me about his life. He said he was sixteen, and had been at school until a few months ago, when he had got a job as a printer with one of the five local newspapers. But he had only been six weeks at it when the five newspapers began to "amalgamate," and his paper—the oldest in the island—having been "amalgamated" with the youngest, he had been "laid off." A sad Fleet Street touch which made the whole world seem kin. I offered him my sympathy, but he was undaunted and said cheerfully that there was a good future for hand type-setters in the island, since there was only one linotype and it had long ago ceased to work. How this little community supports three newspapers, let alone five—some of them bi-weekly and even tri-weekly—was more than the boy could tell me.

Our talk passed to the terrible eruption of the volcano, La Souffrière, which I had seen from the sea as we coasted along the island. It was long before the boy was born, but he had all the figures by heart, the 2000 lives it cost, the number of houses it destroyed, and the acres it laid waste. But the people, he assured me, were all back on the devastated area, and the wise men who know all about volcanoes had done a sum which proved that there would not be another eruption for fifty years, when most of them would be dead anyhow.

The boy dealt with cyclones in the same cheerful spirit. There had not been a really bad one since he was born, but there had been three close together just before, from which he deduced that there "needn't be another really bad one for fifty years." Fifty years was everywhere the optimistic figure about these visitations.

From this he passed to the greatest and most glorious memory of the island—its victory over the visiting team which a great cricketer brought out from England. He showed me the cricket ground, which had little clusters of wooden houses on two sides. When he went in to bat the great cricketer wanted to know who would pay for the windows he was going to smash—and then he was bowled first ball by the island Spofforth. I regret to say that I omitted to take down the name of this hero, but it will be a name to resound for ages in this island. I hope the story is true, but I feel justified in repeating it as the boy told it to me.

. . . . . .

January, 1933.

A few days ago I wrote that Dominica was the perfect tropical island. A day or two later I was inclined to revoke this judgment in favour of Grenada, and at the end of the week I am not quite sure whether both should not be deposed in favour of Trinidad.

Grenada has a charming individuality in that its little town is built on the side of a steep hill instead of on the flat shore, and its roofs top one another and its streets race downhill as in the little seaside towns of the west of England. The resemblance is limited to this, for all else is tropical and the mountains in the background are unmistakably volcanic. For a comparatively small island the scale of the scenery is immense. From the Governor's drawing-room one looks on one side over an imposing coast-line with jutting promontories enclosing wooded bays; and on to the other side into an enormous valley hemmed in by mountains rising some 2000 feet, all of it richly cultivated or densely wooded, and dazzling in colour where the sun strikes the open spaces or a passing cloud throws a purple shadow over the woods. It is an enchanting scene whichever side one looks out, and, as so often on this journey, one passes on regretfully with the thought that one will never see it again.

On the map Trinidad is no bigger than several other islands, but it leaves on one an impression of size and importance in which Jamaica alone is its rival. Geographically it is all but continental, for only a narrow passage cuts it off from the Venezuelan mainland, and the gulf which it encloses on the east is in fact the estuary of the Orinoco, which pours its silt into the harbour of the Port of Spain, compelling all big ships to anchor some three or four miles from the shore.

At this distance you get one of the great West Indian views. The Trinidad mountains—about 3000 feet at their highest—sweep down to the sea in a succession of jutting promontories, between which are deeply wooded bays, and beyond them to the east, and, so far as the eye can see, in a continuous chain, are the high ridges of the Venezuelan mountains, a pale blue in the distance. There are many little islands near the shore, some of them with rich-looking villas and gardens on them. Trinidad extends in a vast arc round the gulf, and all but meets the Venezuelan coast on the southern side as well as the northern side.

There are probably more different races gathered together in Trinidad than in any similar space in the world. Of its 350,000 inhabitants nearly a third are East Indians from Bengal, who, or their forebears, came originally as indentured labourers, and obtained land and settled in the country when

203

their indentures expired. They provide labour for the sugar and cocoa plantations, and though their wages are small, the island gives them in abundance what they want, and their little villages, with their mosques and temples and their rice-fields, are corners of India. They send a great deal of money back to their relations in Bengal, but they have apparently no desire to return there. They keep themselves apart from the blacks, as the blacks do from them, and the efforts of the Trinidad labour leaders to join the two races in the same trade-unions have so far ended in tumult. Of the remaining two-thirds of the population, the blacks of African descent and coloured people of mixed race are of course the great majority. They go up or down the scale from pure-blooded negro to all manner of types and colours, and include some of the most picturesque and charming varieties of the human race to be seen anywhere. Trinidad, it seemed to me, is well justified in boasting of its beautiful girls; and their soft voices and the slight drawl of their speech add to their charm. All the European races contribute to the small pure white population; English, French, Spanish, Portuguese, German, Italian, are all represented, and all intermarry, making the white Trinidadian a composite European seldom found in Europe. The sight of him would drive Hitler or Goering out of their minds.

Port of Spain is a town of nearly 70,000 inhabitants, and reflects all the qualities of its people. It has a beautiful public park and botanic gardens, sumptuous houses and gardens in which the wealthy live, broad streets with European shops, narrow streets with timbered houses and shacks where the poor blacks and mean whites have their abodes; long avenues of bungalows, many of them of excellent design, which might well be copied nearer home. It has country clubs, golf clubs, cricket clubs, race-courses and one good hotel.

Its industrial life is as varied as the products of the island, which produces everything tropical and has for its own speciality an unlimited supply of asphalt from the famous "Pitch Lake" which fills itself as fast as it is emptied. Great

fortunes have been made here, and even now it looks prosperous and remains cheerful. "We can just about make ends
meet" is the report one usually gets when one makes inquiries,
but it is said with a smile which encourages one to hope that
there may be room in this formula for a modest profit.

I ought to have attended a discussion on the economics of
sugar, instead of which, the thermometer being just over
90°, I took a car and drove twelve miles along the shore,
through vast plantations of cocoa, coconut, lime and sugar,
to a lovely wooded beach where I plunged into a cool green
wave breaking on a white sandy shore. A large crane-like
bird with long bill and grey wings kept me company, flying
very close to my head, and he and I had it all to ourselves for
the next hour.

An hour of pure delight, in which Fleet Street and the
fiscal controversy and the American debt seemed very far
away.

XI

THE BRITISH METHOD AND THE FRENCH

MUCH capital is no doubt being spent on improving and increasing the cultivation of West Indian products, but this is, so to speak, behind the scenes, and there is little evidence of enterprise or development in the outward show. There are very few deep-water docks or harbours; municipal buildings, business offices, school buildings are generally mean and insignificant; the smaller towns seem to straggle anyhow and look as if nothing has been done to them for a hundred years.

We have withdrawn our garrisons, leaving in many places deserted barracks and military headquarters which ought either to be demolished or converted to other uses, for they impart an air of decay which is unpleasing to the eye and a bad advertisement for the islands. There are numerous cathedrals and churches of all denominations—a few dating from the eighteenth century, of real distinction—but here, as in India, and indeed all over the Empire, one is left wondering whether the British religious spirit need manifest itself in such exceedingly ugly buildings.

All this may be the British way, but it is in sharp contrast with the French way, which is to set up a glittering apparatus of modern life in even second-rate colonies, and to do it, if necessary, at public expense.

The French way I saw on my return voyage at Casablanca on the west coast of Morocco. I remembered the police incident which suddenly flared up in the autumn of 1908 and seemed for a few days to threaten a first-class crisis between France and Germany, and heaven knows what other consequences in that year of trouble. A little to the south of it is

Agadir, where three years later, there arose another and more dangerous crisis between us and Germany. In those days our Admiralty considered it a matter of first-class importance to prevent Germany, or for that matter any strong naval Power, from obtaining a port and potential naval base on the Atlantic coast of Morocco.

But with these memories I expected to see no more than the old Portuguese and Moroccan town on the sea-shore, with a few modern buildings and offices to mark French occupation. Instead, I saw a great flashing white city of steel and concrete spreading for miles along the shore with all that there is of the most modern—an immense breakwater enclosing the Bay, naval docks and commercial harbour within, towering granaries, great phosphate works, factories and office buildings, churches or cathedrals—all brand new and obviously built on an ambitious, comprehensive plan. And when I went ashore I found great boulevards with arcades and Parisian shops, big bank buildings, theatres, cinemas, music halls, elaborate public park beautifully and expensively laid out, and beyond a garden suburb with charming villas, the abodes apparently of rich or well-to-do people. The old Arab city is still there, but so built in and hemmed round that you have to search it out. It is worth finding, for the bazaar keeps its character, and there are a few old Moorish and Portuguese houses and bits of wall and bastion which are worth looking at. But the Sultan—a carefully preserved relic of the old times—lives in an ambitious new modern villa, and for such of the Moroccan population as cannot be housed in the old quarter, there is a new quarter of little square houses of steel and concrete with an aggressively sanitary appearance.

A broad road sixty miles long and asphalted the whole way connects Casablanca with Rabat, where also there is a brand new modern quarter consisting of houses and offices and serving as headquarters for French officialdom. From Rabat there are other excellent roads connecting with Marrakesh and Fez, and at the chief centres first-class hotels enabling the whole region to be opened up to the motor and charabanc tourist. '

All this or nearly all is the work of the last twelve years, and, so far as I know, there has been no enterprise like it in all the world. Certainly there is nothing like it in the British Empire, which has left its towns to develop gradually through individual enterprise in the usual planless way with anybody's capital, British or foreign. I asked how Casablanca had been financed, and was told, by a French guaranteed loan secured on the taxes of Morocco. How many millions of francs have gone into it I don't know, but anyhow an enormous sum, all laid out under French official guidance and, incidentally, through the provision of material, giving employment to a large number of people in France.

I asked how much money had been spent on working minerals or irrigating the surrounding lands, which, presumably, are to produce the cereals to fill the granaries and provide trade for the port, and was told, so far, hardly any.

I asked how many non-official French colonists there were in the town or up-country, and was told again comparatively few, though there is apparently a considerable number of other nationalities trying their fortunes.

I asked whether there was any certainty that the Moroccans would be able to pay the taxes required to provide interest and sinking fund on the loan, and was told that nobody knew, but officials were confident that this beautiful new apparatus would so enrich the country that its inhabitants would easily be able to bear this or even a greater burden.

I express no opinion, but it sets one thinking. It is all exactly the opposite of our time-honoured method of standing aside and letting things grow, and the nearest approach in modern times to the Roman method of employing the legions to build new cities. I risk challenge when I say it, but I can think of no other example of a whole city being laid out and deliberately built up in a few years unless it be the Jewish city of Telaviv in Palestine, which is, or was, on a much smaller scale.

We have spent vast sums in Egypt and India on irrigation, railways and engineering works of all kinds, and have sent out large numbers of non-official Englishmen to seek their own fortunes and develop the new countries in their own way. The French begin at the other end, and, according to our theory, they put the cart before the horse, providing the apparatus for a life that has yet to be created. It looks dangerous and even reckless to us, but it also makes our Colonies look drab and antiquated compared with theirs, and raises the question whether we are doing enough on this side for our possessions.

For one other impression I bear away. The French are amusing and entertaining the Eastern and African world in a way that we are not; and this materially helps them to keep down the unrest which is afflicting all the other nations in their dealings with their Colonial possessions. This object may not be economic, but it has a very real political import-ance and, combined with the almost complete absence of race or colour feeling among the French, paves the way for a more cheerful co-operation between French and native than the rest of us are able to establish in our Colonies. The gaiety and glitter which the French take with them when they go over-seas are much more attractive to the Oriental than our cold northern civilization.

PART IV

SIDE ISSUES

I

SOME MODERN POEMS

THE other day I rashly chopped into a debate on modern poetry with a letter of three lines hinting that some of the practitioners of this art might suffer at times, as indeed we all do, from an eclipse of the sense of humour. This seemed to me to be a more rational explanation than others which had been offered of the appearance of bathos in some of the pieces under discussion. I was foolish enough to put my name and address—does not Heine say that inferior authors should always give their address?—and during the next few days a little shower of letters descended on me, asking who I was that I presumed to judge of these high matters. It was intelligible and even pardonable that I should know nothing about them, but what was inexcusable and unpardonable was that I should be unaware of my ignorance and incompetence.

In this spirit a young man sent me a volume of poetry with a polite covering letter in which he said that he knew I should not understand it, and therefore did not propose to enter into any argument with me about it, but he would like me just to see what was going on in the real world of modern writers. This implied judgment on my intelligence was entirely justified. Indeed, one or two of the pieces in the young man's book—pieces of which the keynotes were "self" and "self-expression"—got on my nerves and so disturbed my slumbers the following night that I found myself composing pieces like them between waking and dreaming. To the best of my recollection I got through half a dozen between 5 a.m. and 8 a.m., but there were only two I could distinctly remember, and I wrote them down before breakfast. They were deeply metaphysical, as the reader will see :

ME

Yesterday I woke untimely
At five a.m.
But seizing the opportunity
I reflected on ME,
ME the mysterious, ME the profound,
Melancholy incarnate, destruction personified.
Joy of all joys—ME.

Plangent nouns and verbs
Ululate within ME
Saying release us or you burst.
I feel the grey cortex of the brain
Becoming red,
I see red, the whole of ME is red,
The all-red ME.

From the window I see clouds,
Clouds chasing clouds, over hills,
They are very like whales, wombats, turtles, frogs and mice.
So I say to myself, and the imagery wells up
Till I am breathless in pursuing it.
But they are all bits of ME,
ME the universal, ME the all-absorbing;
You are a bit of ME,
But I am not a bit of you,
The miracle of ME.

YOU

Ectoplasmic projection of ME
Chimera phantasmal,
I see through you!
Through your heart, viscera, lungs, liver, kidneys, pituitary gland
    and alleged brains,
Through your complexes, inhibitions, reflexes, reactions, reper-
    cussions,
And all other subliminal contraptions and gadgets,
With which Freud, Yung, Pavlov, Croddeck, Kafka, Marx,
    Wikimitch and Pumperdohl,
Have replaced your obsolete soul.
I know them all, and I know you,
You! You! You!

214

Grinning façade, caricature of ME.
Taking air and earth that belong to ME,
There is only room in the world for ME,
Sun, Moon, Stars and Milky Way are food and drink for ME.

This in my dream was set to music, somewhat in the style of Hindemith, rising in the last line on a tremendous crescendo to C in alt.

Now, an odd thing happens when one falls into this vein. One sees poetry everywhere, poetry growing on every bush, so to speak. Our newspapers, especially the popular ones, with their short crisp paragraphs, are full of it. What is this, for example?

AT THE OVAL

A pea-green day at the Oval,
Sinfield sends up vertically a dolly catch,
No one accepts it.
The first over recedes into the mist.
The light is abominable.
Sinfield is plumb leg-before to a straight one,
He recedes dimly into the Pavilion.

Watts sends Neale's off-stump into hysterics,
Barnett is caught behind the sticks off Gover.
Anyone who scores fifty today is a hero.
No one does.
Gover is becoming positively violent,
Watts too is quite on the rampage.
Dead is Page from a slip-catch off Gover,
Crapp clean bowled by the terrible Gover.
The light is now autumnally normal.

The rhythm of this seems to me admirable; the language is vivid, modern and untraditional. The Gover climax—mounting up to the "terrible Gover"—is a stroke of genius. Here is another by the same hand, written on the ground at Sydney during the second Test Match, 1936:

Remember Ames. He is
A keeper of the highest class
Quiet as a nesting thrush
Magically quick in taking the return.

I unreservedly withdraw
My suggestion that Sievers is a rabbit,
He is behaving like a true kangaroo,
Men are deceivers ever.

The gaming spirit that both makes and mars him
Suddenly tore the cloak of safety
In which the Don had wrapped himself
The greatest run-getter made the worst stroke
In the history of cricket.
To expect a man to score two hundred
Every time
Verges on thickness.

If these two were included in a volume by one of our modern poets, the distinguished critics would, I am confident, pick them out as masterpieces of delicate observation and original expression. So no doubt they are, for the author is Mr. C. B. Fry, the famous cricketer—and, though he tries to conceal it, an accomplished scholar as well as cricketer—and they are taken at random (with very slight rearrangement) from his articles in the *Evening Standard*, articles which he writes every day at flying speed and sends hot off the pitch to the press. Mr. Fry does ten like these in the course of an afternoon and in this way makes the game live for thousands who are unable to see it.

I turn to another paper and in ten minutes have discovered these two :

Adler knows people,
He knows how they react to outside circumstances,
He is not greatly interested in their insides,
Their Subconscious and all that.

He knows how unhappiness, neurosis,
Drunkenness, crime,
Arise in people whose social interest is
Insufficiently developed.
Adler knows people.

Yesterday at luncheon in London.   Vigorous oratory,
    It was not about politics,
    It was about the Russian ballet.

216

Madame Follette next to me,
Described ballet in America,
Isn't it awful? I said,
She offered me a cigarette.

Here, it seems to me, is an almost perfect example of the
sudden-transition method so much in vogue among the newest
writers. It would need a footnote after "awful" just to
explain that this ejaculation had nothing to do with the
ballet in America or Madame Follette, but was hitched on
to some suppressed thought which had interpolated itself
between the beginning and the end of this stanza—if stanza
is the right word to apply to it. But that too would be
following the best models.

In fact our daily newspapers simply overflow with the
new poetry. A week's issue of almost any one of them
would, I believe, provide a most beautiful anthology of little
poems by unknown authors who would leap to fame at the
hands of distinguished critics, if their names were known.
These authors are in such intimate daily contact with the
great realities of crime, cricket, and the social life that their
imagery has a warmth and power which no literary man
working in a study can expect to achieve. They do in
five minutes and in the lightness of their hearts what the
literary man does with the sweat of his brow in hours of
fatiguing concentration. I suggest to all our modern poets
that they make a careful study of newspapers, especially the
more popular ones.

II

A QUESTION OF TERMINOLOGY

I HAVE just been reading a long wail in one of the higher periodicals about the "commercializing of literature." Much of it seems to me great nonsense. If a thing is literature it will not be hurt by any tradesman, and I should rejoice to hear that the author was getting a good price for it. Starving authors are no more likely to do good work than underfed workmen. If the thing is not literature, again no harm is done. It will be no worse and no better for being efficiently marketed. The trouble comes from the confusion of legitimate and profitable book-making with the quite different product which is called literature. What we need in this connection is a new and neutral word to save books of the former class from the false position in which they are placed when they are supposed to be literature, and their authors from opprobrium for failing in what they never pretended to do.

A few days ago I read a long and caustic article in which a clever reviewer demonstrated to his complete satisfaction that a certain popular novel was contemptible as literature. He flayed the author alive and held him up for an impostor and a quack, on the quite gratuitous assumption that he was trying to be a Balzac and ludicrously failing in the attempt, whereas the unhappy man was not dreaming of Balzac, but merely endeavouring to supply his public with an article that they want—a quite legitimate and respectable article requiring a great deal of a certain kind of skill for its manufacture, but not literary skill as the critic understood that word. Manifestly, that book, if reviewed at all, should have been reviewed by a good average specimen of its own public, who could have told us whether it was well or ill done for its particular purpose, and perhaps let us into the secret of the peculiar and intimate affection which that writer inspires in his readers.

The truth is that the great majority of the products lumped together as literature have nothing in common with one another except that they employ the medium of words. Now, words are used for an enormous number of purposes, and the use of them for literature is exceedingly rare. My butcher's bill, unhappily, contains a great many words, but I do not regard it as literature. The public, however, will have it that anything printed in a book must be, or at least ought to be, literary, whereas the vast majority of books merely use words, as they are used in my butcher's bill, for the purpose of communicating different kinds of fact or fiction to a public which presumably wants these things. This is a perfectly legitimate trade, and, for the life of me, I cannot see why any literary man should be offended if its votaries succeed at it—as, by the way, they very seldom do. The best-seller is born rather than made, and he is only born once in a blue moon. He (or she) is a genius at his (or her) business and deserves the corresponding credit.

The need of a new terminology is felt over the whole field of art and letters. For instance I myself, to take a humble example, am most anxious to appreciate the new forms of poetry, painting, sculpture and music. But it would help me enormously and save me from getting tangled up with false analogies and traditional prejudices if only new words could be found for the new things. When the word poetry is uttered, I think instinctively of Shakespeare, Homer, Sophocles, Shelley, Keats, etc., and then when the new thing is presented to me labelled "poetry," I am tempted to say, "either that is poetry, or this is poetry; they can't both be poetry"; whereas if the new thing had an appropriate new name, I should bring a fresh and unprejudiced mind to its study and perhaps in time be able to share the emotions which it kindles in the minds of people like Miss Sitwell and Mr. Herbert Read.

Again, when I go to an exhibition of the late-Picasso non-representational school and find it labelled "painting," I instinctively think of Titian, Rubens, Rembrandt, and again the same mental process is repeated. Either that was not painting, or another word must be found for the thing before me. Again I am put off the scent. Similarly, when I listen to the works of H. and W. and hear their compositions introduced as "music" I think of Beethoven, Mozart, Handel, and the old harmonies come thrumming into my head when I ought to be concentrating my attention on the new discords.

One doesn't blame an orchid for not being a rose, or put either in the same category as cabbages on the simple ground that they are all vegetables. We want the same sort of classifications in the arts as one finds in a nurseryman's catalogue. How helpful it would be if there were standard catalogues with which literary editors and critics were provided as a matter of course! A novel would then be sent out labelled X3, which, when looked up in the catalogue, would be found to signify "Freudian high-brow." Or it might be C1, which would mean "light, best-selling." Similarly with the different kinds of verse. One would be Y3, which would signify "non-metrical, Eliotesque"; others V4, "heavy traditional"; K6, "popular gush"; V10, "alogistic incantational"; V12, "anarchistic propagandist." Music, painting and sculpture would be classed in the same way. Thus, if I were going to an exhibition of Modern Sculpture, I should look it up in my catalogue, and if I found it labelled S1 ("sophisticated nursery") or S3 ("atavistic pre-Aztec"), I should be saved the disappointment of discovering that it was not like Donatello. In the first case, I should think of serious bearded men trying to produce the same effects as I have seen a child produce in ten minutes with a lump of clay, and not judge them harshly if they fell short of perfection in this—for adults—very difficult business; in the second case, I should realize the tremendous imaginative effort it needs for a modern man to get back into the mind of a savage, and be willing to applaud even a moderate degree of success, if it were the result of a conscientious endeavour.

For lack of these classifications and the appropriate terminology, criticism gets more and more at cross-purposes with modern art and poetry. Everything should be applauded which is good of its kind. It is far better to be a good popular novelist than an inferior high-brow. Nothing is sillier than the assumption of the high-brow that he must be superior because he is a high-brow. But in the absence of the necessary *apparatus criticus*, as the learned call it, the kinds get hopelessly mixed, and the inexpert reader finds himself in a world of jargon which seems specially invented for his confusion. Take my own case, that of a person of average, or not much below average, intelligence who, as I have said, does honestly desire to understand the new forms of poetry. I have spent hours over the business; laborious, conscientious hours reading and re-reading. Now and again I think I have got it, and I say to myself, this is really good. Then I read a review, and find my choice selected by the reviewer as an example of deplorable back-sliding, and something else enthusiastically praised which I should have supposed to be a deliberate leg-pull, if so vulgar an expression may be used in this connection. In the end I fall back exhausted upon Bentham's definition of prose and poetry:

> Prose is that which goes on to the margin except at the end of a paragraph; poetry is that which stops short of it.

But even this fails me in much that is now labelled poetry.

III

WHAT'S WRONG WITH THE WORLD?

By Chester K. Gilbertson

1906.

By some obscure process of the reasoning faculty the word "boot" has become associated in the human mind with the word "foot." Yet the essential thing about a boot is that it never by any chance fits a foot. It is a suitable and handy implement for knocking in a nail; it may, as in the mystical tale of the old woman in a shoe, provide convenient shelter for an unmanageably large family; it is unrivalled as a means of swift expulsion, it has a sacramental use in the case of the newly married, but it is always and everywhere at war with the foot. All the boots that I have ever known cause corns, blisters, deformities, and are an impediment to the free wild movement of the human limb. One may even say that a boot makes excellent headgear, but execrable footgear. Turn it about and you have a hat which protects the neck in its most sensitive part, and at the same time shades the face with a projecting eave which is infinitely more serviceable than any brim. There is nothing whatever in the etymology of the word "boot" which requires it to be associated with the word "foot"; and just in proportion as we free ourselves from the servitude of false and fantastic associations imposed upon us by Darwinians, charity-organizationists and undenominationalists, so shall we rediscover the uses of that exquisite wild word. What's wrong with the world is precisely that the world will conceive of boots as associated with feet; I invariably conceive of them as associated with heads.

With the same perversity the world associates a river with

wetness; whereas to me the river is the supreme and mystical image of dryness. If there were no rivers, everything would be wet. If there were no rivers, the rain would stand foot deep in my back-garden, instead of passing through dim caverns to the Thames and the sea. If there were no rivers we should be all one river. If there were no rivers there would be no dry land. It is singular how the mass of mankind have missed this obvious and massive truth. Yet if we once grasp it, it changes our whole attitude towards life and rivers. We shall not think of rivers as wet and shining gods, we shall think of them as fantastic housemaids drying the brown earth with mop and pail and emptying their burdens into the sink of the sea. What's wrong with the world, I repeat, is that it will think of rivers as wet, whereas the river is truly but a mystical ministry of dryness.

I have said elsewhere that the home, which is commonly thought to be tame and domestic, is in reality the one and only free wild spot in the world. But I have by no means exhausted this idea. Many consequences follow from it. It follows, for instance, that homeless men and tramps are the only tame and domestic men in the world; and that the British ideal of domesticity can only be perfectly realized where man is absolutely and utterly homeless, a nomad of some wild wood, probably arboreal, but not so arboreal as to shelter himself twice in the same tree. Such a man would of necessity be prim and conventional, and the slave of rule and habit. The free savagery of the British parlour would be impossible to him, for the simple reason that he would have no British parlour to be savage in. It follows again that the burglar who breaks into the home is not, as vulgarly supposed, invading the inviolable privacy of another man: he is merely breaking out of his own cramped, limited, and intolerably conventional life into the free wild life within. If we believed the criminologist and the evolutionist, the criminal is a wild man who has resisted the taming process of civilization. In reality he is exactly the opposite. He is a tame man who is driven by an irresistible impulse to seek the wild freedom of the home. The act of breaking into a house is a supreme act of self-enfranchisement. The world will continue to go wrong in its treatment of the so-called criminal classes until it grasps this simple but generally ignored truth.

It is commonly said that things are other than they seem. This is not the case. Things in general are exactly the opposite of what they seem. All images are what we call upside-down on the retina; it is only by an arbitrary and quite irrational effort of the brain that they become what we call upright. Hence it is that revolution consists in turning things upside down; by that process alone we get a wild vision of reality. By a divine paradox the writer who stands on his head is alone in a position to see things straight. What's wrong with the world is that it is the wrong way up.

IV

NATURAL HISTORY

February, 1910.

I HAD just been reading Prof. Lankester's account in a monthly magazine of his work as Director of the Natural History Museum, South Kensington, and it had filled me with a vague enthusiasm for science. The picture which it brought to my mind was that of patient students poring over the million and eighteen thousand specimens of six-legged insects that are arranged in cabinets; of biologists and morphologists taking notes; of eminent foreign visitors being shown round the galleries by learned members of the staff, and except for the hushed consultations of experts and specialists, silence profound and impressive. Well, it was Saturday afternoon, and wet at that, so I felt I could do nothing better than go and see for myself. And now, having spent two hours in the place, I feel impelled to record my impressions, in the hope that they may prove to be in the interests of science.

I found the building in full possession of an enthusiastic multitude of both sexes, of whom the great majority were, I should say, between the ages of ten and fifteen, and not a few between five and ten. The work being done at the specimens was of various kinds, but all of it important and interesting. Several experts of twelve and upwards were holding an animated consultation about the birds' eggs exhibited in the central hall, and there appeared to be a rather marked difference of opinion; but apart from this there was little evidence of that concentrated specialism which, as Prof. Lankester tells us, is the sign of the expert. The brains of these students appeared to work as rapidly as

P   225

their feet. They passed at great speed through whole orders and families of living and extinct animals, and the observations that they made were entirely committed to their memories, for they carried no note-books or pencils. I watched them for long, and tried to ascertain on what principle they would pass one thing and stop before another, the latter being generally, to my untrained eye, of a rather repulsive outward aspect. The principle eluded me, but it was plain that certain objects exercised exactly the same fascination upon successive groups. Silence, I found, was not enforced. Conversation, loud and cheerful, was carried on in shrill treble voices, with a freedom from pedantry and scientific terminology which I had scarcely expected to find in the place described by Prof. Lankester.

Looking closer, the next point that struck me was that a considerable number of those present appeared to be occupied in losing one another and their elderly guides. These, I found on closer inspection, were engaged in what is scientifically termed crypto-zetics, which greatly resembles what is vulgarly known as hide-and-seek. The place has great, but not quite perfect, facilities for this purpose. I learnt on inquiry from some youthful experts that the drawbacks are mainly two; first, that the galleries do not communicate with each other; and second, that all the staircases are broad and visible from the central hall. Thus you cannot make a circuit of the building and come out at another place, and you run great risk of being seen when you have to descend from one level to another. That manœuvre has to be executed with great rapidity, hence the hurried pit-a-pat with which the museum resounds on a Saturday afternoon. There are good chances, however, for the really scientific child who knows the ground. The great thing is to draw the pursuer to the far end of one of the lateral galleries and then double back round one of the bigger glass cases. There is abundant cover, if it is judiciously used. But only those galleries should be chosen where the cases are high and the animals in them solid. Skeletons are a snare, and even tall animals should be avoided (for the pursuer can see under their legs), but bears are excellent and tigers will do. The whole art consists in not hurrying except on the stairs, for it is undesirable to attract the notice of the attendants. Ejection from the museum spoils this branch of science and is mortifying.

Other pursuits, however, are still possible, if the young student is not feeling up to this. Thus I went into the room where that great beast, Diplodocus, is set up to remind us how fortunate we are to live in a comparatively late stage of the world's existence. I found two boy students measuring it with a tape-measure which they had clearly brought for the purpose. That puzzled me very much, and it puzzled me still more to find that they only measured a certain section of it, the middle section, excluding a considerable part of its preposterous neck and silly tail. They did it several times with immense care, and the mystery of it struck me profoundly. At last I hit upon it. *They were measuring twenty-two yards of the beast!* Of course! They wanted to know exactly how much of it would stand on a cricket pitch, and how much of it would be left over at each end. Having exactly laid down the space, the elder boy proceeded to bowl an imaginary ball, and his inscrutable boy-nature was satisfied. The seriousness of this pair and their complete absorption in their self-imposed task were altogether fascinating. When it was finished they walked straight out of the museum with an air of triumph. The incident, I divined, was not ended. Pride was going to be lowered elsewhere—the presumptuous pride of parent or big brother who had scouted the idea of Diplodocus spanning a cricket pitch.

I passed on into the butterfly room, and there I found a variety of serious pursuits going on. A young scientist (*aetat.* 12) had brought specimens to compare—specimens in large pill-boxes, stuffed rather perilously into waistcoat pockets. Here was a born naturalist, if ever there was one. He had already the square forehead and incipiently beetling brow of the tribe. Most praiseworthy youth; but more interesting to me was another group of three who had laid themselves out for the afternoon at a neighbouring case. Each had with him an old envelope containing fragments of coloured chalk, and with these they were solemnly drawing butterflies on greasy half-sheets of notepaper spread on the glass above the specimens. One—a sad and gentle child wearing a large pair of spectacles—had done his little picture quite beautifully with these poor tools. The outline was accurately drawn, and he had used his chalks so as to give the effect of shot colour on the wings. That boy was clearly more artist than naturalist, whereas his companions had made their little pictures in the diagram manner. I couldn't help looking over his shoulder and saying I liked it. That seemed to frighten him out of his wits. His voice stuck in his throat, and he could only make a little hoarse sound. My first impulse had been to give him ten shillings and tell him to buy a box of coloured chalks and a drawing-book, but his fright infected me and I fled, feeling that I had been guilty of a vulgar intrusion. After all, the ten shillings would have spoilt it, for the virtue of the effort lay precisely in the poverty of the tools.

I next passed into the stuffed-fish room, to find it in pos-session of a family clothed from head to foot in hygienic wool —father, mother, boy (about twelve), two girls between thirteen and sixteen, and another little girl about five. The last wore sandals and her big toe was carefully separated from the rest and placed in the correct physiological position. The two older girls had violent green cloaks of the kind of material which is laid down in theatres to represent grass. The boy had a nice grey cloak of Harris tweed, but I hate boys who wear peacock-blue stockings. The parents need not be described—the mother had a whole wool hat with a wool-work chrysanthemum in it, and the father was intersely sanitary about his cuffs—or where the cuffs should have been.

The boy was asking intelligent questions about the sword-fish. He said truly that it was a wonderful thing to be able to preserve those brilliant iridescent colours in long-dead fish, and he wanted to know how it was done. I blush for the hygienic father. He knew nothing about the management of the museum, and still less about the preservation of fishes after their death. He, nevertheless, did not scruple to tell his innocent children that the embalming of these creatures so as to preserve the full beauty of their colouring was a speciality of the museum, a speciality for which it was famous all over the world, and which required the services of the most eminent naturalists and chemists. I, who had just read Professor Ray Lankester's article, knew that some of these fishes were models, and that all of them, whether models or carcases, had been deliberately painted to resemble the vivacious appearance of the animals in life. One of them, I think, is the handiwork of Prof. Lankester himself.

After this I followed the hygienic family into the stuffed-bird gallery; and there I saw the parent furtively sidling along the cases, so as to read the labels before his children came up. This, I think, is legitimate within limits. Adults must, in these days, do something to maintain their self-respect when children are too intelligent. But it is an abuse of this legitimate practice to invent silly stories about animals whose names you have learnt for the first time from the museum label. That abandoned man did this with careless volubility and mendacity till I could stand it no more. I tremble for the reaction which must come when those unhappy children cast off their grass-green cloaks and peacock-blue stockings and discover the unscrupulous falsity and silliness of their hygienic parent.

I took my way back past the reptiles and turned the corner sharply to find a guardsman and a nurse adoring each other beneath the giant lizard. But that opens up a whole new branch of the subject, into which I will not enter now. I will only say that the museum, like its neighbour across the road, has many advantages as a trysting-place, and that its ancient skeletons appear to have a peculiar attraction for young love.

V

IN PRAISE OF THE ANONYMOUS

A FEW weeks ago a judge in the High Court remarked from the Bench that he always put a letter into the wastepaper-basket unread when the writer of it had not the courage to sign his name. The observation earned hearty approval as the last word of solid British common sense, and I suppose that nine people out of ten regard its wisdom as self-evident. Yet is there anything at all to be said for it? Is it not even a quite stupid misunderstanding of the part which personality should play in the relations of human beings?

If a man writes to another, making a charge against a third person, and does not sign his name, by all means let him be branded as an anonymous coward. It is a perfectly healthy instinct which objects to a stab in the dark. Even here one can conceive circumstances in which an anonymous letter ought to be read, whatever one may think of the anonymous writer. For instance, a judge seems to me bound to pass on to the police, even if he refrains from reading it himself, any anonymous letter which professes to give information for the purpose of public justice. But, apart from these special cases, there is a wide field for anonymity which is perfectly blameless, and may even be benevolent. For my part, I should like most candid friends to be anonymous. We should then all of us get the benefit of their inestimable advice, and they would be saved the painful necessity of making themselves odious. What the candid friend says to us is very often true and wholesome and, if we did not know its source, might even do us good. I who write remember once making a speech which seemed to me a quite admirable performance. The next day I received an anonymous letter pointing out the extreme inelegance of certain postures which I had assumed, the unpleasant quality of my voice in delivering a certain high-flying passage, and half a dozen little mannerisms of speech of which I was profoundly unconscious. My correspondent said truly and sensibly that none of these observations depended in the least for such value as they might have on the mention of his name, and that for him to declare himself would be merely to cause unnecessary embarrassment to him and me, and to give an air of impertinence to his well-meant advice. As a concession to prejudice, however, he gave me a pseudonym to which I might address a letter at a neighbouring post-office, and added that, if I insisted on it, he would then reveal his true name.

Could anything have been contrived with more charming tact? Criticism which would have been extremely annoying if delivered point-blank by my friend Brown, who makes worse speeches than I do (and doesn't know it), became at once a subtle form of flattery. Who was this mysterious unknown who took enough interest in my performance to put himself to this elaborate trouble, who made the delicate assumption that I was an orator in the making and capable of being wrought to a high perfection? I wrote a note to my anonymous friend, at the address named, to say that I was greatly flattered, that I wouldn't dream of embarrassing him by seeking to discover his identity, but that I was sincerely grateful for his kind instruction. Could I have behaved thus to the candid friend in the flesh? Candour obliges me to say "No."

This is only one of a hundred cases properly covered by the anonymous letter. I seem to see the beneficent unknown sitting in one of the galleries of the House of Commons, attending public meetings or dinners and taking notes for his nightly task of gentle correction. If you are a performer at any of these, you will get a letter from him the next morning telling you in the most charming language all the things that a wise man should most wish to know, but which he would hate to hear from a visible critic. There is a word or a phrase which you keep repeating till your audience is in a state of suppressed titter, and you can't make out why. You become inaudible just when you want to be impressive; you clutch at your waistcoat, fumble with your watch-chain, or do any of the half-dozen irritating unconscious things which mar your effects. The beneficent unknown will tell you of these, and on extreme occasions will add certain things which the most impertinent of journalists will scarcely dare, say: "Your head grows too big, you are getting a bore with all your cleverness, you don't know when to stop; your last speech was intolerably conceited, your jokes have ceased to be funny, and your epigrams are tiresome." How many a clever man now become incurable, and puzzling hopelessly over the causes of his failure and the unkindness of the world, might have been saved if, at a timely moment, he had received just this little spur to self-criticism!

But the greatest sphere of all is the home. Here the candid friend is not merely odious but generally useless. He—or more often she—takes pleasure in telling the kind of truth which is unprofitable as well as unpalatable. The beneficent unknown, on the contrary, will say all the profitable impossible things which petty candour avoids. Mercifully but firmly he will remind the woman of advancing years, dropping just a hint that the hat of seventeen begins to look silly after the fortieth summer, that the change from skittishness to dignity is overdue, that the frock should be a trifle more sedate, the manner a shade more demure! Hundreds of blameless women with no touch of coquetry in their natures drift into a foolish conflict with old age for lack of this little bit of guidance, and find themselves irretrievably committed to a golden wig and a painted face which they dare not change when the truth has dawned too late. "If only someone could tell her," is the comment of daughter or sister, but always with the hasty addition that "of course no one could." For the life of me I cannot see why she should not be told—but told anonymously.

Not long ago I walked through a public park in company with a doctor friend of mine, and with his observant medical eye he took stock of the children whom we passed in our walk. This girl, he said, has spinal curvature, obviously neglected. If it isn't treated at once she will probably be deformed by the time she is twenty. That boy has every symptom of lung trouble; he ought to be sent right out of the town and fed on milk and cream. A year hence it may be too late. That other little boy reading the picture-book on that bench and looking at it slant-wise about six inches from his face has astigmatism with a peculiar axis and needs glasses at once. He will suffer horribly and get no good out of his education unless he is taken in hand immediately. "Good heavens, man," I said, "if this is true you ought to ask the nurses for the addresses of the parents and write to them at once." He shook his head at my innocence. "They would tell me to mind my own business, and they would believe that I was inventing the maladies so as to be called to cure them. And if my medical brethren were to hear of it they would strike me off the roll of my profession for 'infamous conduct.'" "Well, then," I said impatiently, "do you mean that nothing can be done?" "Nothing whatever," was the answer, and we walked on. Yet here, surely, are just the cases for the benevolent unknown.

Perhaps some day there will be a new kind of *société anonyme*—a very secret society with no office or discoverable membership—which shall undertake this duty of benevolent intervention. How exactly it is to be organized I don't know; perhaps its headquarters will be in Tibet, and its medium of communication a Mahatma. At all events, I seem to see its missives fluttering down from the sky or the ceiling with a faint peal of mystic bells to announce them. And then I open one to learn that I have been making a great ass of myself but didn't know it; the intimation, however, being conveyed with such tact and delicacy and such obvious disinterestedness that I recognize the truth without a murmur and inwardly bless the benevolent unknown. Possibly such a missive will descend on my breakfast table tomorrow, when some kind friend has read and considered this article.

VI

OTHER PEOPLE'S TRADES

When the ladies had left, my friend, the F.R.C.S., came over to my side of the table and began talking to me in a strain which, I suppose, is familiar to all journalists. "How ever you can go on doing it," he said, "is inconceivable to me. Day after day that article to write, and that paper to bring out, whether you are well or ill, or there is anything to write about or nothing to write about—why, it would kill me within a month. It's a positive nightmare even to think of it." He held up his hands in horror and looked at me as if he thought me an abominable and incredible piece of human mechanism.

I lay stress on the word "mechanism." If the man had said that I wrote my articles well I should have felt gently flattered. But, as I well knew, he was quite capable of crossing over to my neighbour opposite, who happens to think me a pernicious firebrand, and saying that he never read such shocking nonsense as appeared every day in my paper. And clearly what impressed him was, as Dr. Johnson said about the dancing dog, not that I did it well but that I did it at all. Herein, as I have long discovered, he merely echoes the average non-journalist opinion. Yet, as every journalist knows, there is nothing miraculous about these supposed mechanical feats. The journalist does his day's work like other men; his hours are not necessarily longer than other people, nor always so long; he is not generally in a state of furious excitement, nor, like some politicians, is he called upon to "speak at any length on any subject." Of course he must be prepared to write fast at a pinch, but on many of the jobs that fall to him, he can take abundant time and, if he is a conscientious man who writes slowly as some very good pressmen do, he will take it. I am as ready as most men to magnify my calling, and if my friend will only be kind enough to say that it takes a keen brain and alert intelligence, added to a great deal of hard work, to make a good journalist, no one will assent more cheerfully; but this perpetual harping on the supposed physical horrors and nervous strain of the profession is a tiresome convention which corresponds to nothing that I recognize as true.

"F.R.C.S.", however, would not let the subject go, and with much head-shaking over the "extraordinary strain" of my existence, began to offer me medical counsel as to the best means of avoiding the early and inevitable catastrophe. So, at length, I turned on him and asked what sort of existence he led? What, for instance, were his engagements for tomorrow? He took out a little pocket-book and began reading: "9.30 a.m., operation on Mrs. B. ('dangerous, abdominal,' was his comment); 12 noon, amputation, nursing home, Bentinck Street; 2.30 p.m., hospital, two operations (one 'very critical and difficult'); 4.45–7.30 p.m., visiting patients operated on in the last few days." "Good heavens, man," I cried when he had finished his list, "you actually sit here and eat your dinner and talk to me about the strain of my existence, when tomorrow at this time you will have the life of a fellow-being and her immortal soul trembling in your hands, and day by day you live in these scenes of carnage and suffering with a crushing load of responsibility on you to your patients, their friends, and your own conscience! And yet you eat and sleep, and pretend to be a sane man, and cover it all with an atrocious calmness!" I too lifted hands in horror.

He seemed to be pleased, and smiled at me indulgently. "It is a merciful thing for my patients," he went on, "that I don't fall into a panic about their immortal souls when I am going to operate on their abdomens. Heaven help them if I did. I tell you, I'd rather do twenty 'abdominals' than write one leading article."

235

The rest of the company had gathered round us as we talked, and we were soon taking an informal census as to the callings we thought most impossible and undesirable. I am bound to say that, in spite of my pleading, journalism got most votes. All the non-writing men were persuaded that it was an incredibly awful feat to have to write "at any moment, on any subject, at any length," as they insisted on saying, and one large and breezily healthy man protested at the top of his voice that it would kill him in a week. I was pleased, however, to find that the surgeon came next on the list. A suggestion that to be a packer at Chicago would be worse than doing operations or writing leading articles was negatived by a large majority. "At all events," said my breezy friend, "packing wouldn't absolutely kill you, like sitting up all night and writing leading articles and, if you did make a mistake, it wouldn't kill someone else." I ventured to say that the second of these propositions was at least doubtful, but he made the atrocious answer that "at all events you wouldn't know if it did."

Finding it impossible to shake this opinion, I begged my friends to put surgery and journalism out of the question and consider the next worst. For my own contribution I launched out against acting, and dwelt movingly on the horrors of having to earn your living in the glare of the footlights. "Think," I said, "of the daily nervous anticipation, the cruel excitement at critical moments, the mortification, when applause is denied, the thirst for more and more when it is given, the constant sense of daily public competition with the newspapers on your trail, and all the world witnessing your failure if you fail—think of having to endure this day after day, in sickness and in health, in——" Unfortunately my eloquence was cut short by a loud "Bosh!" from Roscius, the tragedian who, since it was Sunday night, was of our company. "My dear fellow, you haven't the faintest notion what you are talking about. Nervous? Who ever was nervous except on a first night? When you have been going three nights the difficulty is to get up any excitement at all,

and when you have been going fifty you've got to shake
yourself every night before going on not to be hopelessly
bored by it. Once a play's running it's the easiest job in the
world. Now rehearsals, I grant you, are an infernal nuisance,
and one or two of them have given me a downright bad
illness. But that's just because the author's there and the
public isn't. The public positively soothes us. If you ask
me what the real bad and unhealthy trades are, I'll tell you.
They are the sort of thing that our friend Jackson pursues"—
Jackson was the breezy man, and he was something in the
City, and tremendously rich at it—"and when I think of the
daily tragedy of his life, his horrible business with ledgers
and office stools, his unceasing anxiety about his profits and
losses, and his dreadful responsibility for the orphans and
widows who have invested their savings in his companies,
and the probability that he will be banished from Mayfair
to some provincial gaol if he loses a penny of it—why, the
thought positively unmans me, and I congratulate myself that
I follow a quiet, humdrum and commonplace profession!"
Roscius wound up amid applause by saying that he'd rather
write leading articles than be in the City. So, at length,
I got one vote.

VII

ON EPSOM DOWNS

I WAS once rash enough to confess to an old friend, whose advice I am accustomed to take, that I had never been to the Derby. He took a very serious view of the matter.

He pointed out to me that I was advancing in years, and begged me to consider, before it was too late, how I should feel if I had to confess, when I passed into another world, that I had never seen—never troubled to see—that British glory, that unique expression of our race and its finest instincts which is displayed every year on Epsom Downs. I had never thought of it in that way before, but I promised on the spot to make amends and to do so that very year.

I am grateful to my friend. He has enabled me to perform a pious duty, and at the same time to have a first-class outing—two things not always combined. I have seen crowds of all sorts all over the world, but never anything quite like the Derby crowd for either quantity or quality. Epsom Downs are very familiar to me, but I never realized till I saw them full how beautifully the rising ground on each side of the last stretch lends itself to the massing of humanity, and makes the masses aware of themselves and the thing they have come out to see. This leads to an immense concentration on the supreme moment.

Crowds watching pageants, Durbars, football, cricket, have their attention spread out over hours, but the Derby crowd is strung up to one tense minute or even a few seconds. It expresses itself as a whole in a deep unanimous silence, or great indrawn breath, a vast Oh! and a long muffled murmur when the winner is past the post. All my neighbours had "something on," and seemed to be delighted

238

when their chosen animal was badly beaten. This is the true spirit.

My companion and I won £25. We backed a certain horse because it belonged to a friend of ours. It was one of two horses that he was running, and the one which, as we learnt afterwards, he had not "declared to win." But it did win.

In general I have three rules for backing horses, founded on experience gained at many delightful little race-meetings which I have attended when on my travels, chiefly in India and Egypt. These are, never to back the favourite, for he hardly ever wins, and, when he does, you get very little for your money; second, never to back the horse you admire most, for the horses you admire—at all events which I admire—never win races; and third, after eliminating the first two, back the horse ridden by the jockey whose general appearance and facial expression most inspire your confidence.

Comparing notes with my neighbours I have found that this method yields as good results as any.

VIII

CORRECTORS OF THE PRESS

May, 1906.

THE authors of *The King's English* (Messrs. H. W. and
F. G. Fowler) are perfectly right to keep us poor journalists
in order, and I bear them no grudge because specimens of
my own handiwork as a leader-writer serve them as awful
examples in their ingenious red volume. Nevertheless they
tempt me to retaliate by applying their own methods to
their own writing.

Here, for instance, is the very first sentence in their book:

> The compilers of this book would be wanting in courtesy if they
> did not expressly say what might otherwise be safely left to the reader's
> discernment: the frequent appearance in it of any author's or news-
> paper's name does not mean that that author or newspaper offends more
> often than others against rules of grammar or style; it merely shows
> that they have been among the necessarily limited number chosen to
> collect instances from.

This sentence exemplifies, as anyone will perceive who has
read the book, some of the leading theories held by the
authors about the proper way of writing English. In its
use of stops it illustrates what they think to be the correct
use of the colon and semicolon, and in its abrupt ending
with a monosyllabic preposition it carries out the theory
upon which they repeatedly insist in the course of the
following chapters, that it is a pure superstition to avoid this
order of words in either the written or the spoken language.
Within limits I agree with them on this point, but nature
itself cries out against that Teutonic and cacophonous "from"
at the end of their sentence; and as for the colon in line 3,
I have a strong prejudice against it. One might almost as

well have written, "The compilers of this book would be wanting in courtesy if they did not expressly say *the following* :" as illiterate writers do. The colon to my ear has exactly the same effect—the effect of a town-crier making a pause after his preliminary flourish in order to call attention to the portentous announcement which is coming.

This is the method of the advertiser, not of the writer. The writer must weave the sentence together into something modest and graceful. "The compilers of this book would be wanting in courtesy if they did not say that, etc." is the natural way of beginning, and I can imagine all sorts of ways of avoiding a second "that" as well as the complication of negatives ("did not expressly say," "does not mean") in which the sentence is involved. It will be observed that I leave out the parenthetical sentence "what might otherwise be safely left to the reader's discernment." I leave it out because it is partly superfluous and partly meaningless. If the thing can "be safely left to the reader's discernment," why should the authors be held "wanting in courtesy" unless they "expressly say" it? If it can't, why say that it can, and then proceed to reflect on the reader's discernment by saying it? And in any case what is the meaning of "otherwise"? Finally, in the last sentence, what does "they" refer to? What the writer means is "he" or "it," *i.e.* author or newspaper mentioned in the previous sentence. If this is correct writing, I can only say that it ought not to be, and I hope no one will imitate it.

Let me hasten to add, lest in spite of my disclaimer this outburst should be attributed to spleen, that in several of the sins attributed to myself I am in hearty agreement with the authors and will endeavour to mend my ways accordingly. The remaining cases are matters of taste, in which the usage is good or bad according to the context and the general nature of the writing. Thus, while it would be absurd for me or any other journeyman of the press to write a leading article in the style of Tacitus or Carlyle, it is not absurd for Tacitus or Carlyle to write that style on fit occasion. Some of these "airs and graces" would, as Bacon says, "do better in poetry where transcendencies are more allowed," but they are not to be excluded from prose if the emotional pitch is such as to make them appropriate and significant. It puzzles me again that Emerson should be pilloried for "cheap originality" because he wrote "the faster the ball falls to the sun, the force to fly off is by so much augmented." It is awkward, if anyone likes, but why "cheap" or "original"? Almost everyone gets into a tangle in trying to express this meaning, and Emerson, it seems to me, is just floundering.

While they are strict in some things the authors of this volume seem to me dangerously indulgent in others. Thus, in spite of what they say, the good rule about the split infinitive is one of total abstinence. In nine cases out of ten it is abominable, and though there is a tenth case in which it is perfectly right, the thing requires as much thought as the rule about the cretic in a Greek Iambic. Again, there is a rather perilous passage about mixed metaphor. The authors quote and defend the following passage:

> Sir Wilfrid Laurier had claimed for Canada that she would be the granary and baker of the Empire, and Sir Edmund Barton had claimed for Australia that she would be the Empire's butcher; but in New Zealand they had not all their eggs in one basket, and they could claim a combination of the three.

This, say the authors, has been wrongly denounced as an example of mixed metaphor: "It is nothing of the kind: *they* in New Zealand are detached from the metaphor." Strictly speaking, there may not be a "mixture," but the succession of images is so grotesque that no good writer or speaker could perpetrate it. Similarly, no good speaker would begin a sentence by talking about "moorings," and end it by talking about "ruts," as in another passage which the authors defend, even though the two images were detached from each other. It is nearly as bad for metaphors to jostle one another as to cross one another.

I strongly advise the reader to avoid the sections on "And who" and "And which." It is a good enough rule for most writers to avoid the "and," unless there is a previous relative. "The essential to co-ordination," say our authors, "is that the co-ordinates should perform the same function in the sentence." I can't stop to explain what this means, but it is a paradoxical rule which permits us to say:

> "Unambitious men and who have no experience,"

and condemns Thackeray for saying,

> "in the best French which he could muster, and which in sooth was of a very ungrammatical sort."

Neither is elegant, but it demands a sublime courage to write the first and hold up your head. But this, it appears, is a "patent co-ordination," *i.e.* you pretend that the adjective "unambitious" is the equivalent of a relative sentence (who are unambitious), and then proceed to co-ordinate it with a second relative sentence. The practice is morbid and should be strictly eschewed by young writers. On the other hand, excellent advice is given about the use of participles. There is no surer sign of a failure in the sense of logical construction than a loose use of the participles:

> The lovers sought a shelter, and, mutually *charmed* with each other, time flew for a while on downy pinions.
> Having acquired so many tropical Colonies, there is the undoubted duty attached to such possession of, etc.
> While hesitating to adopt this terrible indictment, it must be admitted, etc.

We all write like that at times, but if the habit becomes frequent we had better make up our minds that we need a holiday and take it quickly.

I join hands in sympathy with all that the two authors say about "elegant variation" (*Anglice* journalese), and none the less because I find myself pilloried, as I think unfairly, for a sentence in which the variation of the words was not "elegant" but practical. However, since an obvious printer's error has exposed me to a second charge in the same indictment, I will forbear a defence which would be hopelessly complicated.

243

The plain rule is that the word should not be varied, even "for the sake of euphony," as the Latin grammar says, unless the meaning is varied. If you are speaking of the sea, don't call it the "ocean" the second time it is mentioned, unless you desire to make a distinction between the two things. Lying on my table beside me is an unpublished paragraph about Mr. Joseph Chamberlain which is extremely "elegant" in its variations:

> Here is a story about the senior member for Birmingham which, whether or not it really happened to the magnate of Highbury, is at any rate highly characteristic of the pushful champion of Fiscal Reform.

If I had no other source of information but this paragraph I should naturally conclude that the "senior member," the "magnate of Highbury," and the "pushful champion" were three separate persons, and when finally Mr. Chamberlain is mentioned by name, as he is in the next paragraph, I should suppose him to be a fourth. This kind of writing was much admired twenty years ago, and the masters of it were highly ingenious people who must have compiled their own dictionaries of synonyms for the purpose. But the present generation of readers is altogether too busy and too practical to find leisure for this literary hide-and-seek. They want to know at once what you are talking about, and you play with them at your peril.

Indeed, there is no more dangerous vanity for the daily journalist than to have a style. The daily article is like the daily bread. It must be bread and not cake or jam-tart, for no one can eat cake or jam-tart every day of the week without nausea. Nothing is sadder than to see how quickly the stylist, with his pretty tricks and turns, is worn out in the daily baking. For a week or a month he gives a pleasant seasoning and is much admired. Then his admirers turn on him, and, after a year or so, begin to talk of this "tiresome man" and his "affectations." In all probability he is just as good as ever he was, but the reader is sick of his pastry. The stylist must be very sparing of himself and rest content with one novel or one book of essays in a year. The one thing he must not be is a journalist. But the making of daily bread is none the less a fine art, and the advice given in this volume will help the journeyman not a little.

We all sin very often, and should be grateful to our correctors. Yet we have something to say in excuse. The art of writing is subject to an occasional paralysis of the faculties which nothing can quite cure. You get a thing wrong in your mind, and so firmly is it stuck there that you are blind to the manuscript, blind to the proof, blind even to the printed thing that faces you all day. And yet the next day consciousness will return, and you will feel a sense of abject disgrace. Sometimes the choice is between sucking your pen, like sentimental Tommy, in the vain pursuit of the right word and making the best of a bad one for the supreme object of getting to press. The first course is very expensive to the newspaper proprietor; and, human nature being what it is, he generally resents the missing of trains and the piling up of "returns." The second course is deeply wounding to your own literary conscience. I must leave it to casuists to decide what is the ethically right thing to do in this dilemma, but most of us, I am afraid, elect to stifle our consciences and catch our trains.

IX

AN ENCOUNTER

IT was exactly what I wanted—a group of cypresses, backed with olives, filling a gap in the hills; an old grey wall in front making a kind of pedestal; the ground running away steeply below, with a broken foreground of hemlock and myrtle, the straight stalks of the hemlock tufted with bunches of the green-yellow flower which isn't a flower, but which anyhow made a nice splutter against the dark green of the myrtles. Tomorrow I would come and bring my paint-box. I walked round it, revelling in the smooth warm grey of the cypress stems, which basked in the sun against massive bunches of copper-green foliage. Then I spied a nook to sit in at the right distance, with a flat stone left by Providence to hold paint-box and water-tin.

So much for the reconnaissance. I came next day at 3.30, approaching from the other side, so that the olive was in front of the cypress. As I turned the brow of the hill I became aware of a strange commotion. The olive, apparently, had gone mad. It was jumping and dancing in a great silver bonfire, through which I dimly descried its waving brown arms. The cypress in the meantime had turned blue-black and stood with rigid dignity, as if reproving these antics. The dazzle was blinding, and the hemlock and myrtle foreground had become a mere muddle against the light. Painting was obviously absurd, and I stood awhile gaping in amazement, and then retired beaten.

Next day I came an hour later and found affairs comparatively normal. The olive had calmed down and looked quiet and decorous in pale grey. The cypresses were taking the sun with a sleek air of luxury, their smooth stems full to the light, their massive paunches delightfully burnished. The myrtle did its duty as discreet background to the hemlock, and everything else fell into place in the pleasant arabesque which had first caught my eye. Now was my time; so I settled myself in my corner, laid box and brushes on the flat stone, scribbled in an outline, dabbed in a sky, measuring its tone at the point where the shadowy side of the cypress impinged on the grey of the olive, and then set to work at the serious business of mixing a wash for the olive—vandyke brown, cobalt blue, yellow ochre, a dash of carmine, a touch of emerald green—too blue, too brown, too green, a thought more carmine—surely just right!

I look up, my brush poised, just at the critical moment when the sky is wet enough to take the next wash softly. A second later it will be dry and hard. As I look, the infernal tree begins to laugh at me—really there is no other way of expressing it. Right and left, all over its surface, it breaks into little ripples of silver light, ἀνηριθμὸν γέλασμα, if ever there was such a thing. The manœuvre is wholly successful. Once more I am struck with the absurdity of attempting to subdue this sparkling fairy to a grey wash on a piece of white paper. She trembles into a thousand silver spikes, vanishing and reappearing with incredible speed. I wash out my brush, let my cunning mixture go to waste—and turn to her brother the cypress.

He—I must make him masculine, though Horace, I admit, does otherwise—retains his composure as yet. The imperceptible breeze which had set the olive dancing and sent the sun to her head is beneath his notice. His pendulous bunches shine like burnished metal on the sunward side and are thrown into high relief by dense shadows making irregular circles on his tapering front. A long velvety shadow descends from the top of his spire on the side nearest the olive, and the colour of it, I swear, is blue—at all events, something dark and purple, with never a touch of green in it. Here was plain sailing—the wettest wash with the biggest brush for the greens, and the shadows plunged in before it dried—

a breathless, exciting two minutes in which half the colours in my box were brought into the fighting-line. Not so bad, or so I thought in my vanity. The blue and purple shadows did nicely against the sky, the greens had a flash in them which seemed not quite amateurish. But the top of my tree—or, rather, the tops of my four trees, for I had dabbed them all in—hung suspended in mid-air, and now I must start on those shining stems, which, as the least expert reader will perceive, led me straight back to the olive. This sounds irrelevant, but the connection of the two things was intimate and compulsory.

In real life things shine of themselves, which makes them infinitely simple. In pictures they only shine against something else which is darker than they are. There are masters of the brush who know how to flash light upon light, and one of these might be able to bring a grey cypress stem fronting the sun into bright relief against a sparkling silver background. My humble design was to disengage it from a comparatively dark background, and I looked to the olive to help me. Never for a moment should I have committed myself to this adventure had I not seen it with my own eyes playing this sober, necessary part of foil without fuss or ostentation.

And truly it seemed now to follow my thought. Visibly, as I looked at it, it began to calm down. The sparkles disappeared, the agitated motion ceased; and it clothed itself in a veil of tender grey—a grey with a heart to it of the most bewitching mystery, passing at the upper end of the scale through emerald green to pale yellow, and at the lower to a warm brown. Mistily through it one saw the gaunt, gnarled skeleton which makes so forbidding a structure for such a sylph-like creature. The olive has a peculiar trick with this queer skeleton. Whereas other trees will show you leaf and bough alternately, breaking the line here, continuing it there, now clothing a limb luxuriantly, then letting it go bare for a space till it plunges into the next wave of green, the olive will reveal either the whole of her anatomy or none. True, the outline is slightly blurred by the film of grey, but as I look into the tree I see the whole of it, trunk and branches of rich brown, with beautiful curves breaking abruptly into sharp angles—brown assuredly; but a second look shows them grey towards the light, with here and there a singing accent of lichen yellow. Where and how to begin on it? Grey the foliage must be and tolerably dark, for the cypress stems demand it; but no flat wash will ever hint at it—it must be shot with green and brown and yellow and carmine, and subtly graduated towards that right-hand corner which lunges out of the shadow and emerges pure silver in the sunlight. I am sore and beaten as I pursue the thing in frantic haste, but something goes down—the least said about it the better—and at all events I have got my cypress stems drawn by the simple expedient of leaving them white, and the four trees are standing on ghostly pale legs. Then, while the olive wash is still glistening, I take a dry brush of vandyke brown and dash in the olive skeleton, letting it sink softly into the background. This is not so bad, and, crude as the whole performance is, I am rather proud of this part of it.

My pride is short-lived. I am feeling about for a warmer tone to get a heart into the tree, when I become aware that the olive is up to mischief again. A slight breeze, imperceptible to me, is stirring on the far side of the hill, and instantly she is all of a flutter with it. Her sensitiveness is incredible and maddening. Every single one of her innumerable leaves is in the act of turning. For a moment they show a thousand little javelin points in immensely serried ranks, each catching the sun on its tip and throwing its neighbour into shadow. An instant later the manœuvre is finished, and this wicked tree is unashamedly buff—I had almost said yellow—and grossly opaque. Trunk and branches are clean gone; the silver bonfire and the pale grey mist seem to be figments of my imagination. Here she is as hard and solid as the caruba on the opposite side of the hill, and her colour is positively ugly. I could swear she scoffed at me. Manifestly this was her revenge on me for having presumed to imagine that I saw her bones. She would show me that,

249

if she chose, she could be as decently, as soberly clad as any other tree. That might be, but the livid yellow of her last costume was detestable.

She gave no further sign, and had apparently settled down into that ugly mood for the rest of the day. So I gave her up in disgust and turned again to the cypresses. But the task of painting their stems was cruelly complicated by the fact that they now stood against this obstinate yellow-brown background. It changed their colour and took all the sheen out of them. Moreover, there was a certain agitation on foot even in these sedate trees. The neatly arranged patterns of their foliage were changing shape, the shadows spreading, the light contracting. The sunlight on the stems was now but a bright line on the outer edge. I looked behind me and saw that the sun was perilously near the mountain crest which would shortly eclipse it. For two hours on a bright after-noon there is a sort of solstice, and, if there is no wind, the outer aspect of things remains much the same. Then there follows a half-hour of bewildering transformation. The shadows race up the hillside, sweep across the trees, changing their form and colour, turning the round into the flat, obliterating the detail, throwing tides of grey and purple over green and yellow, and in other ways miserably defeat-ing the unhappy sketcher who is caught at that moment. Wisdom says flee, and begin again tomorrow; yet you stay and fight furiously, recalling a bit from memory, taking another bit from nature, and coming away finally with a muddy and muddled compromise. I will spare the reader what happened in the next half-hour, though the unhappy record is before me as I write. I played the fool's part of interloper in this struggle between the powers of light and darkness; I dabbed and smudged and swore between rage at my own futility and delight in the beauty of the scene. One glorious moment I remember when the olive blazed up again from its dull yellow into silver and then as suddenly sank into a cold grey. Then I took off my hat to acknowledge defeat and turned home through the wood.

X

THE EMPTY PEW

1912.

I AM tempted to cut into the debate which has been revived, for about the tenth time in my life, about the empty pew. People go to church, or don't go, for a great many different reasons. The devout Churchman or Churchwoman, the Church-going communicant, will go to any church within his or her reach, regardless of what is called the "appeal" of the clergyman who ministers in it. There is nothing to be said about these. I have heard a highly respected bishop argue that it would be far better for the Church of England if it confined itself to them and relied on influencing the rest of us through the example of an "intensive Christianity" which they would present to the world. But that is not the opinion of his episcopal brethren, or of the mass of the clergy who daily lament the decline in the habit of church-going, and would be less than human if they did not feel some sense of mortification and defeat at the sight of the empty pew, the pew stubbornly remaining empty, for all their toil to make themselves and the ministrations acceptable to their parishioners.

During some part of my life I was in the habit of attending Anglican churches and Nonconformist chapels alternately on successive Sundays, and a few observations occur to me which I will set down for what they are worth. The Church rests on devotion to an institution, the Chapel on the power and influence of a man. It is impossible to get away from that. The two church clergy—vicar and curate—whose ministrations I found quite adequate in their own setting, would kill any chapel in about a month. Neither of them has

51

any gift for preaching and they would probably be quite unequal to the extemporized devotions which form so large a part of the Chapel service. Certainly the Chapel congregation would not for a minute tolerate the little essays which they read from manuscripts, and if they could not do something different and better, their career in the ministry would come to a speedy end. They fill their church, nevertheless, passably well with the aid of a good choir and an orderly, though by no means advanced, ceremonial. The liturgy is their stand-by, and their constant appeal to the Church as an institution and to the Sacraments as the means of grace takes the load off their backs and renders the priestly office independent of the man.

The sermons I have heard in these weeks might lead one to suppose that it is thought "bad form" to speak eloquently or effectively from an Anglican pulpit. What strikes one especially in going to churches where there are two or more clergymen, is that none of them is any better than the others in the pulpit. One would suppose that if a vicar had no gift for preaching, he would take care to choose a curate who had; but that, I am told, is most unusual. Vicars, it seems, are human like the rest of us, and it is not thought becoming that they should be outshone in their own pulpits by eloquent young men. Whether this is the explanation or whether it is pure accident I don't know, but it almost invariably happens that when the vicar is a bad preacher the curate is a worse. I gather that warnings against being "pretentious" or "ambitious" are apt to be delivered to those who develop unsuspected gifts.

Preaching in these circumstances becomes extremely conventional. The seasons come round, and there is a sermon or service for every season, the assumption being that your mood will always be attuned to "the lesson for the day," and with the observations on it which from year to year are made with mathematical accuracy by the vicar or the curate out of that little morocco-bound case with the cross on it, which contains the thrice-delivered sermon. These hard-worked clergy, so busy with their parish organization, have no time to write new sermons, and, if they had, their minds work in grooves which are not encouraging to new ideas. Their congregations, accordingly, tend to become predominantly of one sex—congregations of good women, who are susceptible to church discipline, and who attend the church as the fountain of sacramental grace and the centre of an organization into which they are caught up.

But now go to any of the leading Nonconformist chapels—Wesleyan, Congregational, or Baptist. You will find that the men in the congregation are generally equal to the women, and very often outnumber them. The minister depends wholly on his own efforts to hold them. He has none of the coercive powers which the least of Anglican curates can bring to bear upon the devout churchman. He cannot say that here, and here alone, are the acceptable means of salvation, or that the church orders you to attend his ministrations, appoints certain rites and ceremonies which are administered in his chapel. He has no secure living which will enable him to earn his bread by ministering to an empty church, if his congregation deserts him. Minister and congregation stand or fall together, and their relation is mutual and personal. If the congregation gets no benefit and refuses to attend, the minister has no reason for existing, and he enters the ministry with the full knowledge that his success or failure will depend on the power of his appeal. This is a condition which applies to all other professions and businesses, and must apply to a church so soon as you banish the notion that the minister has priestly tasks apart from his relation to his flock. It is for that reason, I think, that Nonconformists regard the establishment as necessarily sacerdotal. They see it descending from the time when the beneficed priest was endowed for the serving of altars; and they believe with all their hearts that the endowment of a ministerial caste is fatal to the right relations between minister and congregation, and calculated in practice to make the minister a dull man.

That at once makes a remarkable difference of atmosphere

between Church and Chapel. However unpriestly the Anglican clergyman may be, he has behind him a system and tradition which make him a sacerdos in spite of himself. He walks in procession, wearing cassock, surplice, and stole, one of a company engaged in a prescribed ceremonial, which will go on year in and year out, whether the church is empty or full. Choir and clergy are removed from the congregation, and beyond them is the altar, which holds the place of honour in the church. The Nonconformist minister goes solitary to his rostrum, which commands the congregation. There is a prescribed order of service, but everything in it depends on his improvisations. The hour and a half which follows is for him a time of intense effort, intellectual and spiritual. He delivers an extempore prayer lasting a quarter of an hour, and a sermon lasting three-quarters of an hour. Commonly he has nothing with him but his Bible. No doubt he has meditated over his prayer, but his congregation expects him to catch the impulses of the moment, and he will have had sudden requests for special kinds of prayer just before his service begins. Very seldom does he venture to read a sermon from a manuscript; in the great majority of cases he preaches extempore from the open Bible, and his congregation expect that his sermon should last three-quarters of an hour. It follows almost as a matter of course from these conditions that the Nonconformist knows the business of preacher and speaker as the clergyman does not. He is in these respects a professional where the other is an amateur, and I think the Anglican clergy might learn a good deal if occasionally they would condescend to attend the ministrations of some of these gifted preachers. One thing that strikes me when I pass from chapel to church is that the average Anglican pulpit is much more difficult to preach from than the Nonconformist rostrum. If we were not so hardened to it by custom we should rebel against seeing a man in a surplice projecting from his waist upwards out of a round box. And nothing can make a short surplice compare in dignity with the black gown which is still the vestment of the chapel.

My ideal church would give me an Anglican cathedral service followed by a first-rate Nonconformist preacher. Brought up an Anglican, I am not yet subdued to the chapel service. The extempore prayer generally tries to combine two incompatible things, supplication and instruction. Much of it is meant to edify the congregation, and yet in form it is addressed to the Almighty. It requires rare tact on the part of the minister to steer between the dangers on either hand. Some few do it supremely well, but it is sometimes hard for those who have not been brought up to it, and who are accustomed to Prayer-book English, to quench the critical spirit.

When it comes to doctrine, I am frankly an eclectic. Both ministers and clergy seem to me to say some totally impossible things; but the urbanity and calmness with which they assume my consent keep me in a suitable frame of mind. This is the secret of the orthodox churches.

XI

SOWING AND REAPING

March, 1932.

ONE day last week a friend of mind gave me a touching account of a visit he had paid to Briand a fortnight before his death. He found him in a state of great despondency about his own career and work in life. He thought of himself as a failure and spoke of his work being in ruins.

A man must not be taken too tragically when he is in the grip of a mortal sickness, and Briand, I hope, will be judged hereafter to have deserved the high eulogies pronounced over his grave. But what my friend told me set me thinking about the discouragement which befalls so many of the great and eminent at the end of their days.

According to his latest biographers the last utterance of the younger Pitt was not "My country, how do I leave thee!" but "I think I could eat one of Bellamy's meat pies." He did, nevertheless, die at the evil moment after Austerlitz, when all Europe seemed to be at the mercy of the French, and the great English effort, of which he was the leader and inspirer, to have been in vain. In the next generation Castlereagh died by his own hand, leaving the credit for most that was good in his policy to be reaped by his rival, Canning, and the execration for what was bad for himself.

Peel had better fortune in that he saw the accomplishment of his policy, but he too died in political exile, bitterly estranged from his former friends. Thirty years later his rival and supplanter, Disraeli, passed away when the reaction from his policy was at its height and he, the hero who had returned bringing "Peace with Honour," was a broken old man in opposition.

256

Twenty years later his great opponent, Gladstone, passed from the scene when the fortunes of his party were near their lowest and the cause to which he had given the last years of his life seemed to be irretrievably wrecked. Sixteen years later the same fate befell Joseph Chamberlain, and after another fourteen years Asquith.

I remember hearing John Morley and Joseph Chamberlain say, on the same evening at the same dinner table, that they cared nothing for what posterity might say about them; they wished to see their work accomplished and enjoy their triumphs while they were on the scene. I do not think this was the real thought of either of them, or has ever been that of any considerable man of affairs. No man who plays a great part can ever think of his work as limited to his own mortal existence.

For those who do not, disappointment becomes a mere incident, and the moral is: "Fear not to sow because of the birds." The harvests are not regular; the reaping may come years after the sowing, and, when it comes, it is generally so mixed that no one can say for certain whose was the sowing. But the labourer in this field must hold to the belief that the good seed bringeth forth good fruit.

Young men start out in life thinking of the world process as a drama which will be completed in their lifetime. They will see the curtain fall on a scene of questions answered, problems solved, happy reconciliations effected. Old men know that the utmost they can expect is to play their part creditably in one moment of one scene in the human or divine comedy.

The rest is faith.

INDEX